An Introduction to
Kant's *Critique of Judgement*

D1598749

For Catherine, with love

An Introduction to Kant's *Critique of Judgement*

Douglas Burnham

Edinburgh University Press

© Douglas Burnham, 2000

Edinburgh University Press Ltd
22 George Square, Edinburgh

Typeset in 10 on 12½ Sabon
by Hewer Text Limited, Edinburgh, and
printed and bound in Great Britain by
MPG Books Ltd, Bodmin

A CIP record for this book is available
from the British Library

ISBN 0 7486 1353 6 (paperback)

The right of Douglas Burnham
to be identified as author of this work
has been asserted in accordance with
the Copyright, Designs and Patents Act 1988.

Contents

Preface

Immanuel Kant is often said to have been the greatest philosopher since the Greeks. Certainly, he dominates the last 200 years in the sense that, although few philosophers today are strictly speaking Kantians, his influence is everywhere. Moreover, that influence extends over a number of different philosophical regions: epistemology, metaphysics, the philosophy of science, aesthetics, ethics, politics, religion and history. The *Critique of Judgement*, written near the end of the eighteenth century, when Kant was in his mid-60s, addresses itself in important and coordinated ways to all of these topics. However, the book has been rather neglected until recently, and even now, during a period of relative renaissance for the text, it is often read and taught selectively.

This book is introductory, but is intended for readers who do have some knowledge of philosophy or the history of ideas. The aim is to give a clear but non-reductive and non-modernised exposition of the whole of the *Critique of Judgement*, warts and all, placed in the context of Kant's philosophy in general.

In the attempt to achieve this aim, I have had to cut out most of the scholarly 'apparatus' and contemporary debates internal to the field. I also felt it necessary to give a systematic overview of Kant's critical philosophy in the Introduction to this book, which some readers may wish to skip or skim. I have also included, as aids to the reader, both section and chapter summaries, and a brief glossary. The bibliography is selective.

I am indebted to a number of people who had an important role in the writing of this book. All of my past and current colleagues at Staffordshire University were generous with their support, occasional editorial advice, and innumerable conversations (not *all* in the pub). Of these, five in particular stand out: Dr Catherine Burgass, Dr Darrell Hinchliffe, Dr Tony Gorman, Mr Peter Shott and Dr David Webb.

Note on
Abbreviations and Editions

Throughout this book, I have used Werner Pluhar's admirable translation of the *Critique of Judgement*, but I have occasionally used alternative translations of key terms and phrases. These (along with other commonly used alternatives) have been indicated at the first few mentions. All references to the text are given by section number (§49, and so on) in order to facilitate the use of alternative editions.

Prior to completing the *Critique of Judgement*, Kant wrote a long introduction, which was then rewritten in a much briefer version, partly on the advice of his publisher. This first longer draft is referred to throughout this book as the 'First Introduction', while the revised, published version is referred to as the 'Introduction'.

Only three abbreviations have been used in the notes: CPR for *Critique of Pure Reason*, CPrR for *Critique of Practical Reason*, and CJ for *Critique of Judgement*. The *Critique of Pure Reason* went through two editions with significant changes (1781 and 1787), and it is standard practice to designate these as A and B. Where the editions overlap (that is, where B is the same as A), the convention is to give page references in the form of, for example, A147=B187.

For other texts, it is a convention to make references to Kant's text by means of the page numbers in the Akademie edition of the complete works. I have followed this convention where it will be of use to the English reader, and this is denoted as, for example, Ak. p. 9.

Introduction: The Issues Behind the *Critique of Judgement*

Immanuel Kant and the Eighteenth Century

Kant's students at the University of Königsberg, from the 1750s on, had two required lecture courses with him. They were Logic and Metaphysics, with the former providing both the conceptual language and the main structural distinctions for the latter. The logic lectures, then, were Kant's way of introducing both himself and philosophy in general to his students. Near the beginning of the lectures, Kant has this to say:

> The field of philosophy in the meaning it has for the citizens of the world[1] may be summed up in the following questions:
> 1. What can I know?
> 2. What ought I to do?
> 3. What may I hope?
> 4. What is man?
> The first question is answered by *metaphysics*, the second by *morality*, the third by *religion*, and the fourth by *anthropology*. At bottom all this could be reckoned to be anthropology, because the first three questions are related to the last.
> [W]ithout knowledge one never becomes a philosopher, but knowledge alone will never make the philosopher, unless there is added a purposeful joining of all cognitions and skills into unity, and an insight into their agreement with the highest ends of human reason.[2]

Kant clearly does not just mean that these are the 'eternal' questions, the ones that human beings have always asked themselves. His point is stronger: these are the essential questions, the ones that human beings *must* ask themselves. For we are 'citizens of the world'; it is in this world that we think and feel, live and die, act and hope.

Moreover, although these questions are 'answered' by different branches of philosophy, that philosophy is to be unified. This unification takes place in two ways. First, insofar as all of the questions seems to relate to the last one: 'what is man?' In other words, encompassing all of philosophy is anthropology in the broadest sense. That would be a *fundamental* anthropology[3] which encompasses not just those generalisations that can be made through empirical accumulation of data about humans, but the study of what is essential to the human, beyond all historical or cultural contingencies. Secondly, all of the knowledge and abilities of philosophers (including fundamental anthropology) are pointless and valueless unless they are directed to the highest end or purpose of all human reason. In this world, even knowledge has to be understood in terms of the good, for oneself or for others.[4] The highest purpose, Kant consistently claims, is morality. For morality concerns what *ought* to be, and thus also what other philosophical concerns – so far as they are able – *ought* to be concerned with. Morality, Kant says, unifies the various questions and branches of philosophy with respect to their *purpose*, and to that extent also organises a fundamental anthropology.

All of these ideas are thoroughly distinctive of Kant, but are also intimately related to the major intellectual themes of the eighteenth century.

Kant was born in Königsberg, Prussia (now Kalingrad in Russia) in 1724 to Pietist Lutheran parents. Königsberg was a significant and affluent seaport and for that reason more cosmopolitan in some ways than larger cities inland. Even so, it was something of a backwater with respect to what we now see as mainstream eighteenth-century intellectual, political and cultural life. Kant's early education first at a Pietist school and then at the University of Königsberg was in theology, but he soon became attracted by problems in physics, and especially the work of Isaac Newton. In 1746 financial difficulties forced him to withdraw from the university. After nine years supporting himself as a tutor to the children of several wealthy families in outlying districts, he returned to university, finishing his degree and entering academic life, though at first (and for many years) in the modest capacity of a lecturer. (Only in 1770 was he given a chair in logic and metaphysics.) He continued to work, lecture and publish widely on a great variety of issues, but especially on physics and the metaphysical issues behind physics. He rarely left his home city, and gradually became a celebrity there for his brilliant, witty but eccentric character.

Kant's working life spanned the second half of the eighteenth century, a formative period in the history of Europe. In so many ways – politically, scientifically, economically, intellectually, even in some ways culturally – this period marks the emergence of the distinctive characteristics of the modern world that we now take for granted. With the exception of his complete inexperience of wider travel, Kant's life is quite exemplary of his period. Indeed, despite the lack of travel, and despite living in the north-east corner of

Europe, Kant was a typically cosmopolitan figure, reading works from all over Europe, and having his works read just as widely. The eighteenth century, as a period in intellectual history, is often called the Enlightenment, and it is characterised above all by an optimism in the human ability to think or reason. This ability was seen as the key to a progressive knowledge of the natural world (the sciences, especially physics as the paradigm of human thought becoming a science), including human beings (psychology, sociology, economics, politics, even revolutionary politics). Reason was applicable even to the moral world and to God (resulting in 'deism', an entirely rational religion entirely separated from the dogma and practices of any church).

Kant's intellectual development parallels almost exactly this wider, European adventure. He starts out as a student with the emphasis still firmly on theology as the centre of philosophy. But it is not long before he is forced to address the issue of science (particularly physics, and within this, the work of Newton) and the relationship of science not only to religion but also to the nature of human being and human values. Kant's early work was in the tradition (although not dogmatically) of the great German rationalist philosopher Leibniz, and especially his follower Wolff. However, by the mid-1750s, he was increasingly in the orbit of Leibniz's great scientific rival Newton. These philosophers certainly were optimistic about rational thought, but in a manner that Kant later characterised as 'dogmatic'. That is, they were unwilling to consider that the rarefied thinking of human beings might have essential limitations, which did not indeed stand in the way of man's intellectual progress, but meant that one's concrete experience of the world had to be taken into consideration.

Newton was hardly a typical empiricist. However, the success of his physics certainly made plausible, for example, his quite realist conception of the nature and existence of space and time, which were directly contradictory to the Leibniz/Wolff tradition. Moreover, the Newtonian conception of the natural world as entirely subject to the interaction of basic forces made the determinism of that world – that the natural world was subject to inescapable natural laws – increasingly plausible. Kant was not alone in recognising that this exacerbated the age-old philosophical problem of free will. How could human beings – who are obviously at least partly *natural* beings – act freely in a Newtonian universe? And, if free will is impossible, what happens to morality?

Furthermore, Kant was coming under the additional influences of two great eighteenth-century figures, Hume and Rousseau. Hume was a committed empiricist and reluctant sceptic, who condemned as illusion the pretensions of metaphysics, and especially those concepts (such as substance or cause and effect) often taken as the foundations of natural sciences. Any reasoning that was not entirely subservient to our experience of things was bound to be utterly worthless. Hume was not saying that a science of nature, or of human beings as natural beings (including sociology and morality), was thereby impossible, but that it had to be founded on an entirely and thoroughly empirical basis. He was therefore the figure most antithetical to Leibniz and Wolff's subject matter and style of philosophising. Kant famously claims that Hume 'first interrupted my dogmatic slumber and gave my investigations in the field of speculative philosophy quite a new direction'.[5]

Rousseau influenced Kant in a number of ways, in particular with his condemnation of reason (and similarly culture and society – because of their constraining artificiality) not as an instrument of scientific knowledge, but as an instrument of ethical or political advance. Rousseau had in mind reason in all its exterior and institutionalised forms in the modern world. Too often, he thought, this 'reason' distorted or eliminated the *natural* virtue and liberty of humans – our ability to rule over ourselves – rather than enhancing it. Kant saw both Rousseau and Hume as raising the most profound challenge not merely to this idea or that, but to philosophy itself. For if reason was to have any role in philosophy, then some way of answering Hume and Rousseau – without simply ignoring them, as Kant saw most of his contemporaries doing – had to be found. Above all, a correct understanding of the relation between scientific reasoning and moral reasoning was at stake. One can imagine that Kant saw Hume as collapsing this distinction, and Rousseau as widening it to the point where there was nothing but antagonism. Moreover, these influences begin to make it clear just how and why Kant was always concerned with the systematic inter-relationship of various, often separately considered, branches of philosophy, and the 'faculties' or 'powers' which make them possible.

Scarcely any intellectual figure in the second half of the eighteenth century was not influenced by Rousseau and Hume, but what is so significant about Kant is the utterly original way in which he tried to treat the issues those philosophers raised. It was Hume in particular who forced Kant to investigate the validity of metaphysics, rather than assume it. It was Rousseau who forced Kant to undertake a critique of pure theoretical reason and to elevate in its place practical reason. During the 1760s, Kant produced a series of works attacking Leibnizian thought. In particular, he now argued that the traditional tools of philosophy – logic and metaphysics, all in the service of reason – were severely limited with respect to obtaining knowledge of reality. Moreover, the claims of reason to be able to know the theological foundations of virtue were destructive, distracting from humanity's own 'native' resources for grasping and acting upon the good – namely, freedom. He argued that reason had be to reconceived such that its fundamental basis and purpose was practical (moral) rather than theoretical.

Nevertheless, in Kant's works of the 1760s, there is still a kind of frustrating inconsistency to his ideas. He seemed, for example, to be unable either to accept a mere empiricist account of knowledge, or to reject it entirely. Similarly, in considering how to understand morality, he contradicted himself on the origin of moral principles, and the relation of those principles to the divine being. Finally, he achieved no solution to the problem of free will. Sometimes, in this period, he would hit upon a way of dealing with one of these issues that would also be the solution he settled upon later in his 'mature' or 'critical' period – only to retract it in the next work.

These problems were pressing precisely because of the conception of philosophy with which we began. A philosophy could hardly be considered complete if it did not answer all four of the questions. Moreover, such a philosophy could not be considered satisfactory if it did not show its own unity, both by enclosing all the questions in the question 'What is man?', and by at least showing that it was possible to coordinate all the branches of philosophy towards the highest purpose: morality. That Kant was unable to settle on solutions to the nature and limits of human knowledge, and of human morality and freedom, meant that he had not yet reached a fundamental characterisation of the nature of the human. Similarly, that he prevaricated on the subject of morality and its relation to both freedom and the world meant that his philosophy was by no means as organised as it ought to be.

At least in the philosophy of scientific knowledge, however, Kant began to move – in the late 1760s, and especially in his *Inaugural Dissertation* of 1770 – towards the ideas that would make him famous and change the face of philosophy. In the *Dissertation*, and with primarily Hume in mind, he argued three key new ideas. First, he argued that sensible and conceptual presentations of the world (for example, my seeing three horses, and my concept of three) are not at all the same kind of thing, but are two quite distinct sources of possible knowledge. Secondly, it follows that knowledge of sensible reality is only possible if the necessary concepts (such as substance) are already available to the intellect. This fact, Kant argued, also limits the legitimate range of application of these concepts. Thirdly Kant claimed that sensible presentations were only of 'appearances', and not things as they are in themselves. This was because space and time, which describe the basic structure of all sensible appearances, do not exist in things in themselves, but are only an effect of things upon our organs of sense. This exacerbates the limitation imposed above by proposing a whole realm of things in themselves which necessarily lies beyond knowledge in any ordinary sense. These were new and often startling ideas, although here they are only fragmentary with respect to the overall conception of philosophy Kant was pursuing. Nevertheless, with slight modifications, they would turn out to form the core of his philosophical project for the rest of his life.

After publishing quite often in the preceding fifteen years, the *Inaugural Dissertation* ushered in an apparently quiet phase in Kant's work. Kant realised that he had discovered a new approach to philosophy. He now needed rigorous demonstrations of his new ideas, and had to pursue their furthest implications; he even needed to find a new philosophical language to properly express such original thoughts. This took more than a decade of his life. A remarkable correspondence survives from this period, but Kant published virtually nothing until the massive first edition of the *Critique of Pure Reason*, in 1781 (revised second edition, 1787). Over the next two decades, however, he furiously pursued his new philosophy into different territories, producing books or shorter publications on virtually every philosophical topic under the sun. This new philosophy came to be known as 'critical' or 'transcendental' philosophy. Of particular importance were: the *Critique of Pure Reason* (1781/1787), *Critique of Practical Reason* (1788), and the *Critique of Judgement* (1790). These are often called the 'first', 'second' and 'third' *Critiques*.

How do these texts answer the four questions from Kant's own *Logic* lectures? The *Critique of Pure Reason* concerns itself primarily with the first question ('What can I know?'), although with some very important overlaps into the others. The *Critique of Practical Reason* concerns itself with the second ('What ought I to do?') and, to a limited extent, the third ('What can I hope?'). He even published his lectures on anthropology, although these are predominantly empirical in method, and thus not really an attempt to grasp the four essential questions as contained in the last ('What is man?'), or what we call a 'fundamental anthropology'.

However, Kant did write one book which has the unity of philosophy as its explicit and central theme. It is his *Critique of Judgement*.[6] The book contains a great deal of rich material in more specialised fields – especially aesthetics (the philosophy of beauty and art) – and we shall be discussing this material, but throughout what follows we shall always have one eye, so to speak, on this larger question: the systematic unity of philosophy. Although by no means the last work Kant published (he was productive almost up to his death in 1804), the third *Critique* was conceived of by Kant as the 'completion' or unification of his work as a philosopher.[7] Having read the passage from the *Logic* with which we began, we now know what that might mean: it means uniting all of philosophy, in the sense of giving a fundamental characterisation of the nature of the human, such that the basic features of philosophy are discoverable within that characterisation. It also means showing the possible coordination of all the branches of philosophy towards the highest purpose of man: morality.

Kant quickly became famous in the German-speaking world, and soon after elsewhere. He was, and still is, staggeringly influential, largely because he created a new type of philosophy to deal *systematically* with a set of questions that go straight to the heart of our modern world, to the extent that the history of philosophy is often divided into pre-Kantian and post-Kantian phases. This fame did not, however, bring universal praise. Kant's work was feverishly debated in all circles, and his work on religion and politics was even censored. And by the time of his death in 1804, philosophers such as Fichte, Schelling and Hegel had already struck out in new philosophical directions – directions, however, that would have been unthinkable without Kant. The next few sections of this book are an attempt to give a systematic overview of Kant's 'critical' or 'transcendental' philosophy. This overview is given from the point of view of the *Critique of Judgement*, that is, from a point at which Kant felt he had completed his critical work, and could look back and provide an 'Encyclopaedic'[8] (and perhaps quite shaky) account of it. Accordingly, I have structured this discussion after the rather unfamiliar and perhaps over-complex manner in which Kant conceives of the 'faculties' or 'powers' of the mind. Any reader who has come across Kant's work before, either the epistemology or the ethics, will already be familiar with the main lines of this overview.

A Systematic Overview of Kant's Critical Philosophy

What is Meant by 'Critique'?

Kant wrote a great number of books and shorter pieces, but the three most famous, most widely read and studied, and taken to be the core of his philosophy, are the three *Critiques*. These three have very different subject matters, ranging over knowledge, morality, freedom, sense of the beautiful, and faith in God, as well as trying to put forward a vision of what philosophy itself is and should be. In order to get a grip on the third *Critique* we need to have a sketch of how Kant thinks all these various topics hang together. The obvious place to begin, because it is the one element that all the titles have in common, is the notion of 'critique'.

'Critique', in Kant's sense, can be defined provisionally as follows: 'An analysis which attempts to determine the legitimate range of application of a concept.' As we saw above, this problem was already introduced in the *Inaugural Dissertation* of 1770, but Kant had glimpsed it earlier, for example in *Dreams of a Spirit-Seeker*.[9] If I try to apply some concept (for example, the concept of a horse) outside its range, that is to some other but inappropriate concept (for example, the idea of 'colourless') the result will be nonsense ('that colourless is a horse'). Usually, we can tell immediately when this has happened – everyone laughs. In this example, however, the problem is basically grammar. More interesting would be those propositions that make grammatical sense, but are still nonsense from the point of view, for example, of any possible knowledge of the world. When concepts become very abstract – that is, are not so clearly related to real objects in the world – it may be less obvious when nonsense is produced. For example, is it, or is it not, nonsense to say 'God is the cause of the universe', or 'space is infinitely vast'? Notice that it is not, at least at first, a question of establishing whether such statements are true or false – that is, in what way the statement belongs to *knowledge*. The statement 'that colourless is a horse' is neither true nor false, and is therefore unrelated to knowledge. It doesn't make enough sense even to be called properly false. A useful first approximation to what Kant calls 'critique' is the process of deciding when the use of a concept such as 'cause' or 'infinitely large' is appropriate. The process of critique is to determine what kinds of abstract statements make sense, such that we can then go on to determine whether they are true or not – that is, whether they contribute to our knowledge of the world.

It is thus necessary to group concepts (and other mental presentations such as intuitions of particular things in the world) together according to what uses of them might conceivably make sense. Kant does so in a fairly traditional way, according to the *origin* in the mind of the concepts or other presentations. Thus, he is less concerned with what individual abstract concepts we may have, and the appropriate range of their application, than he is with the various *mental powers* we have which produce or make use of these abstract concepts. He is therefore investigating the appropriate *use* of these powers. So, our definition of 'critique' above should be amended to read: 'An analysis which attempts to determine the legitimate range of application of *some type of mental power.*' By investigating the source and purpose of our concepts (i.e. the mental power upon which they depend), Kant means to investigate their validity with the greatest possible thoroughness and precision.

> SUMMARY: The distinctive character of Kantian philosophy is *critique*. This is defined as an analysis which attempts to establish, for a mental 'power' or 'faculty', the range of applications of that ability which make sense and thus are legitimate.

The 'Faculties' and Critique

I have talked above about mental 'faculties' or 'powers'. Kant's word for the things that our minds can accomplish or do is *Vermögen* (or sometimes *Kraft* in compound words). This is often translated as 'power' but also commonly (and historically) as 'faculty', in the sense of a capacity for doing something. Trying to understand human thinking in terms of its basic 'powers' or 'faculties' is a common eighteenth-century idea.

Earlier philosophers using the idea of a 'faculty' were doing what we might now call psychology. They were asking what kinds of real parts the mind or brain consists of. In the eighteenth century, the natural sciences and, above all, physics were making rapid strides forward, and for most intellectuals in the period, the person most responsible for this, or at least symbolic of the whole trend, was the physicist and mathematician Isaac Newton. The dominant form of explanation in these sciences was mechanical. Phenomena were explained in terms of mass, energy, momentum, and perhaps also forces acting at a distance such as gravity. Since this procedure was so successful, many felt that the same basic ideas should be applied to the study of the mind. The mind – or rather the brain – was to be understood either as a physical object entirely governed by either the same laws as any other physical object, or at least by laws of its own which are nevertheless closely modelled on such physical laws. For example, we ought to be able to explain the phenomenon of aesthetic taste in such terms.

In studying the mind 'mechanically', one must first catalogue and sort all the phenomena that need to be explained. Each distinctly different phenomenon (products of the imagination, the judgement, and so on) will require a distinctly different physical explanation. We might be tempted to think of Kant's work on these same lines: an analysis of the different real 'powers' of the brain. But for various reasons, Kant believed this approach would lead to a dead-end. He was certainly happy to admit without argument that many mental phenomena *might* be explained in this physical way. But prior to and independent of this physical or mechanical element, there was something in the mind which had its own laws, which was thus independent of such physical causation. If that was the case, then an analysis of the functioning of the brain could only be superficial. In this way, Kant was one of the first philosophers in history to have distinguished sharply between what we now call 'psychology' and the proper domain of 'philosophy'.

This distinction is at the root of his philosophical method. At stake in Kant's idea of a 'power' or 'faculty' is not a real thing or a real physical process, but simply a capacity or function of doing this or doing that. The scientific explanation of these functions is impossible in principle. This means that Kant can give what he calls a 'transcendental' account of the faculties and their interrelationships while at the same time avoiding the metaphysical pitfalls of trying to achieve a truly fundamental account of them in terms of psychology or physiology.[10] We shall return below to the notion of transcendental philosophy.

Given their importance to the idea of critique, coming to some understanding of these faculties is necessary. We will also see that the list of faculties will provide Kant with clues for the task of critique, as well as helping us to understanding the structure of his philosophical work as a whole.

Unfortunately, depending on what he is writing about, Kant gives several different analyses of the various faculties, often contradicting himself. Furthermore, he will often call many other things 'faculties' – these will be things the mind certainly does, but in a derivative instead of a fundamental way. In his Introduction to the third *Critique*, Kant tries to systematise his idea of faculties – that is, to give those fundamental few activities or accomplishments to which all the other things he sometimes call faculties can be reduced. I will base the following discussion on the analysis given in the Introduction to the *Critique of Judgement* (especially sections I, III and IX; and also First Introduction II, III, XI). However, I will expand the treatment given there in order to take account of a few other issues. We would be very lucky if the following discussion held for, and mapped out, all of Kant's writings, but Kant is not a mindless automaton, following his distinctions to their ultimate conclusion. Rather, he is constantly rethinking, recasting, and discovering new issues and undreamt-of avenues for philosophising. At best, any such 'map' can only orient us initially, and perhaps help to keep us from getting too terribly lost.

In a sense, all Kant is doing is asking 'What kinds of thinking are there?' or 'What can the mind do?' In answer to this, he begins with a distinction between the 'mental faculties' or 'faculties of the mind' (or sometimes 'of the soul') and the 'cognitive faculties'. Roughly, the former are the basic achievements or products of the mind while the latter are the activities, or sources of the presentations, that are necessary to achieve the former.

The 'Faculties of the Mind'

Each of the 'faculties of the mind' can be in a 'higher' or a 'lower' form. Higher means 'independent' [*Unabhängig*] of, or having 'spontaneity' [*Spontaneität*] with respect to the natural world and our experience of it.[11] 'Lower' means locked into that world, and conditioned [*bedingt*] by it. Kant is primarily interested in the higher forms, because this 'independence' is both their advantage, and danger, to philosophy. So, what is it that our minds can achieve?

Table 1   *The Faculties of the Mind*

HIGHER	LOWER
Theoretical cognition of nature	Subjective associations
Legislative faculty: understanding, with laws of nature	
Aesthetic feeling for nature & art	Corporeal feeling
Legislative faculty: judgement, with principle of purposiveness	
Pure desire in the exercise of freedom	Corporeal desire
Legislative faculty: reason, with principle of morality, and of the highest purpose or Good	
Non-legislative faculty: sensibility, especially productive imagination	

Kant identified three 'faculties of the mind', each with a 'higher' and 'lower' form.

First we think about things. On the 'higher' side, Kant calls this ability the *faculty of cognition* [*Erkentnisvermögen*]. Cognition could be, for example, about things that exist in nature (in which case it is, or aims to be, knowledge). For Kant, the 'natural world' includes the human world as well, to the extent that the latter is seen to obey the same scientific laws as the rest of nature (for example, as objects of the sciences of medicine, psychology, sociology, economics and so on). Or cognition might be about things that are only possible objects in nature (hypothetical scenarios or examples, fiction, and so on); or even about things that could not possibly exist in nature – not because they violate its laws, but because they are its ground that does not itself appear (what Kant calls the supersensible, for example God). In the last case, Kant will try to prove that knowledge in such cases is strictly impossible. On the 'lower' side we can have mere *subjective associations* or habits, being the contingent connecting together of various sensations, such as the appearance of the fireplace with the sensation of warmth. One might consider these the sole source of more complex thoughts, as many eighteenth-century empiricists did, but, as we shall see, Kant believes that these lower associations are insufficient to explain our full relationship to the world.[12] That is why he focuses on the higher side.

Secondly, we have feeling [*Gefühl*]. Feeling in general, according to Kant, is an immediate awareness of our activity of being alive, or of the general effect of something upon that activity. Kant defines 'life' as a being able to act according to desires or purposes.[13] Where, therefore, my desires or purposes are furthered or impeded, or where my general sense of my ability to act is furthered or impeded, I will feel respectively a certain kind of pleasure or pain. This awareness is also a direct incentive to act so as to prolong pleasure or discontinue pain.[14] The higher faculty of feeling, called *aesthetic feeling*, is the pleasure (or pain) felt in the presence (or absence) of the beautiful or sublime. Lower, *corporeal feelings* or *gratification* [*vergnügen*] are the recognition of satiety or accomplishment, or of the lack of these; for example, the pleasure felt in eating a doughnut. Again, Kant argues in many places that the lower feelings are not up to the job of accounting for the full range of our feelings, especially our relationship with art and beauty.[15] (Why we should believe, and how it can be the case, that there can be a higher faculty of feeling at all is a problem we shall return to.)

Thirdly, we have desires and act upon them. We can call the higher side of this faculty *pure desire*, which is our free will [*Wille*] determined by the moral law. Pure desire also has a purpose to its action: the 'final purpose' of man, or the highest Good (Summum Bonum).[16] By this, Kant means the most perfect imaginable state for rational beings: that they are fully happy, and that their happiness is morally deserved. The lower aspect is *corporeal desire*, determinations to act in concrete ways, in order to achieve certain purposes.

Although we sometimes have some choice [*Willkür*] in this respect, that choice is always at least partly determined by inclinations, or emotions and passions.[17] For Kant – and again in contradistinction to many previous philosophers such as Hume – the lower desires alone cannot account for morality as we know it;[18] thus he concentrates on what we have called pure desire.

The 'Cognitive' Faculties

The 'cognitive faculties' fall under each of the aforementioned three higher faculties of the mind as basic operations that make them possible. They are the distinctive source of principles, concepts, ideas and sensible images – or activities involving these – which enable the achievement of the the faculties of the mind. These concepts, images and so on Kant lumps together as 'presentations' [*Vorstellungen*], also translated as 'representations'.[19] So, these cognitive faculties are the source of presentations, or perhaps they perform activities with or on these presentations. Again, there is a distinction between higher and lower. Here, we will deal only with the higher cognitive faculties and do not attempt to describe fully the lower cognitive faculties.

There are three higher cognitive faculties (as we shall see below, there is a fourth faculty that is also very important, but it does not correspond to any 'faculty of the mind, and therefore should be treated separately). They work together in different ways depending upon which faculty of the mind they are serving. In particular, for each of the faculties of the mind, a different cognitive faculty will be dominant – or as Kant puts it, 'legislative' or even 'constitutive' (see Table 1 on p. 10, which is mostly a re-arranged version of Kant's own diagram at the end of his Introduction to the *Critique of Judgement*). We have already asked 'What can our minds do?' now we are beginning to ask 'With what tools can it do these things?'[20]

First, there is *understanding* [*Verstand*], which is the source of concepts for our knowledge of nature. In particular, understanding is the source of *a priori* formal concepts or 'categories', and through these provides the legislative principles of the cognitive faculty of the mind.

Secondly, there is *judgement* [*Urteil*] which in ordinary terms, as we saw above, is the source of our decisions as to whether things are this or that. All judgements are defined as the thinking of a particular under a universal – that is, a presentation that applies to more than one particular (Introduction IV). For example, 'That is a cat' places the particular cat to which I refer under the universal concept of 'cat'. But where do the universals and particulars come from? From other cognitive faculties, especially the understanding, Kant answers. So judgement does not seem to be a faculty on its own and independently, but rather a kind of coordinator or connector of the other cognitive faculties (First Introduction II). Thus, judgement is a very general notion. Virtually everything we think that 'has something to say' is to be considered a judgement, but usually judgement in the service of the under-standing. Nevertheless, this coordinating faculty might still have a legislating principle precisely for such coordination (rather than for objects). Kant argues that it does, namely the 'purposiveness' (also translated 'finality') of things in general with respect to our cognitive faculties. This principle shows up in certain more specialised cases of judgement, which are thus the topics of Kant's *Critique of Judgement*. In one of these cases, aesthetic judgement, this principle is legislative for the faculty of feeling.

Thirdly, there is *reason* [*Vernunft*] which has several significant dimensions. In the ordinary sense, reason is the ability to relate individual acts of the understanding together, in order to prove or demonstrate things. In such rational proofs, we are always moving to and from more universal and less universal propositions (such as, in the famous example, to prove from 'All men are mortal' and 'Socrates is a man', that 'Socrates is mortal'). Reason in its theoretical sense is the attempt to string cognitive propositions together in order to consolidate or extend our knowledge of things. In some cases this 'stringing together' goes even beyond the bounds of our experience of nature, in which case Kant often calls it 'speculative' reason. This activity of speculative reason is also the source of *ideas* [*Ideen*] which are formed in complete abstraction from any possible real thing. These include, above all, the concept of freedom. Kant calls 'practical' reason (based upon the Greek root of the word 'practical', which means simply 'to act') that faculty which can determine the will to act.[21] Practical reason is the legislative employment of reason in general. It is legislative for the faculty of desire, meaning it determines the free will according to the formal principle of the moral law. In this determination, the purpose of the faculty of desire is the 'final purpose' or simply the 'Good'.

The three faculties above are explicitly 'legislative'; that is, they are each linked to a corresponding mental faculty, and provide *a priori* rules for its achievements. There is also a fourth but non-legislative faculty which should be mentioned, the faculty of *sensibility* [*Sinnlichkeit*].[22] Sensibility can be loosely defined as the source of *particular* presentations. But sensibility itself has several components. We have already seen the distinction between 'independent from world and body' (higher) and 'bound to world and body' (lower). If we add another important distinction, namely between abilities that are in themselves *passive* or *active*, then we have a complete four-part list of the subordinate parts of sensibility:

1. *Sensation* [*Empfindung*] Kant understands to be both passive and lower or dependent. In sensation we are presented with colours, sounds, feelings of warmth, hardness and so on.
2. Pure *intuition* [*Anschauung*] (passive, higher or independent), does not refer to some kind of 'sixth sense'. Rather, the faculty of intuition is Kant's name for the source of our *a priori* presentations of the *form* of

space and time. Importantly, Kant argues that this form is quite different from the 'content' of sensation.

3. Reproductive *imagination* [*Einbildungskraft*] (active, lower) is our ability to see things, hear things, touch things, and soon, when they are no longer there. Reproductive imagination also allows us to form associations between different things we have experienced at different times. For example, the colour of this room resembles that of a room in which I once stayed in Paris.

4. *Productive* (or sometimes 'free') *imagination* is both active and independent. The imagination in its higher aspect turns out to be very important in the first half of the *Critique of Judgement*, as well as elsewhere.[23] However, it is not always clear what Kant means by productive imagination, except that it is not bound to *previous* sensations or intuitions, or at least not to the laws of association that govern the reproductive imagination.

Excluding sensibility for the moment, the other three cognitive faculties are legislative for the corresponding faculty of the mind. By 'legislative', Kant means that the cognitive faculty governs how the accomplishment of a corresponding mental faculty can happen.[24] Thus, for example, for theoretical cognition, the understanding is legislative. This legislation, Kant argues, involves two things. First, it involves a set of concepts; a concept being a *general* presentation of a thing. Secondly, it involves a set of principles; a principle being a proposition laying down the law of how concepts are to be used and also, therefore, laying down the law of what possible objects those concepts might have.[25]

In the case of the understanding, the concepts are called the *categories*, such as the concept of cause and effect. The principles determine how these categories are to be used: for example, a straightforward principle is the familiar logical one of non-contradiction.[26] More interesting are the principles that govern how a concept like cause and effect works. One of the things that the principles of the understanding state is that a concept like cause and effect could only be valid when applied to sensibility. Now, according to the structure of Kant's table, sensibility (in its higher aspects) is marked out as distinct because it is the only higher faculty that has no faculty of the mind for which it is uniquely legislative, presumably because it deals with particulars rather than universals.[27] This is slightly disingenuous on Kant's part, firstly because he certainly speaks of principles following from higher sensibility;[28] more importantly because sensibility is the condition under which the understanding can exercise its legislative powers. However, this ambiguity in the above structure does no harm, so long as we remember that sensibility both 'realises' and 'restricts' the categories of the understanding.[29]

That the understanding should be legislative for theoretical cognition may seem straightforward enough, until we realise that both of these are termed 'higher' – that is to say, faculties that are independent with respect to experience of the world. Immediately, then, we see that Kant cannot be a simple empiricist, for whom all knowledge arises from our straightforward sense-perceptions of the world.

In the list of the cognitive faculties, judgement and reason also have legislative aspects. For aesthetic feeling, judgement supplies the legislative *a priori* principle, which Kant claims is the principle of the 'purposiveness' or 'finality' of nature. Without this principle, Kant will argue, it would be impossible for us to judge (and indeed to feel) something to be beautiful in the way that we do. And for pure desire, reason is legislative, determining the will according to the moral law and toward the Good. This is a fundamental idea in Kant's ethical philosophy and also the key topic at the end of the *Critique of Judgement*.

For each mental faculty, the other cognitive faculties may still have important roles, but they are non-legislative. So, for example, as we shall see below, reason is not legislative for theoretical cognition, but does have what Kant calls a 'regulative' role there. Similarly, the understanding cannot legislate for higher desire, but is certainly helpful for figuring out *how* to achieve our desire for the Good.

Of course, in this discussion of the faculties of the mind, and the cognitive faculties, we have not required Kant to prove his account. He has given us a list of faculties, and a set of relations between them (such as legislative). We do not yet have any reasons for accepting this account. And even if we supposed Kant's map to be an adequate explication of all the various achievements and presentations that we apprehend in ourselves, that would not prove it to be the *uniquely correct* account. Of course, in the above explanation, in order to give an overview of Kant's system we have started at the end, giving a completed map of faculties and their inter-relationships. Kant does not assume these; rather his whole 'transcendental' or 'critical' philosophy consists of attempts first to prove that all of us must have just such abilities to think, feel, reason and so forth and that these are inter-related in just such a way; and second to show the implications of our minds being constituted in this way.

If 'critique' is the study of the proper boundaries to a faculty, then critique is simply unnecessary for lower faculties, because the boundaries are obvious and fixed (the natural world). A lower faculty could, in itself, no more break its boundaries than a table lamp could turn on before it is plugged in. As we suggested above, the higher side is of greater philosophical interest, and requires critique to discover and explore the boundaries to its validity. It is precisely the 'independence' or 'spontaneity' of such faculties that means that the proper relation between their principles, and what they know, judge or act upon may be unclear, and subject to abuse.

SUMMARY: What *basic* faculties are there; what is it the human mind can do? We can think about the world around us (theoretical cognition), we can have feelings, we can have and act upon desires. These Kant calls 'faculties' or 'powers' of the mind. But how are these achievements reached? Kant claims that they are made on the basis of certain activities or sources of 'presentations' that Kant calls the 'cognitive powers or faculties'. There are three of these linked to the above three achievements, respectively: understanding, judgement and reason. A fourth cognitive faculty is sensibility which includes the imagination. Each of the above is split into lower and higher parts. 'Lower' means that the faculty is entirely a function of nature and subject to its laws, for example the laws of psychology. 'Higher' means that the faculty is independent of natural determination, thus functioning in some way 'prior' to natural laws. The process of critique, then, requires the investigation of how one cognitive faculty (perhaps together with the others in a merely supporting role) achieves one of the faculties of the mind, and thus also what kind of validity and range of application the result has.

Transcendental Philosophy and the Notion of *A Priori* Conditions of Possibility

So, how does Kant perform his critical analysis? It would be no good to investigate a number of *particular* uses of reason or judgement, because that would not reveal the *general* range, for now and always, within which reason or judgement can be properly used. But there is a more pressing difficulty than this. In asking whether something is nonsense or not, we may in effect be asking whether it is 'reasonable' or a 'good judgement'. But how can we use the notion of 'reasonable' to investigate the nature of reason? It would be like lifting yourself up by pulling on your own shoelaces. In other words, we may be asking a mental ability to judge itself, which for obvious reasons puts the reliability of the whole enterprise into doubt.

Kant's answer to such difficulties is to invent a new type of philosophy, which he calls 'transcendental' philosophy. As much as his *answer* to any philosophical question, this new *method of answering* such questions has been enormously influential. Transcendental philosophy is distinctive in that it attempts to discover the *a priori* conditions for any mental faculty (such as reason or judgement) to function at all. What does that mean? A condition of possibility is something which must be the case before something else can possibly take place. For example, a condition of a basketball player scoring is that he or she has the ball. Without the ball, the player cannot score any points.

'*A priori*', however, is a philosophical expression that means something is *absolutely* independent of any 'ordinary' event or thing, that is, independent of any event or thing which can be observed or studied as being either within my conscious mind, or in the world around me. So, a basketball player having the ball may be a condition, but it is not an *a priori* condition, because having the ball is a perfectly ordinary event (no matter how rare for some players!). A more fundamental condition of a basketball player scoring is that there is a game called 'basketball'. This is obviously prior to all basketball teams and games. But it is still not *a priori*, since the invention of new sports, although perhaps rare, is also an ordinary event. By an *a priori* condition of reason, Kant means: the field of logical and formal conditions that must be understood to be in place for reasoning ever to happen. That which supplies *a priori* conditions has to be completely independent from any 'ordinary' thing, like a physical thing.[30] This is not yet an argument that could prove his point, because we have not yet proved that there are these things called *a priori* conditions. But at least we are getting closer to understanding why Kant's description of the mind is not just psychology as ordinarily understood, because all psychological events are ordinary events.

To the extent that such *a priori* presentations are known to make something else possible, Kant calls them 'transcendental'. So he will often talk about the 'transcendental conditions' or 'transcendental principles' for some mental activity. The type of philosophical argument which seeks to establish the existence and nature of such transcendental principles is, not surprisingly, termed a 'transcendental argument'. Over and over again in his work, Kant will employ such arguments, which have the following form: X is some obviously universal experience (such as the awareness of my own existence); Y can be proved to be the necessary *a priori* condition for any such X; therefore, Y.

For example, the *Critique of Pure Reason* has for its basic issue the investigation of the conditions under which the mental faculty of cognition (That is, the theoretical cognition of nature) can be achieved, and in particular, what, if any, role does the cognitive faculty of pure reason have in this. Kant suggests that it is, in fact, the cognitive faculty of understanding that supplies the categories and makes use of then according to *a priori* principles, which are transcendental conditions for the achievement of any theoretical cognition of the world. He supplies a set of transcendental arguments to show the necessity of this suggestion. The plan is that these principles, in making such cognition possible, will determine the essence or form of what our theoretical cognition of the world is and can be, and will also form the basis for a critique of that faculty and the faculties that enable it.

However, here we ought to distinguish between (1) our 'transcendental' or 'critical' knowledge about the existence of *a priori* conditions or principles for the understanding; and (2) our *a priori* knowledge of nature that those conditions make possible. The former is the job of the critical philosopher, and is perhaps of interest to him or her only; the latter Kant calls a philosophical doctrine which actually says something directly about nature (see, for example, First Introduction I). It may be the case that critique will contribute something to doctrine (that the critique of pure reason might have something to say about physics, for example).[31] But for the most part, the latter is left to natural scientists, the important part being to understand how anything at all can be said about nature, and what limits there might be to this.

Kant then goes on to consider pure reason – that is reason considered entirely on its own. We all have the ability to think in the abstract, we can 'use' our reason, and in doing so, Kant says, we produce 'ideas' distinctive to reason. Does reason, however, have a legislating or constitutive theoretical role – does it accomplish theoretical cognition also? And if so, what? Because such abstract theoretical reasoning is often associated with what philosophers do (usually under the title of 'metaphysics'), Kant is in effect asking: what is it that philosophy can actually do? This is a big question for philosophy, and that is why so many philosophers – in Kant's day and now – pay attention to Kant's work. Thus, Kant writes of a critique of reason:

> By critique of pure reason, however, I do not mean a critique of books and systems, but I mean the critique of our faculty of reason as such, in regard to all cognitions after which reason may strive independently of all experience. Hence I mean by it the decision as to whether a metaphysics as such is possible or impossible, and the determination of its sources as well as its range and bounds – all on the basis of principles.[32]

However, we have just seen Kant link *theoretical cognition* with the cognitive faculty of *understanding*. And, in the 'map' above, we said that for every faculty of the mind there will be one legislating cognitive faculty. Therefore, we can anticipate that the answer to the question of the legislative role of reason in knowledge is: 'nothing at all!' The ideas of reason have no legislative role with respect to theoretical cognition. As a non-legislative faculty, theoretical reason merely has what Kant calls a 'regulative' or 'hypothetical' role. This conclusion greatly annoyed many of Kant's contemporaries. Remember that above we concluded that the process of critique was in effect asking 'what is it that philosophy can do?'. For a long time, many philosophers had felt that pure reason alone could 'do' something in the sense of 'answer all our questions'. Kant now claims to have proven that this is impossible. Thus, his conclusion severely curtailed the ambitions of philosophy. Nevertheless, there is more to be said on such topics because, of course, theoretical cognition is not the only faculty of the mind.

The only faculty which *is* able to provide *a priori* principles which contribute directly to possible legitimate cognition or knowledge of nature is understanding. As we saw above, its *a priori* principles do make possible knowledge of the world according to the categories. The understanding, however, is quite limited, because unlike reason it is not a thinking that is completely abstracted from any worldly thing. Rather, its concepts only function validly if they can be 'exhibited' [*darstellen*] (sometimes translated as 'presented' in distinction to 'represented') in things that are in space and time and are thus a part of *nature*. That is, what the understanding understands are things that are given to us by the faculty of sensibility, by which we mean roughly 'things sensed in space and time'. These 'sensible intuitions' of the world are not in themselves knowledge or even experience: through them we are presented first and foremost with a mere 'manifold' or 'multiplicity' of relations of space or time ('to the left of', 'before' or 'after'), that are 'filled' with sensations (blue, warm and so on). Experience of the world, and thus any possible knowledge, requires the action of the understanding upon such sensible intuitions. Without the understanding's action, we would have no sense of a world 'out there'. But the reverse is also true: the concepts of the understanding only make possible theoretical cognition with respect to intuitions. Famously, Kant writes, 'Thoughts without content are empty, intuitions without concepts are blind'.[33]

Suppose we define metaphysics as the attempt to have theoretical knowledge of things that are not 'in front of our senses' and thus not in space and time (Kant sometimes calls such 'things' the 'supersensible'). It follows from the above that such metaphysics is impossible philosophy. But the understanding still makes possible *a priori* knowledge, within this much more limited realm of the 'sensible'. The understanding, in its spontaneity, is able to anticipate certain key structures of the natural (sensible or intuitable) world. 'Making possible' such knowledge has the strange, disorienting implication that *the basic features of nature or the world do not 'belong' to nature originally, but belong first to the mind* which contemplates nature, and thus can be known 'prior' to experience of nature. This is Kant's 'transcendental idealism'. He writes that 'we can know *a priori* of things only what we ourselves put into them'.[34] That is why, again, Kant is not an empiricist. Yet these 'basic features' of the world are very broad – we find Kant writing at length about classic philosophical problems like substance or causality – and thus do not say anything yet about particular objects like plants or stones. There is still plenty of need for empirical knowledge.

The understanding can make possible knowledge *a priori* because it is the source of the categories. But above, we said that the understanding only applies properly to intuitions. So intuitions too must be *a priori* if there is to be *a priori* knowledge. Kant argues that we have available to us *a priori* intuitions of space and time. Thus, pure intuition is included as a higher though passive aspect of sensibility in the list of faculties above. This is the other half of Kant's transcendental idealism: a material thing is not, for example, three-dimensional because that is the way it is 'in itself', but rather because that is the way that I, as a human being, apprehend things. How it is 'in itself' is unknown and unknowable. Just as the basic concepts of nature or the world are provided by my understanding in order that they may then be 'discovered' within my experiences of the world, so space and time are features of my human manner of intuiting in order that things might be encountered in space or in time. For Kant, it follows from his transcendental idealism that underlying all these sensible and cognitive appearances [*Erscheinungen*] will be something entirely unexperiencable and unknowable. He has a number of approximately equivalent expressions for such a realm: thing-in-itself, noumenon, supersensible, intelligible.

Above all, this does not mean that what I experience is *mere illusion* [*Schein*] – Kant's word 'appearances' might seem to suggest this. On the contrary, space and time are indeed 'transcendentally ideal' – that is, they have their origin 'in the mind' – but they are nevertheless 'empirically real'.[35] We live, act and think, all the time, in the realm of appearance – how more real and objective can you get? All our knowledge, and it really is knowledge, pertains to this empirical reality. Hence Kant's famous and startling result, that this transcendental provision of the categories and pure intuitions is that which uniquely guarantees the objectivity of my experience, thus making experience of the world or nature possible for me. With its access to both the categories and to *a priori* intuitions, the understanding is able to anticipate (or, from another point of view, legislate for) – and make possible for us the experience of – the basic law-governed structure of nature. The anticipation of nature is 'higher' theoretical cognition.[36] The understanding, together with sensibility, are thus the *a priori* conditions of the possibility of experience. (This also explains why 'lower' faculties are of so little interest to Kant: as 'lower' they are determined by the natural world, which in turn is legislated for through the higher faculty of theoretical cognition.)

SUMMARY: Kant's transcendental philosophy is a search for the *a priori* conditions of certain basic phenomena, such as our experience of the world. Critical philosophy – deciding, for a faculty, the range of legitimacy (or of sense) – can only be done transcendentally. However, it turns out in the *Critique of Pure Reason* that reason is not constitutive of any knowledge, and that if this is forgotten, reason produces a number of philosophically dangerous illusions. Thus, a purely rational metaphysics is impossible. However, the negative evaluation is not the end of the story. Only the understanding is constitutive for theoretical cognition, and then only within its critical limits, that is only for sensibility.

Deduction and Dialectic

So far, this 'anticipation' is just a fascinating and bizarre story. Like the list of faculties, we have no reason to believe it to be anything but a fiction. But Kant of course believes that he has proof of his transcendental idealism. A number of arguments are provided throughout the book and elsewhere – in particular there is one for each of those principles governing the use of the categories. However, one of the key arguments is contained in a lengthy and infamous passage entitled the Transcendental Deduction. It is a transcendental argument, but of a particularly broad generality. Kant had already identified a list of abstract concepts called categories, which he believed were the basic forms of the faculty of understanding. But he had not yet fully proved that these concepts were *a priori*, rather than merely abstracted *from and after* our ordinary experience. And even if they were *a priori*, he could not be sure that they also formed the transcendental conditions of the understanding: they could be concepts that, though *a priori*, just loiter in the mind not doing very much for us. Kant expresses this question with a famous legal metaphor: why should we believe that the categories have 'jurisdiction' over our understanding of the world?[37]

To complicate matters, the Transcendental Deduction comes in two versions, because Kant rewrote it in 1787 for the second edition of his book. For simplicity, we will only discuss the second (called the 'B') version. Here, Kant introduces the notion of the *transcendental unity of apperception*, which is the principle that governs the possibility of any experience whatsoever, by any subject whatsoever. The unity of apperception simply states that all experience must be one experience, and all subjective consciousness must be similarly unified across its various experiences. He then proves that the demand of this principle can be realised if, and only if, the categories are the instruments of unification of all our experiences. The categories function as the rules of the various synthetic acts which unify our experience, and with it, our apperception. Kant thus claims to have proved that both experience in general as an experience of one world, and our sense of self as one self would not be possible without *a priori* concepts of the understanding. Since we are clearly capable of having such experiences, and since we clearly have a functioning sense of self-identity, there must be these concepts. Moreover, they must be the conditions of *any* possible use of understanding. This establishes their validity. Kant can then legitimately ask how they function in our experience and knowledge of nature (that is, what more particular principles govern the individual categories).

In this way, the *Critique of Pure Reason* involves two main parts.[38] The first, called the Transcendental Analytic, is an analysis of our mental ability to achieve theoretical cognition, which consists of the higher cognitive faculties of understanding (together with higher sensibility). The analysis reveals the transcendental concepts and their principles which underlie all cognition, and also supplies proofs of the necessary role of those principles in the cognition of nature. The second, called the Transcendental Dialectic, is a critical analysis of our mental ability to reason, which yields the unexpected result that pure reason, on its own, cannot contribute to theoretical cognition. If reason tries to put across its supersensible results as cognition of nature, the result is pure nonsense. Kant calls this nonsense in general 'illusion'. (Such illusions take several particular forms, depending upon the structure of reasoning involved; one that is important for the *Critique of Judgement* is called 'Antinomy'.) This whole structure will reappear in the *Critique of Judgement*: it too will have an Analytic (two, actually: one for the beautiful, one for the sublime), and a Dialectic, including an Antinomy, and it will incorporate a Deduction. Kant is claiming that this structure is part of the methodology of any critical philosophy.

To return to the *Critique of Pure Reason*, however, the negative claim about reason producing dialectical illusions is not the end of the story. This is for three reasons. First, reason does produce, of its own accord, what Kant calls 'ideas'. These ideas – of, for example, God or freedom – do not produce any possible knowledge; they are in other words not legislative or constitutive for theoretical cognition. To claim that they do so would be to pursue the metaphysical nonsense discussed above. However, the dialectic does demonstrate that these ideas have a certain indeterminate possibility – we *also* cannot have knowledge of the *non-existence* of such objects! This claim is made more strongly in the Antinomies section: there, the positing of the supersensible in some relation to the sensible was the critical solution to the antinomies. For example, Kant can now claim that freedom is *only* intelligible if we assume a supersensible ground of the human subject. This notion will become increasingly important in Chapter 3 of this book onwards.

The second reason is that the ideas (however 'hypothetical' they may in themselves be) do guide or, as Kant puts it, 'regulate' investigation by the understanding. For example, these supersensible ideas always make us unsatisfied with whatever scientific knowledge we achieve, not because that knowledge fails to explain something, but because it fails to explain *everything*. It falls short of the 'idea' of an absolutely complete knowledge. By way of its demand for the fulfilment of its idea of the totality of our cognitive grasp, reason thus compels us to 'keep going' in our search for systems in nature. The Holy Grail of modern physics since Einstein – a unified field theory – is a perfect example of this. Seen in this limited way, and only in this way, the ideas of reason are not nonsense for the understanding.

The third and most important reason is that in our characterisation of critique as sorting out sense from nonsense, we defined 'sense' too narrowly. We said that something makes sense if it *could be* true or false when applied to the world. But this definition is relevant to one and only one of the mental faculties: theoretical cognition. It may be that reason *is* a source of something that makes sense – *on reason's own terms*, if not for the understanding. In other words, that reason is, after all, legislative.

SUMMARY: The transcendental functioning of sensibility (especially intuition and imagination) and understanding, together and only together, make possible any experience (and thus cognition) of the world. Kant's attempt to demonstrate this famous thesis is called the Transcendental Deduction. This deduction, like any transcendental argument, works by showing that if a given concept were not valid according to a principle, then a certain type of experience (which we obviously have) would not be possible. Reason has no constitutive role in knowledge, and if it attempts to make for itself such a role, then the result is dialectical illusion. However, the ideas of reason have a *regulative* role which spurs us on towards the completeness of our knowledge.

The Legislations of Reason and Judgement

What kind of 'sense' might be appropriate to reason? Recall that in the list of faculties, Kant asserts that the proper *legislative* area for reason is not cognition of nature, but free or pure desire. Reason determines desire to follow practical (that is, moral) law, and to act towards the Good. Thus, Kant's *Critique of Practical Reason* attempts to discover the transcendental conditions for our practical reason. If desire is pure, then there must be an *a priori* principle guiding it, and that principle will be absolutely in advance of any psychological or physiological compulsion which makes as want to do this or do that. That is, such an *a priori* principle pertains to our 'freedom', and such a desire is 'free'. Kant calls such desire 'good' or 'moral'. So the study of practical reason is the study of the *a priori* principle that legislates for free ethical action: what we ought or ought not to do, but are not compelled to do by any natural condition. Our morality must originate in a 'place' that is outside nature, because all natural things are governed by natural laws, especially the law of cause and effect (otherwise, there could be no science). But freedom is precisely *exemption* from natural law. The production of the *a priori* principle which obligates pure and free desire is thus the appropriate legislative use of reason.

Similarly, the *Critique of Judgement* will begin by saying that we all have the ability to make judgements about things, and that this entails judgement having some kind of *a priori* principle of its own. According to the table on p. 10, in aesthetic judgements, this principle governs the activity of judgement so as to legislate for the faculty of feeling. The critical questions are: first, what is this principle; and second, what are the limits placed upon what judgement can achieve with this principle? This question is answered through a transcendental analysis of the conditions of the possibility of judging. The critique will provide an understanding of how judgement can happen at all with respect to, for example, fine art. We will return to all these issues in more detail below.

'Critique' must always proceed by giving a *transcendental analysis* of whatever is undergoing critique; and it is systematic to the extent that it analyses one by one all the faculties in all their inter-relations. So, in understanding Kant's philosophy as a whole, we are understanding a method of analysis (transcendental philosophy) as applied to a comprehensive critique of the forms of thought, feeling and action that belong universally to human beings.

In addition to the all-important ideas of critique, faculty and the transcendental, we now have a new idea which will prove important for understanding Kant's account of judgement and its place in critical philosophy. This is the distinction between (1) 'theoretical' philosophy[39], which can only deal with the conditions of theoretical cognition (or in other words, provide principles formally legislative with respect to 'sensible' things in nature) and (2) 'practical' philosophy, which can only provide principles legislative for the pure desire of 'supersensible' (free) things, that is, human beings insofar as in our freedom we are capable of moral action. The former deals with the transcendental analysis of mental abilities insofar as they may contribute to our experience of the world. The latter deals with the transcendental analysis of mental abilities insofar as they yield *a priori* moral law. As we have seen, these are the subjects of the first and second *Critiques*, respectively. But what then is the relation between theoretical and practical philosophy? Not surprisingly, it turns out that the third *Critique* (the *Critique of Judgement*) takes just this question as one of its main topics.

At the end of the *Critique of Pure Reason*, Kant explores the implications of his work (thus far) for both the methodology and the true scope of philosophy. These sections were written for the 1781 edition, and not revised in 1787. By 1790, Kant's overall conception of critical philosophy has slightly altered. In our survey of Kant's philosophy, we will draw attention to just one key point Kant makes here. For Kant, the practical interest or function of reason is the higher interest of human rationality. It is the 'whole vocation'[40] of man to act in accordance with moral law, and thus to bring about what he calls the 'moral world'.[41] The purpose of theoretical/speculative reason (to discover systematic and complete knowledge of all possible objects) is indeed essential to that aspect of our rationality, but with respect to reason as a whole – with respect to human beings as rational entities – it is a 'subsidiary' end.[42] The purpose of knowledge of nature is to facilitate moral action. The ultimate purpose even of the ideas of pure speculative reason – beyond their regulative value for systems of knowledge – is for their objects to be posited as the *necessary prerequisites of morality*. Freedom of the will, Kant claims, is obviously the first of these. The immortality of the soul is required such that there is guaranteed to be an indefinite future for the 'moral world' to be realised. And the existence of a God is required as the 'Supreme Reason'[43] that guarantees that the moral world is actually possible, in other words, that moral action and natural law can entirely converge. (This latter thesis is developed in much greater detail in the second half of the *Critique of Judgement* – see Chapter 5). None of these requirements is knowledge, but they are, Kant argues, postulates logically connected to – and thus of as high a degree of conviction as – my belief that I am at least capable of acting morally.

In one sense, none of these ideas is modified in the *Critique of Judgement*, but by then Kant had noticed an additional problem. In the earlier work, Kant does not see the connection between theoretical/speculative philosophy and practical philosophy to be a problem, or at least not so worrying a problem as to require a volume of critical philosophy. Nor does he see it thus in the second *Critique* in 1788. This connection seems to be soluble without the mediation of the third party, but once a problem of the unity of philosophy, and thus of the human faculties is discovered, then a solution is urgently needed. And finding a way to harmonise all the faculties so that their ultimate purpose can in fact be a fulfilment of man's 'moral vocation' is exactly the overall problem of the *Critique of Judgement*.

SUMMARY: Reason has a 'sense' of its own, and in this case is called 'practical reason' to the extent that it is also legislative for the faculty of desire. The principle of this legislation is the moral law. (Similarly, judgement as a cognitive faculty legislates in aesthetic judgement for the faculty of feeling.) The difference between the legislations of the understanding and of reason forms the basic Kantian distinction between the theoretical philosophy of nature, and the practical philosophy of being free for the law. But are these two realms entirely separate? Is there nothing which makes a transition from the one to the other?

The Basic Issues of the *Critique of Judgement*

The *Critique of Judgement* explores what *a priori* 'principles' might lie in our ability to *judge* things – that is, which 'principles' are transcendental conditions for that ability. On this basis, Kant wishes to explore the proper place of judgement, and thus the limits of sense and nonsense in our judgement. We will be seeing several examples of transcendental arguments which are designed to reveal the transcendental conditions which make any act of judging possible.

What is Meant by 'Judgement'?

Above, we gave a brief definition of judgement. Now, we need to add detail to this picture. Judgement is always a coordinating faculty with respect to other cognitive faculties. For example, a scientific judgement receives its concept from the understanding, and applies that concept to sensibility. A moral judgement receives its concept of, say, virtue or guilt, from practical reason and seeks to apply it again to some sensible particular. Judgement, then, is a general phenomenon; a judgement happens every time we think something about something. As we shall see, Kant focuses on two particular types of judgement: aesthetic and teleological judgements, both of which are distinctive by being 'reflective'.

In the Introduction to his *Critique of Judgement*, Kant makes a set of distinctions between various types of judgement in general. Although he never lays them out quite in this way, in order to identify all the problems that he wishes to work on, he needs five types of judgement. The first he calls determinate (also sometimes translated as 'determinative') judgement, which consists of the application of something well-known and general (a 'concept') to a given object or situation: 'If the universal (the rule, principle, or law) is given, then judgement which subsumes the particular under it, *is determinant*' (Introduction IV, translation modified). For example, in judging distances, we have a well-known situation or thing in advance of the judgement, either from practical experiences such as tying shoelaces, or from the algebraic counting of unit-lengths such as metres. It is therefore a question of seeing whether the given particular thing or situation matches up to our concept. Kant says that the concept then 'determines' the thing as this or that ('too far away', 'exactly three metres', and so on). Through the concept, this determination has validity beyond the precise situation in which it is formed. Other people can come along and, using the same concept, judge again whether my judgement was correct. Of course, in some situations, the 'matching-up' need not be exact, while in other cases, the 'matching-up' should be as mathematically exact as possible, for example, if we are measuring whether someone has broken a long-jump record. Part of my well-known concept will be just how exact the matching-up process has to be.

A second type Kant calls 'indeterminate' judgement. In this case, the object or situation is quite new to me, and I have no well-known concept in advance. Instead, I have to come up with a new concept in order to perform the judgement. In the *Critique of Pure Reason*, the Transcendental Analytic proved, claims Kant, that our ability to understand the world and thus attain knowledge would not be possible without the principled application of transcendental concepts such as unity, necessity, or cause and effect. Thus, whenever we try to understand anything in the world, these concepts will already be there, making that world intelligible for us. But precisely because these few concepts function transcendentally for *all* experience, they outline the range of all possible understandings and reasonings in very broad brush strokes. They will never have much to say about the particular detail of real empirical experiences. Thus, we have to form empirical concepts in the course of ordinary experience. But how? If ever we want to move from a given experience to a new concept – one we have not come across before – then the type of judgement involved will be quite different from the determinate type. Such a judgement Kant calls 'indeterminate', and its job is to discover new concepts.

Imagine, for example, that a botanist working somewhere remote discovers a new species of wildflower. This will involve several determinate judgements: determining that the plant is indeed a plant according to the well-known concept of 'plant', and that it belongs to this botanical family and that genus. But because the species is new to the botanist, there will be no concept for it at that level. In creating the concept, the botanist reflects upon the specific differences of this species *vis à vis* other flowers in the same genus. The formation of the judgement ('This is . . .') and the creation of the new concept are thus the same activity. It is important to realise that the fact that the botanist invents the concept does not mean that it is arbitrary. Just like a fully determinate judgement, these indeterminate judgements have wider validity.

The third type of judgement Kant calls 'teleological judgement'. Consider a living organism. Biological science quite naturally takes the organism to be a set of cells or organs, each of which is a straightforward cause of some quite separate function. These functions together keep each of the cells or organs alive. There is, in an important sense, no living organism at all, just a heart, two lungs, a stomach, and so on, and the various separate, specialised cells that make them up. But, despite all this, it is difficult not to see the organism itself, as a whole, as the main thing – the thing that is truly alive – and the cells and organs subserviently organised by that pre-existing sense of the whole as purpose. In other words, the whole organism appears as if it had been 'designed' as an elaborate active structure for creating and sustaining the whole. This latter attitude is a teleological judgement: seeing organisms 'caused' by their *telos* (purpose), the completed and whole form. Thus, teleological judgement happens when we judge something to have been produced according to an idea of it, but where this judgement is at odds with the way that object is 'naturally' and determinately judged. In the second half of his book, Kant will go to great lengths discussing this issue, its possibility and limited but important range of validity (see Chapter 5).

The fourth type Kant calls 'aesthetic judgement'. Here, I not have a well-known concept in advance, but in addition the situation is such that I also must judge without forming a new concept either. In order to form the judgement, it is as if I am 'thrown back' entirely onto my own resources as a thinking subject. This case is like an extreme version of the 'indeterminate' one; as is, Kant claims, the teleological judgement.[44] Kant calls both the aesthetic and the teleological judgements 'reflective' to indicate that a determining concept (which accords with the principles of the understanding) never enters the equation.[45] Aesthetic judgements are about things we call 'beautiful', or some other aesthetic category (such as 'sublime'). Such things include art.[46] In saying whether a novel is 'great' or not, it would seem that I had a well-known concept of 'greatness', and was applying it to a particular novel. But this, Kant says, is not the case. If I had such a concept, I would be able to give a set of rigorous criteria, with which everyone could agree, for that novel – and any novel – being 'great'. But in centuries of discussion concerning novels, this has proven extremely difficult to do. After all this time, it is perhaps not unduly pessimistic to give up the chase.[47] In the case of a concept such as how to tie one's shoes, although it includes inexactitudes in some areas, we can nevertheless pin down very clear criteria in other areas (exactly two loops, exactly two loose ends, and so on). But no concept can be thoroughly inexact in all areas. My judgement about beauty does not follow or produce a concept, but takes place by way of *feeling* – the feeling of pleasure in the beautiful.

Certainly, I can say other things about the novel that are less indeterminate. I can claim that it was 257 pages long, a very determinate judgement indeed. But insofar as I am judging it as *art* (as having that peculiar kind of literary value that seems to be named by 'great'), then the judgement is 'aesthetic', and neither has nor invents a concept. 'Greatness' in novels only names a set of individual judgements (this novel, that novel, are great), but has in itself no determining content.

However, it might appear that other judgements which are not about art behave in a similar way. Suppose I am ordering my dinner in a restaurant. My taste in food can be different to that of my dining companion; so, we certainly have in advance no concept of taste or of 'good-tasting food' in general, nor do we form one. Moreover, my taste may even differ now from yesterday or tomorrow: I just get pleasure from certain foods at certain times, and displeasure from others. None of these situations causes us any philosophical problems, however. We just call the judgement entirely subjective, and its validity belongs uniquely to the person who makes it, when he makes it. This is the fifth type of judgement Kant describes, which he calls judgements of sensual 'interest'.[48] So, perhaps what Kant calls 'aesthetic judgements' are really just entirely subjective judgements of sensual interest, which is exactly what important traditions in eighteenth-century aesthetics claimed.

It is essential to Kant to demonstrate that this is *not* the case. Aesthetic judgements are not subjective in this sense; they have a 'wider' validity. However, in every other case of judgements that have a wider validity, this is because of the existence or creation of a stable, determinate concept. Using that concept, different judges can come to the same conclusions in different circumstances. Here in aesthetic judgements, however, we have a judgement that both has wider validity *and* has neither a well-known concept in advance, nor produces one in the act of judging. How can such a judgement happen? Or, in other words: what *does* happen when I, for example, feel a novel to be, and call it 'great' – or a sunset 'beautiful', or the mountain range 'sublime'? This *particular* problem occupies Kant for much of the first half of his book. We might add that he was among the first to discover, describe and discuss this problem – and certainly his way of treating it is utterly original. (We will return to these issues in Chapter 1.)

Furthermore, however, this particular problem serves Kant as a mode of entry to a larger, more general and, he thinks, more important philosophical problem. This is the problem of the 'unity' of all philosophy. He sees judgement as being at the very centre of philosophy, capable of unifying it. This is the issue we first raised at the end of the previous section (see p. 25).

We have now explained how a book of which more than half is about aesthetics, and which since Kant's day has been widely read as a book *essentially* about aesthetics, came to have a title which makes no mention of aesthetics. Nor is this information irrelevant, a bit of historical trivia. On the contrary, we will never understand Kant's aesthetics unless we understand why he felt it necessary to provide an analysis of judgement per se, and also why it was necessary to give an analysis of this type (that is, a transcendental analysis). Of course, Kant has much to say about aesthetics, and much that is of continuing relevance. But when we look more carefully at Kant's analyses, we will find again and again that we must return to the more general topics we have just discussed.

SUMMARY: A 'judgement' is a mental act which in some way decides whether a thing is this or that. But there seem to be different types of judgement. A 'determinate' judgement is one that has a concept in advance and simply applies it to a thing. An 'indeterminate' judgement is one that creates the concept in the same act as making the judgement. A judgement of sensual interest works on the basis of my entirely subjective tastes. A teleological judgement sees the holism of a living organism in terms of purposes and not in terms of the straightforward cause and effect relations of natural science. Finally, an aesthetic judgement judges a thing (such as an alpine meadow, or a novel) to be of aesthetic value. The last two types function in peculiar ways: they neither have, nor create, a determining natural concept of the thing; nor are they *entirely* subjective in their validity.

Judgements with these characteristics (teleological or aesthetic) Kant calls 'reflective'. This explains why a book about judgement should have so much to say about aesthetics. Reflective judgements are important for Kant because they involve the judgement doing a job in some way *for and from itself*, rather than relying on some externally determinate concept. These cases therefore might be the place to search for judgement's *a priori* legislating principle. Kant's particular problem in the first half of his book is to discover how aesthetic judgements are possible.

An *A Priori* Principle for Judgement?

Why should we believe that such an ability to judge requires some *a priori* principle in order to function? This question Kant has to answer, and he does so in several different ways.

Kant gives a number of transcendental arguments in this book and even a Deduction (beginning at §30), the purpose of which is to prove the validity of the principle for judgement. We will discuss the Deduction at length in Chapter 2. For the moment, let us look at two other transcendental arguments he offers. In general, he tries to show that reflective judgements of one type or other would not be possible without an *a priori* principle for the judgement.

Section V of Kant's Introduction provides one version of a proof that judgement must have an *a priori* principle. The natural sciences require indeterminate judgements (which Kant here considers reflective) which 'invent' new concepts. If we already had all the concepts we needed to understand the natural world, we would not need to do basic scientific research. Moreover, we must assume that the various empirical observations we make will come together to allow us to discover laws of nature within them, and also that the various laws of nature (laws of biology, motion, magnetism, and so on) are neither infinite in number nor entirely separated from each other, but relate to one another in a comprehensible, systematic fashion that is, as a whole, capable of being grasped by human cognition. That is, they too must converge and science, insofar as we humans have the mental capacity to carry it out must have an end-point. Thus, the assumption must be made that nature itself has a certain purposiveness (also translated 'finality') with respect to our ability to have cognition of it. What is meant by 'purposiveness' or the related notion of 'purpose' (or 'end')?

For Kant, 'purpose' means: 'A thing that is aimed at by way of a concept of it'. Thus, 'purpose' in the sense of the expression 'I had a something *in mind*, and I did it'. The completed section of this book is a purpose, and I am writing it (causing it to happen) through a concept I have of it. Purposiveness (or, again, finality) means roughly 'the property of having been produced according to a concept'. This finished book is 'purposive' (or 'final') meaning that it was produced by me in accordance with a concept of it. Moreover, something is purposive if it is on the way to some further purpose; thus we say that someone striding quickly across a street is 'acting purposefully'. (We will return to the notions of purpose and purposiveness in more detail in Chapter 2.)

Returning to Kant's argument, he is saying that for there to be any point to empirical science, it has to be assumed that nature – insofar as it is governed by a set of empirical laws – exists *as if* it were made for the human understanding. Nature is assumed to be purposive by our judgement, in the sense of being on the way toward something. This, then, is an *a priori* principle of judgement. Of course, we are talking about a principle of judgement here, not the understanding. So this principle does not provide *knowledge* about nature: thus the 'as if' above. Rather, it 'only represents the unique mode in which we must proceed in our reflection upon the objects of nature with a view to getting a thoroughly interconnected whole of experience' (Introduction V). Thus Kant writes, concerning the Swedish scientist Linnaeus who pioneered the principles of modern classification in the natural sciences,

> One may wonder whether Linnaeus could have hoped to design a system of nature if he had had to worry that a stone which he found, and which he called granite, might differ in its inner character from any other stone even if it looked the same, so that all he could ever hope to find would be single things – isolated, as it were, for the understanding – but never a class of them that could be brought under concepts of genera and species.
>
> (First Introduction, Vn)

The principle acts as a *necessary assumption*, which could never itself be proved scientifically, for any scientific judgement whatsoever. As Kant puts it, without this principle, 'the understanding could not find its way about in nature' (Introduction VIII).[49]

But how does this argument about the possibility of science relate to beauty? For Kant, scientific judgements are nothing but exacting versions of ordinary judgements – thus he is still talking about judgement in general. If judgement in general can be demonstrated to have an *a priori* principle, then it seems likely that aesthetic judgements (as a kind of sub-class) must also. However, there are still important differences between ordinary (potentially scientific) judgements and aesthetic (as well as teleological) judgements. So we still have to discover if and how the purposiveness of nature might inform the latter.

The second argument is contained in the main body of Kant's text, but is alluded to in Kant's introduction. We will introduce it here, but we will discuss the various versions of it more fully in Chapters 1 and 2, because it merges with Kant's Deduction. This argument works by way of an analysis of the observed features of reflective judgements. If such judgements are entirely empirical, then one would expect that the results of the judgement would be contingent; that is, the judgements that I form and the judgements that you form will be different, and if they appear to be the same, it is a kind of accident. We do often disagree about art, for example, but then a transcendental principle would not prevent all empirical disagreements. Kant's point is rather that such judgements are *communicable* – I may disagree with you, but we assume from the start that *at bottom* we both mean the same thing by, for example, 'beauty'. Moreover, it does not seem impossible for us to discuss and explain to each other at least some of the reasons for our different judgement. Kant argues that this communication of judgements would be impossible without a transcendental principle for judgement.

Another version of this argument begins by noting again that not all reflective judgements result in a concept. There are certain types of reflective judgement where the judgement precisely *fails* to come up with an adequate concept for the thing being judged (it only comes up with a feeling of pleasure or pain). These are judgements about, above all, natural or artistic *beauty*. In such cases, and despite or even because of this failure, such judgements are not only communicable but even claim to be universal. That is, my judgement that 'This landscape is beautiful' does *not* mean that I can exhaustively identify, according to a concept, what *makes it beautiful*, but my judgement nevertheless comes with the expectation that others will agree with me. Or if they do not agree, one of us is, in some sense, wrong. The judgement of taste demands – but does not necessarily *expect* – assent. Again, would this be possible without a transcendental principle behind the ability to judge? Aesthetic judgements, despite being radically subjective as we have described above, nevertheless claim as a matter of course 'universal assent', just as if they were objective judgements about real things in the world. This must mean that they are not as 'subjective' as they appear. Or rather, that here is another transcendental *a priori* principle, like those of the understanding for example, but one that legislates for a feeling in the subject rather than for a world of objects. Because this principle is both *a priori* and operating transcendentally, the 'subjectivity' in question is no longer in the sense of 'you or I, as individual beings'. Rather, it must mean a transcendental subjectivity that you and I necessarily share.

Clearly, such a transcendental subjectivity – as *part of* the *a priori* conditions of being human – belongs to anthropology (the study of humans) conceived in the broadest and most fundamental sense. Suppose, however, that this transcendental subjectivity as we called it were of a particular generality. That is, suppose that what grounds the aesthetic judgement were in fact a kind of expression of the *essence* of that which grounds all objective cognition of nature (the understanding together with sensibility). Moreover, suppose that the grounds of aesthetic judgement could be shown to have essential links to the grounds of our moral and political being as well. Then this transcendental subjectivity, although it started out as specific to aesthetic judgements, would no longer form just another 'part of' a fundamental anthropology. Rather, it would make a claim to being among the most fundamental features of such an anthropology. In that case, if we return to the four questions from Kant's *Logic* with which we began, the subjectivity that grounds aesthetic judgement, as a fundamental anthropology, would complete and even enclose the other three basic questions of philosophy. It would be well on the way to demonstrating the unity of philosophy itself. Kant is going to make (although sometimes only implicitly) just this series of claims.

That aesthetic judgement should both rely upon a universal principle, and seek universal assent for its results, partly explains what Kant means in saying that judgement legislates for the higher faculty of feeling. The beautiful gives me a feeling of pleasure. My feelings, as we discussed on p. 11, are feelings for the activity of my living being; life means to be able to act upon desires. Normally, my feelings have to do with bodily activities, like the feeling of hunger for example. What might improve that state, and give me pleasure, is entirely subjective. A doughnut might do nicely. I feel pleasure in the beautiful, and pleasure in a doughnut – what exactly is the difference? In proposing aesthetic feeling as a *higher* feeling, Kant is claiming that there can be an *a priori* principle – a principle that is prior to any such individual or corporeal concern – even for feeling.

Briefly, he explains this in the following way (see, in particular, his Introduction VI and VII): feeling (by way of the concept of life as activity) is related to the attainment of purposes, or at least the expectation of such attainment. Thus, any situation wherein we judge the purpose to be attained, or to be expected, will produce pleasure. Normally, this attainment has to do with lower feeling: satisfying my hunger is a purpose, a doughnut is the means. Such pleasure is entirely subjective and has no validity beyond my doughnut eating. Reflective judgement, however, gives itself an *a priori* principle of the purposiveness of nature of cognition. If such a judgement found itself in a situation where this principle was apparently corroborated in an intuition – here is nature apparently organised to our benefit – then that too would give pleasure, and it would be a pleasure universally valid for all judging subjects. Nature presenting itself to me as *generally* purposive for cognition is exactly what Kant means by the beautiful. The beautiful therefore enhances my feeling of life because, through the focused cognitive activity that Kant calls 'contemplation', it presents itself as in general accord with my purposes as a cognitive being.

SUMMARY: The critical and transcendental question concerning judgement is whether judgement has within itself a legislative principle. The principle in question asserts the suitability or purposiveness of all nature for our faculty of judgement. Kant offers a number of arguments to prove the existence and validity of this principle. First, he claims that without such a principle, science (as a systematic, orderly and unified conception of nature) would not be possible. Secondly, he argues that without such a principle our judgements about beauty would not exhibit the communicability, or tendency to universality even in the absence of a concept, that they do. This second argument will be more thoroughly dealt with in Chapters 1 and 2. Insofar as aesthetic judgements will be demonstrated to rely upon *a priori* grounds in the human subject, and insofar also as these grounds are closely related to the grounds both of theoretical and practical cognition, then the study of aesthetic judgements might constitute the fundamental anthropology Kant seeks to unify philosophy.

The Role of Judgement in Philosophy

Kant calls judgement the 'mediating link' between the understanding (the faculty that legislates for knowledge of nature, theoretical philosophy) and reason (as the faculty legislating for desire, thus practical philosophy) (Introduction III). As we suggested above, judgement might therefore be important for discovering the unity of all philosophy.

Theoretical philosophy has as its proper object things that are natural or sensible; practical philosophy has freedom, which is supernatural or supersensible. This latter concept means that freedom, as such, is an impossible object of sensible or natural intuition. Everything we intuit is (indeed, must be, according to Kant) not free in some fundamental sense. Philosophy has these two parts, theoretical and practical; each has its own distinct domain [*Gebiet*] of concepts and objects. However, Kant says,

> [U]nderstanding and reason – have two different legislations over one and the same territory of experience. – Now, although these two different domains do not restrict each other in their legislation, they do restrict each other incessantly in the effects that their legislation has in the world of sense. Why do these two domains not form *one* domain?
>
> (Introduction II)

Practical philosophy is the study of the concept of, and implications of, freedom, which again belongs outside the natural world. But, clearly, practical philosophy must in some sense *also* refer to the natural world, because that is where our moral or immoral actions take place and have their effect. Freedom, and the moral law, would be powerless unless they could change real, sensible things (at the very least, our bodies) and help to bring about their purpose (and, ultimately, what Kant calls the Highest Good). So, although the two have distinct 'realms', these are in one and the same territory, namely the sensible world. The relationship between these two faculties, and thus the unity of the philosophy which studies them, would seem to be inherently a problem. The 'moral vocation' of man is his 'ultimate purpose' (see p. 11), and this relies upon the coordination of these faculties towards that purpose. But it is not clear that this coordination is even possible. Thus, this problem is both the *most important* and the *last* problem of critical philosophy.

Why should we suspect that judgement might be the bridge between these two parts of philosophy? There are two reasons. First, simply because judgement is the only possibility left. If neither of the first two types of philosophical thought can bridge the gap on their own, then it has to be judgement, or nothing at all. But this relies on the validity of Kant's list of faculties, which in one sense is precisely what requires proof. The other more important and more complex reason we will discuss in detail in Chapter 5; for the moment, we will just make a few suggestions.

The key idea, obviously, will be judgement's *a priori* legislative principle of the purposiveness of nature. Now, the experience of a purpose achieved (or anticipated) is linked to the feeling of pleasure and pain (Introduction VI). We get satisfaction from seeing things done – out there in nature, or in here, in our nature. But our faculty of desire is also motivated by the anticipation of pleasure or at least by present pain. Thus, a natural concept of a purpose (such as eating a doughnut) is linked to practical action (obtaining and actually eating a doughnut) by way of anticipated pleasure or present pain (hunger). If judgement is in fact the legislating cognitive faculty for the faculty of feeling, then it will be the mediator (at least at the sensible level) between concepts of nature and practical action (Introduction III).

But as yet that is a superficial understanding of the link, which focuses only on our subjective sensible response, and does not really touch practical reason at all.[50] The real bridge spans, so to speak, a deeper river, and Kant alludes to this bridge in Introduction IX. Very briefly, Kant needs to find a way to make comprehensible the fact that the two different parts of philosophy (theoretical and practical) must pertain to the sensible world. This can be the case, he claims, only if it turns out that nature must be seen (from a certain perspective) as *itself* heading in the direction of the final purpose, the attainment of the highest good. In other words, nature must be seen as purposive with respect to the purposes given by freedom. Since judgement provides the principle of nature's purposiveness in general, it will be judgement that brings the two parts together. We will return to such issues throughout the book, and discuss the manner in which Kant believes they provide a solution to the unity of philosophy in Chapter 5. This bridge and the systematic unity of philosophy it offers, are clearly important for Kant. As we saw above in the passage from the *Logic*, this co-ordination of the various branches of philosophy according to the final purpose of human beings is one of the criteria for a satisfactory philosophy of this world.

All this talk of judgement as the bridge or transition also means that judgements about beauty and other such judgements are not just isolated events. Aesthetics is not a kind of frivolous branch of philosophy, and art has a meaning or purpose beyond just being pleasant, or being the vehicle for the communication of fairly ordinary ideas. On the contrary, all these are essentially linked to the most basic questions, such as the very possibility of knowledge, the nature of morality, or what it means to be human.

Of course, Kant's book will raise dozens of other interesting philosophical issues along the way: the nature of art, science, genius, religion, faith, culture, freedom, and morality, to mention a few. Indeed, for many philosophers, Kant's explicit purpose is a a non-starter, and the real importance of the book is the light it sheds on one or another of these problems. Nevertheless, as we explore its riches, it is worthwhile keeping in mind this explicit overarching purpose to the *Critique of Judgement*. For only this overarching purpose, however obscure it might turn out to be, can allow us to see the book as a whole rather than just a collection of interesting, isolated observations.[51]

SUMMARY: Judgement, Kant claims, forms the mediating link between the two great branches of philosophical enquiry: the theoretical (legislated for by the understanding) and the practical (legislated for by reason). These two philosophies, paradoxically, have as their 'object' the same sensible nature. Kant's solution to this enigma will involve investigating the implications of judgement's principle of the purposiveness of nature. This mediating link is important in order for philosophy to be unified in its purpose by coordination towards the final or highest purpose of man.

The Structure of Kant's Book

Kant's *Critique of Judgement* has a peculiar structure. The reason for this is that Kant fails to mark significant new divisions in the book in any formal way. It is therefore easy to lose one's way in the text. In particular, the Deduction (§30) and all of the miscellaneous problems (especially the problem of fine art) which follow it are included in the 'Analytic of the Sublime', which as we shall see makes little or no sense. It is best to treat them as if they were 'Books 3 and 4' of Division 1 of the text.

The following breakdown of the structure is not by section, but rather by topic, and is included as an aid to following Kant's argument and the coordination of his themes. The structure of the book is as follows:

Preface

Introduction, Section I–IX
I–II	The division of philosophy and the problem of its unity
III	Judgement as possible 'solution' to this problem
IV–VI	Judgement as legislating *a priori*, and its principle of purposiveness
VII–VIII	Aesthetic and logical (teleological) purposiveness
IX	Judgement as 'solution' to this problem

Part 1: Critique of aesthetic judgement
  Division 1: Analytic of the aesthetic judgement
    Book 1: Analytic of the beautiful
      Four 'moments'
        1. §§ 1–5 Concerning *interest*
        2. §§ 6–9 Concerning *universal delight* (or 'satisfaction', or 'liking')
        3. §§ 10–17 Concerning *purposiveness* (including discussions of perfection and ideal)
        4. §§ 18–22 Concerning *Necessity* and *Common Sense*
      General comment on first division (i.e. the 'first book')

Book 2: Analytic of the sublime
  §§ 23–4 Introduction
  §§ 25–7 Mathematically sublime
  §§ 28–9 Dynamically sublime
  General comment upon the exposition
(Virtual Book 3: Deduction of aesthetic judgements, and fine art)
  §§ 30–7 The problem of a deduction
  §§ 38– Deduction and comment
  §§ 39–42 Provisional discussion of the social and ultimately moral
  implications of the universal validity of natural beauty
(Virtual Book 4: On fine art)
  §§ 43–5 Art
  §§ 46–50 Genius and aesthetic ideas
  §§ 51–3 Division and comparison of the fine arts
  § 54 Comment (on gratification)
Division 2. Dialectic of the aesthetic judgement
  §§ 55–8 Antinomies of taste
  § 59 Beauty as the symbol of morality (which we should take as Kant's
  conclusions to the first part of this book)
  § 60 Appendix on methodology
Part 2. Critique of teleological judgement
  § 61 Introduction
  Division 1: Analytic of teleological judgement
  §§ 62–3 The question of an objective purposiveness in nature.
  §§ 63–6 The organism.
  §§ 67–8 The conception of nature as a system of purposes.
  Division 2: Dialectic of teleological judgement
  §§ 69–74 The paradox of thinking nature as purposive.
  §§ 75–6, 78 Objective purposiveness as a critical principle of reason.
  § 77 Implications for our conception of our understanding.
  Appendix: Theory of the Method
  §§ 79–81 Relation of teleological principle and science.
  §§ 82–4 Man as final purpose.
  §§ 85–6 Theological implications.
  §§ 87–90 Moral proof of the existence of God, and discussion.
  § 91 Faith and knowledge.
General comment on teleology

CHAPTER SUMMARY: Kant's philosophy defines itself as transcendental or critical philosophy. 'Critique' means to determine the nature
and limits of a given 'faculty' or 'power'; this is done by means of a
transcendental method which seeks to investigate these faculties by

showing their role as *a priori* conditions of any experience. Certain faculties turn out to be 'legislating' for certain types of experience (understood broadly); this means that they supply the principles according to which that experience is structured and thus possible at all. Does judgement supply such a principle? Kant investigates this problem by way of two particularly interesting types of judgement: aesthetic judgement, and teleological judgement. One of the key reasons for investigating judgement at all is that it may have a mediating role between the theoretical philosophy of nature and the practical philosophy of moral action. The study of judgement would thus unify all of critical philosophy.

1

The Peculiarities of the Aesthetic Judgement

In the Introduction, we discussed why Kant feels aesthetic judgements need studying. In particular, we talked about how aesthetic judgements were exemplary of what Kant calls reflective judgements – judgements which proceed without a concept. These judgements were interesting to Kant for further, and still broader reasons. Aesthetic judgements are the most radical kind of reflective judgements, and have a number of peculiar features which at first sight look like nothing other than paradoxes. The task of this chapter is to begin to describe those features using Kant's conceptual language. This will enable us to ask the transcendental question typical of Kantian philosophy: how are such judgements possible?

In the first two sections, we will talk more generally about aesthetic judgements and what kind of strange properties we can discover just by examining our typical experiences, and our use of aesthetic language. Then we will move on to discuss the 'moments' that Kant identifies as being definitive of what it means to judge aesthetically.

What is an Aesthetic Judgement?

As a first approximation, we will say that by 'aesthetic judgement' Kant means those judgements in which a feeling of pleasure is predicated of (First Introduction VIII) or connected to (§36) our 'merely judging' something (§45). It is any judgement that can be expressed in the following way: 'When I look at or listen to that object or event, I am pleased by the *mere experience* of it, and say that it is beautiful or sublime.'[1] (Kant feels that the sublime presents a different set of issues, and so he postpones discussion of it. For simplicity, we will also postpone discussion of the category of the sublime until Chapter 3, and stick to beauty here.)

Our word 'aesthetics' – meaning something like the experience or study of fine art and perhaps also the beautiful or sublime in nature – was coined by the German philosopher Alexander Gottlieb Baumgarten in the generation immediately prior to Kant. Kant uses it to refer generally to the sensible aspect of our cognition of nature (thus the section in the *Critique of Pure Reason* that deals with the pure forms of intuition is entitled the 'Transcendental Aesthetic'). But he also follows Baumgarten's narrow usage, which is now the standard usage, to refer to those sensible objects valued as art or as being beautiful. Baumgarten's account of art was essentially *cognitive*: although art objects were of course sensible, their value lay in the manner in which their sensible form was actually a type of knowing. Art is therefore judged by reference to its perfection and clarity as such sensible knowledge. Kant's account of aesthetic judgement is to a great extent a reaction against Baumgarten. In particular, since the judgement in question is reflective, and does not proceed by way of concepts, aesthetics has nothing to contribute to knowledge. Kant is concerned to 'loosen up' concepts such as beauty, art, and taste – so that they are not confused with cognition of objects in nature – but without losing the sense that judgements about art and beauty have some validity beyond simply the sensible interest I happen to take in them. (Kant also calls the aesthetic judgement a judgement of *Taste*.)

In effect, Kant is just assuming that there are such things as aesthetic judgements. Clearly, we make judgements about things (paintings, films, symphonies) that we can call 'art'. Clearly, also, we say that natural objects (flowers, a coral reef, the shape of the DNA molecule) are beautiful or sublime. It is possible, however, that what we think are 'aesthetic' judgements are not; they are perhaps just ordinary judgements of sensible interest masquerading as something distinctive. In the Introduction, we saw several arguments Kant uses to try to show that judgements, and especially reflective judgements, really are distinctive types of mental acts (see pp. 30–3). That is, Kant argues for *transcendental* necessity of assuming the existence of reflective judgements at least, and the principle of purposiveness as the legislative principle for judgement in general. But Kant never explicitly sets out to demonstrate the existence of aesthetic judgements against an aesthetic sceptic. Rather, he does so indirectly: pointing to the *empirical* fact of what appear to be aesthetic responses, which are phenomena that require explanation.

In the aforementioned definition of aesthetic judgement, the object or event could be a natural landscape or seascape, a bird's song, or a flower. Or it could be a human artistic production, such as a painting, poem, musical composition sculpture. We might think that Kant is slightly unusual in believing that judgements about natural objects and judgements about artificial objects are not very different. However, this was not out of place in eighteenth-century thought, and in some ways continues today. We will come across some important differences between the aesthetic judgements of nature and of art in later chapters, but their commonality goes right to the heart of the experience, Kant believes. The simple definition given above, then, has already expanded to give us three concepts that need sorting out:

taste, pleasure, and beauty. After that, we have the problem of explaining the meaning of the phrase we used: 'mere experience'.

'Taste' is an old-fashioned word, and it is liable to get in our way when we are trying to understand Kant. As we will see in more detail, by 'taste' we do not mean a sensation in the mouth. We mean something more akin to when we say someone has 'good taste' or 'bad taste' – that is, someone who is good or bad at judging the aesthetic merit of things. However, 'good taste' *could* just mean 'good fashion sense'. Kant thus distinguishes between taste for the agreeable (a judgement of sensible interest) and taste for the aesthetic (an aesthetic judgement), although subsequently, he usually uses 'taste' only in the second, much narrower sense. Thus, by 'taste' Kant meant something very simple: our ability to judge natural objects or works of art to be beautiful (§1n, Introduction VII). For Kant, then, the aesthetic judgement is a judgement of taste – a judgement which says the mere experience of something 'is liked' (or 'delights', or 'satisfies') me (§2) and is thus judged beautiful.

Pleasure or liking (or the opposite: displeasure or pain) is a traditional way of describing one's response to nature or art. In the Introduction, we discussed the meaning of pleasure for Kant, and also said something about why the faculty of judgement might be considered legislative for aesthetic feeling. We will take up this broader topic in Chapter 2. For the moment, let us focus on the 'surface' relationship between beauty and pleasure. For Kant, pleasure is a sign of our being in the presence of beauty. But I can receive pleasure from other things also. Formally speaking, then, aesthetic judgement consists of connecting this sign to its proper 'origin': the beautiful object.[2]

One problem appears immediately: whether we in fact feel pleasure with respect to art. Naturally beautiful objects are less troubling: to feel pleasure in a landscape or a flower is precisely to feel pleasure in looking at, smelling, walking in, and so on. A common enough experience, we might agree. Today, however, it seems we do not always expect to respond with pleasure to fine art, especially to contemporary art. Much modern and recent art is deliberately grotesque, upsetting or repulsive,[3] or else simply emotionally cold, and we accept that. On the face of it, this discounts Kant's aesthetic theory from the outset, as it discounts virtually every aesthetic theory prior to this century. Let us extend the point further to popular culture. We do not go to the cinema or theatre just to be 'grossed out' by a shlock horror film, but precisely to enjoy ourselves while, and indeed because of, being grossed out. How? There is pleasure involved because of the displeasure, and the displeasure is redeemed by the film's being entertaining, interesting, oddly sexy, funny, or part of a 'cult' phenomenon that we enjoy participating in.

What is true for popular culture, however, is also true for 'serious' art (assuming that this distinction can be made reliably). But probably we need to broaden the notion of pleasure to the notion of some kind of sense of 'gain' with respect to our purposes or interests. We may respond with anger and shock to a contemporary work of art, and this first response is certainly not pleasurable. Nor is it yet a response to a work of art. For such anger and shock often come hand in hand with a statement like 'This is not really art – it is rubbish.' Arguments about censorship often proceed in just this way. Precisely to the extent that we accept that something is art – however that may happen – the anger and shock are transformed into something else at least in part. Perhaps the anger and shock have helped me to see something afresh, or have helped me to think about or understand something differently, or change the person I am. This change may be disturbing in itself, but with respect to the fulfilment of its goal or purpose can certainly be described as a 'gain'.[4] Even today, despite our twenty-first-century sophistication, it is difficult to get away from the idea that art must have something redeeming about it, not necessarily to reward the viewer so much as to justify its existence.

Sometimes the arguments needed to link contemporary art to pleasure, even when broadened to 'gain', may be slightly strained. It is precisely at these points of strain that arguments about 'what is art' become most heated, if not always most interesting. But perhaps such arguments are heated and uninteresting, precisely because the two sides are fixed on quite different notions of 'taste', 'pleasure' and, indeed, 'art'. For Kant, pleasure simply means 'the feeling of an enhancement of life'.

The word 'beauty' also strikes us as old-fashioned, and Kant's phrase for 'fine art' [schöne Kunst] assumes beauty [Schönheit]. We are more likely to call a kitten 'beautiful' than a sculpture in a contemporary art gallery. But 'beauty' was merely a current word in Kant's day, just as taste was. For Kant, beauty starts out as simply a name for 'that which pleases in the mere experience of it'. In other words, for the moment, all we know is that for Kant beauty is a name for the 'something distinctive' about art or certain natural things which we discussed above. For the moment, we need not associate beauty with what anyone, in any historical period, happened to call beautiful.

The point is that while there is certainly a minor difficulty to be overcome in Kant's antique language, this is no insurmountable barrier. We have to forget our automatic responses to words like 'beauty' or 'taste' and try to think our way into Kant's mode of thought, or at least not be sidetracked by mere terminology. Of course, before we are finished, the provisional definitions of taste, pleasure and beauty given above are going to be refined in many complex ways; for example, we will see that defining beauty as a 'distinctive' property of an object is precisely not what Kant believes, although it may still be a good starting point.

SUMMARY: An aesthetic judgement (or judgement of taste) means a judgement which 'connects' a feeling of pleasure to the *mere experience* of something, and accordingly calls it 'beautiful', or 'sublime'.

What Counts as an Aesthetic Judgement?

Suppose I judge a painting to be beautiful. This could mean precisely what it says: that the painting itself is being judged as beautiful art. But my judgement, Kant claims, might instead be a misuse of the term 'beautiful'. (This does not necessarily mean that the painting is in fact not art – my judgement could be correct, but for the wrong reasons.) It is important to narrow down what it is, exactly, that is pleasing me in the 'mere experience'. My judgement could mean, for example:

1. The painting reminds me of my grandmother. I have affectionate memories of my grandmother.
2. The colour used to paint the sea is an exquisite and rich green. I find this colour especially pleasing, and therefore judge the painting to be beautiful.
3. I own the painting, and upon having it valued discover that it is worth a lot of money. This pleases me.
4. I painted this work myself, and I am proud of it.
5. The painting depicts some historical act of sacrifice and selflessness. Because the painting expresses a political or moral ideal with which I agree, I say it is beautiful.
6. The painting expresses or embodies some intellectual idea I find fascinating. Contemplating the painting gives me pleasure and I call it beautiful.
7. The painting is new to me, but by an artist whose style I have for years enjoyed and admired. Therefore, I enjoy this one and call it beautiful.
8. Someone else whose judgement I trust thought this painting was beautiful. Therefore, I think it is too.
9. The painting, or the painter, is all the rage. I jump on the bandwagon and say I love it too.

Kant claims all of these are examples of mistakes.

In numbers 1–4 I have a subjective interest in the painting. That is, my response is based upon an emotional or physiological reaction that is peculiar to me alone. I value the painting (have an interest in it) for purely subjective reasons. There is a kind of accidental quality about my response (I happen to like that colour . . .); this, Kant argues, is alien to the concept of aesthetic pleasure or beauty.

In numbers 5–6 I have an intellectual or ethical interest in the painting. It is not the painting itself to which I am responding, but a value entirely outside it (ethical goodness, or intellectual fascination), of which the painting reminds me, or of which the painting is an example.

In number 7 I am being too objective with the judgement. That is, I am treating beauty as nothing other than a property of the object, like its size or weight, or in this case, the signature at the bottom corner. This assumes beauty can be reduced to some concept of a *type* of painting (all the work of one artist, or one period) and ignores that this is also an individual and unique work of art.

In numbers 8–9 I am failing to respond at all to the work, just taking someone's word for it.

There is nothing wrong in responding to things for these reasons. For the moment, at least, we have no reason for saying that the aesthetic way of responding is better than some other way; it is just different. The exclusion of these ways of experiencing an object is part of what is meant by aesthetic judgement being based upon the 'mere experience' of something. In short, that mere experience excludes any experience conditioned by either sensible or intellectual interest, or by any objective concept. (Of course, it could be the case that a judgement based upon the 'mere experience' is thereby rendered impossible.)

One way of understanding what Kant is doing in the opening sections of the book is coming up with four definitions of the 'behaviour' of aesthetic judgements that can be used as 'tests' for a real aesthetic judgement. 'Behaviour' here means, for example, what sort of conditions the judgement permits itself, and what sort it excludes; or how the judgement relates to other judgements, actual or possible. Kant calls these the four 'moments', and the first major part of the book after the Introduction is the four 'moments' of the beautiful. There must be four of these for a precise reason: in logic – at least in *Kant's* logic – there are four basic *formal characteristics* that a judgement can have: quantity, quality, relation and modality.[5] It should be the case, then, that a thorough description of the aesthetic judgement can be given by asking in what particular way such judgements fit into these four broad characteristics.[6] Here, however, we will not deal in depth with this specifically logical dimension of the four moments.

In the preceding two sections, we have tried to explain in a provisional way several of Kant's key concepts in order to provide us with an initial orientation. We did this by talking in general about ideas such as 'taste', and about how aesthetic judgements behave. We will now return to Kant's book itself in order to see how he defends, refines and expands upon these initial ideas. For the sake of clarity, we will change Kant's order of presentation, and discuss Kant's four 'moments' in the following order: second, first, fourth and then third, with the last of these discussed in Chapter 2. Changing the order will allow us to build Kant's account of aesthetic judgement from the ground upwards, rather than having to assume elements of it.

SUMMARY: Not all pleasures connected to my experience of something are aesthetic pleasures. In particular are discounted pleasures that follow from: subjective interests, intellectual or ethical interests, objective considerations of the object, or any other failure to respond to the 'mere' experience of the thing in itself. The first sections of Kant's book (the four Moments of the beautiful) are accounts of how such judgements 'behave'; for example, in what way they include or exclude the above 'interests' or 'objective considerations'.

Universality (Second Moment)

Kant's second moment is *universality*. The judgement of the beautiful is intended to be universal. What does this mean?

When we say 'Something pleases me' we do not particularly expect that anyone will agree with us. If I say 'Something pleases me' and you respond 'Yes, it does', this would be most strange. My pleasure is something only I know about, it is private knowledge, unless I squeal with delight or give some other public indication of my private state. Moreover, my pleasure also tends to be private in another sense. If I say 'The taste of honey pleases me', then you could say 'I don't like honey' and we could both be 'right'.[7] Whether honey pleases you or not is something that presumably depends upon the chemistry of your palate, your upbringing (what you ate as a child) and so forth. Honey only pleases, or does not please, individual people. The pleasure is a *subjective response*. Many people like honey, but not all people; nor do I believe that all people should like it. Of course, if honey pleases me, that may originate in certain facts about honey: take all the sugar out, and I might not like it. But it still remains a merely subjective evaluation, and is not a description. Thus, we do not expect that anyone else *must* agree with us.

By contrast, if I say 'Honey is sweet' – by which I mean merely that it contains sugar – then I am commenting on an objective fact about honey, and I expect you to agree with me. If you say 'Honey is not sweet', then you simply do not understand the meaning of the word 'sweet', or perhaps you do not know what honey is. Although a private sensation, sweetness is still considered an objective *description* of honey, because it refers to the plain fact of sugar content. Honey is sweet, although not everyone will enjoy eating it.

The way Kant has defined aesthetic judgements includes the notion of pleasure. It would be reasonable to assume that aesthetic judgements are like 'The taste of honey pleases me'. That is, it would be reasonable to assume that judgements about beautiful objects (whether natural or artificial) are simply my reports about private and subjective responses to objects, that you can therefore disagree with me (have a different response yourself), and we can both be right. However, Kant says that, despite the fact that such judgements involve pleasure, judgements about beautiful objects instead behave more like 'Honey is sweet'. That is, they behave *as if* the object of the judgement were a real, objective property of the thing judged, and that judgements about this property are therefore universal (this is the point of §7).

At first, then, judgements about beauty seem to be subjective evaluations. However, aesthetic judgements do make an appeal, although often in a hidden manner, to universality, which subjective evaluations of honey do not. In this respect, judgements about beauty behave more like objective judgements, such as 'Honey is sweet'. Kant expresses this strongly, writing that the judge of beauty 'judges not just for himself, but for everyone' (§7). How can this be?

We must be careful here. Kant writes that we talk about the beautiful '*as if* beauty were a characteristic of the object' (§6, emphasis added). Kant certainly does *not* think that beauty actually is a property of the object, so that things are beautiful in the same way that a mountain is 4,000m high, the flower has twelve petals, or honey contains sugar. That is why the basic thesis of the second moment does not just talk about universality, but universality 'without a concept' (§9, Definition). A concept of an object would speak of properties of that object, characteristics which could be described and found elsewhere; without a concept, we cannot speak of such properties. This means, among other things, that an aesthetic judgement is entirely *singular*, for it does not deal with an object as a type, but as a particular. So, beauty only behaves *as if* it were an objective property, *as if* there were a particular concept that we were all using in our judgements. The phrase 'as if' is very important here.

The judgement, Kant says, 'demands the agreement' of others (§7). Of course, we know that people do disagree aesthetically about beauty and art.[8] Kant is quite aware of this. This disagreement could be interpreted as arising from the fact that such judgements are merely subjective. Or, it could arise from the fact that not all aesthetic judgements are well-formed – some are the result of mistakes. Kant claims that, logically, the aesthetic judgement assumes this second explanation: it behaves in such a way as to assert the existence of a correct answer, just as if it were objective. So, judges of beauty sometimes make mistakes, and that is why they do not agree, Kant is asserting.

Of course, when I claim that a natural object or work of art is beautiful, I may not in fact expect everyone to agree with me. Others may disagree with me, and though we may argue about it, we may never agree. But, to the extent I believe I am right, I believe everyone *should* agree with me. Several times, Kant asserts that we do not wait upon or assert the opinions of others, we rather 'demand' or 'require' their agreement (for example §7, 8). In other words, if I claim it is beautiful, and someone else claims it is not – and provided we both mean the same thing by 'beautiful' – then one of us is wrong. This is the crux of the difference between Kant's concept of 'taste of reflection' (referring to the concept of a reflective judgement (§8)) and having the 'taste of sense' for chocolate or honey. Judgements which are in accordance with taste of reflection ('taste' in Kant's distinctive meaning) are presumed universal, although everyone else may not *in fact* agree with you.

Further, if you did not expect anyone to agree with you, or you expected their agreement to be merely accidental, then there would be no point in communicating our judgements. It would be 'foolish' (§7) for someone to wander through life pronouncing 'I like honey' and expect anyone to care! Presumably there is a *point* to saying 'This painting is beautiful'. Ultimately, Kant is saying that our everyday use of the word 'beauty' belies the common saying that 'beauty is in the eye of the beholder'.

Suppose you like anchovies, and you meet someone who says that they hate them. You ask them why they hate them. Perhaps you are trying to understand their dislike, to get inside their head in the act of disliking anchovies. What you could not seriously be doing is asking them to convince you that anchovies are delicious, or expecting to convince them of the opposite. Even if, after a conversation about the merits of anchovies, you somehow understand their dislike, you will still like anchovies. If, however, the conversation was about a natural landscape or especially about a painting or poem, both of you might reasonably expect that an outcome of the debate could be agreement. It follows, Kant claims, that a proper interpretation of what is meant by an aesthetic judgement involves a claim of 'truth',[9] and a claim upon the agreement of everyone else, which the anchovy judgement does not.

In other words, the judgement 'That is beautiful' behaves differently with respect to the judgements of others, than 'That tastes good to me'. It is this difference in logical behaviour that is Kant's first indirect argument for the distinctiveness of aesthetic judgements. Kant describes this difference in several ways that are meant to be ultimately equivalent: that the judgement demands agreement; that it is, or tends towards being, universal; that it behaves as if it were an objective judgement.

Another related argument for Kant's point is that, to the precise extent that some activity is taken to be something like an art form, subjective judgements are not allowed. Sometimes we forget this fact, but careful attention to the distinctions we make in fairly common situations verifies it. If in a cookery contest, for example, a judge downgrades a contestant for using honey just because the judge does not happen to like honey, we would immediately consider this inappropriate. The judge would be biased and a bad judge. Wine experts constantly tell us that it is OK to drink what we like, and yet they are also constantly judging competitions and talking about the 'artistry' of wine-making. For some purposes, then, wine is just a matter of individual taste, but for those whose taste is finely tuned (wine experts), it is more like an art form. The wine taster and the cook must rise above their personal subjective taste. This assumption of the universality of judgements about beauty is just what we mean by saying something is beautiful rather than just agreeable, pleasant or tasteful. Thus, again, 'beauty' behaves like an actual property of the object.

Kant tries to explain what this universality means in yet another way. Any merely subjective pleasures we might feel are just that – subjective. We can only guess exactly how another is feeling. But if the judgement 'behaves' universally – that is, if it contains an implicit claim upon your agreement – then it must also be the case that we can reach agreement upon what it is that we are both judging. Otherwise, the universal claim would not be either right or wrong, it would be nonsense, just as we used that notion in our Introduction when discussing what Kant meant by the idea of philosophical critique. So, what is fundamental to the judgement is that the mental state of pleasure can be communicated, and this is tied up with its universality. We will return to this idea of communicability.

In any case, the property of universality helps to give art its significance. With the exception of beekeepers, nobody cares if you or I like honey. Nobody much cares if Shakespeare or Mozart liked honey, either. Similarly, if I could not communicate my aesthetic judgements, then they would have no social, political, educative, or historical sense; art and beauty in general would be rather pointless. It is partly because art appeals and speaks to us universally that people care about art.

The next moment, 'disinterestedness', narrows the range of aesthetic judgements still further.

SUMMARY: Aesthetic judgements behave universally, that is, they involve an expectation or claim on the agreement of others 'without a concept' (§9). This universality is distinguished both from the mere

> subjective evaluation of judgements such as 'I like honey', and from the strict descriptive objectivity of judgements such as 'Honey contains sugar and is sweet'. Judgements of reflective taste behave *as if* they were objective; also as universal, they are communicable.

Disinterestedness (First Moment)

Moving backwards in Kant's book, the first moment describes the aesthetic judgement as *disinterested* (also translated as 'devoid of interest'). If something is to be judged as beautiful, the object in nature or the work of art must please me, but *not because I have any interest in it*. Interest means that the object becomes desired in some way. This interest could be sensible (i.e. corporeal or physiological), ethical or intellectual. Kant gives several examples, of which the following one is famous and clear:[10] he relates a story of a Native American who visited Paris, saw the great architecture, viewed the great paintings, listened to the great music, and then said that 'he liked nothing better in Paris than the eating-houses' (§2). In this example, such a response to the wonders of Paris is obviously not aesthetic, the desire for food being an aesthetically illegitimate physiological interest (which does not preclude that cookery *can* be an art form). Assigning beauty to something for such reasons would be a mistake. These reasons, we might say, are 'exterior' to the beautiful object itself. This idea of getting rid of such exterior factors is part of what we meant in initially defining the aesthetic judgement as being based on the 'mere experience' of a thing.[11]

The second moment in Kant's description helps us to understand this first one better. If wildflowers on a hillside merely elicit my *subjective* interest (if, for example, I just happen to like the scent), then the pleasure I feel from them, and any judgement I make on that basis, will not be universal. Similarly, again, with honey and anchovies. I have no reason to expect that my subjective interests are, or should be, universal. Kant expresses this when he says that the judgement is 'free' from my various likes and dislikes. However, this notion of freedom does not mean that I am free to choose what I find beautiful. Indeed, it would be better to say that beauty 'chooses' me; it catches my eye, and causes me to linger upon it in contemplation (§12). Rather, by 'free' Kant means that the ground of my judgement is free from the various inclinations which overlay or overrule beauty, so to speak, from the outside, and thus prevent beauty from revealing itself to me. This notion of a free judgement is the first of two ways in which Kant will try to describe what is really meant by disinterestedness.

Kant is also disallowing other interests, such as the ethical, political and intellectual. Now these *do* carry an assumption of universality. I do believe that everyone should agree with my political views. That is why we have election campaigns, debates, political broadcasts, and so forth. Kant's example is of someone objecting (in the spirit, he says, of Rousseau) to the vast and opulent Palace of Versailles because thousands of more or less enslaved workers suffered to make it possible (§2). If I have a political view, then I must have some sense of what is 'good' or 'bad' in politics. And that sense, however admirable as a political or ethical matter, is *exterior* to aesthetic judgement; it is not judging the 'mere experience', and thus counts as an interest. The 'Rousseau' objection to Versailles is not therefore a judgement about the palace as art.

So, we must distinguish between several components in our presentations of objects. First, there is the content considered as mere 'sensation' (see Kant's Introduction VII, and the Introduction to this book). This would include the colours or scent of wildflowers, the sound qualities of a musical instrument, or the analogous properties of a palace (for example, the sumptuous fabrics). Second, there is 'form', by which Kant means the properties that are expressible only as space or time, such as the shapes of the flower, the flow of notes in birdsong or music, the play of forms in the dance, or the mere architectural design of the palace.[12] Third, there are the responses to the above components that are assigned to interest at the level of physiology (I like that colour because it makes me feel warm and cosy). Kant calls this response the 'agreeable' (§3). Fourth, there are the responses that are assigned to interest at the level of any concepts (my pragmatic response to a painting that will form a good example in my teaching duties; or my ethical responses to Versailles). All such responses are to the 'good' (§4), and Kant focuses primarily on the ethical meaning of 'good'. Fifth, there is the *aesthetic* response to the mere form, which has so far been defined as universal and free from my interest in the agreeable or the good (§2). The disinterested judgement of the beautiful, then, must also ignore the sensation-content of the object. One reason for this, of course, is that pleasure which arises on the basis of sensation is necessarily merely subjective, and thus not universal. Pleasure which arises from form has at least the possibility of being universal.[13]

But there is another reason. The second way in which Kant tries to explain what 'interest' means is by considering how the judgement relates to the real existence of the object. An interest involves *caring* for the real existence of the object. Sensation gives us all kinds of information about things (temperature, colour, and so on) but also forms our basic criterion of the present existence of something.[14] 'Pinch me,' we say, 'Am I dreaming?' When something really exists here and now, we have sensations of it. Thus, pleasure which arises from sensation will be linked to the real existence of things, and in this way is linked necessarily to an interest in the object. Indeed, the pleasure I feel relies upon the presentation of such an existence as linked to *my existence or action* (§5). Perhaps I can imagine the taste of honey – even then, that sensation could only give pleasure if I were imagining myself *actually eating* the honey. Accordingly, Kant says that, strictly speaking, aesthetic pleasure refers to no object outside of me. Similarly, for the good, the thought of a moral deed is only pleasing if I imagine it as a possible object of will; the good too is necessarily desired. The aesthetic response is thus *pure* or *free* from any interest, and self-contained with respect to the existence of the object.

The judgement, then, should deal only with the *form or design* of the object (its spatial or temporal structure) and not pay any heed to sensations (content) which lie within that form. It is the delicate and graceful shape of the flower, the arrangement of trees and hills in the view, which comprise beauty. In music, it is primarily the arrangement of notes, understood mathematically, rather than the sound quality, which is our object in judging that the music is beautiful. Thus Kant famously and controversially argues that tonal quality (in music) or colour quality (in painting) are secondary and subservient to form. And, although colour can perhaps *highlight* beautiful form, it is equally likely to get in the way of proper aesthetic judgement (§14). Kant thus becomes the ancestor of every formalist theory of art.[15]

Similarly, Kant argues in the same passage that the judgement should deal only with the 'intrinsic constituents' of the object. This means that any *parerga* (literally, work that is to one side) – for example ornamentation of any kind, such as the gold-leafed frame around a painting, or trills, vibrato and other such flourishes in music – are to be ignored unless they contribute to the beautiful form of the object. Such 'finery' appeals only as the agreeable, not as the beautiful. However flashy or ornate the trimmings, it is the *thing itself* that we are judging, in the 'mere experience' of it.

'Interest' now refers to anything which ascribes value (either positive or negative) to the fact that the object *actually* exists or does not exist (§2). Clearly it would be important for the Native American in Kant's example that the food exists! Similarly, it matters for the moral pain felt by the person objecting to Versailles that the palace was actually built.[16] However, we might think this strange, since if I am viewing a beautiful natural landscape, then surely it must exist! But consider: I could be viewing a video image which was taken days or years ago, since which time an open-pit mine has been introduced. Similarly, I may admire the beauty of a building from the architectural plans before it is ever built. I may even be remembering, years later, architectural plans for a building that was never built – or even just imagining a building!

Still, whether it be a video, a photograph, a plan or a memory, *something* exists and must exist for the aesthetic judgement to take place. What is it, then, that Kant means? Let us distinguish between two ways that an object can be at the beginning of an experience. First, the object can be the instigator or catalyst of an experience – something that must be present, but is not materially the cause of the experience. Because it is pleasurable, I certainly desire to continue such contemplation, and thus may desire to possess the object. But my 'possession' of the object, and my aesthetic contemplation of it, are distinct. Thus 'the judgement is only aesthetic, and refers the object's presentation merely to the subject' (§6; compare also §1). Properly understood, in saying that the presentation is referred wholly 'to the subject', Kant seems to be claiming that our judgement of the beautiful is an activity in some way *self-contained* within my inner mental sphere. This idea of being 'self-contained' is found, for example, in Kant's use of the word 'contemplation' (§5). And this is part of what was meant above by the definition of the aesthetic judgement being based upon 'mere experience'.[17]

The second way for an object to relate to my experience of it, is as the cause of the experience, and thus the object of an interest. Because of the object, I desire the object (in the case of the agreeable); or because of the object, I desire to do something for or against it (in the case of the good). In this case, my pleasure is entirely bound up in having or doing something with respect to the object. The two (object and interest) cannot be separated.

Oddly, however, we can also say that if we take interest in an object, then it is not the object itself to which we are responding, but something else entirely. Before I ever experience the object, I already like certain colours, or already feel passionately about certain political views. The existence of the object matters, but for reasons other than the presentation of the object taken in itself. Therefore, I am not actually judging the presentation of the object itself, *on its own*, and the judgement activity again lacks that peculiar self-contained quality we mentioned above. In §9, Kant accordingly writes that the estimation of the object itself is the ground of pleasure in aesthetic judgement, rather than the other way around. Thus when two judges of beauty disagree, we tend to suspect that one of them has an interest in the object. We might say that, in effect, they are judging two different objects.

This thesis of a response to the mere experience may seem odd, for at least two reasons. First, if I am judging a poem, for example, I must have some information in advance, which is not part of this self-containedness – namely the meanings of the words used, knowledge of grammar, idiom and indications of tone, and so on. The same would go for most other art forms: a certain level of what we might call 'enabling knowledge' is necessarily involved. That is why, when visiting an art museum I might wish to buy a guide book, or read up on the artist or period in advance. Now, certainly, the guide book could not substitute for the experience itself, or the formation of a judgement, but it does help enable that experience. Thus, one might argue that such a judgement cannot be self-contained.[18]

Secondly, Kant himself later says that one's taste can be 'developed' or 'cultivated' (at, for example, §60). That is, a failure to have taste can be changed to competent taste through the proper education. This is a familiar enough idea: we do not expect children, for example, to have very advanced tastes in art. This means that at least some judgements have as a condition (though not an *a priori* condition) the development of taste. Kant goes so far as to claim that 'taste is precisely what stands most in need of examples' (§32). But again, if a particular judgement requires such development, in what sense is it merely contemplative and self-contained?

Perhaps Kant can answer all these objections in this way. If I say that I have, in advance, an interest in good food and in ethically good acts, then – in order for that statement 'in advance' to actually *mean* anything – I must be able to specify in advance what kinds of food are 'good' and what kinds of acts are 'ethically good'. A reliable sign of a non-reflective judgement would be that one could specify in advance the judgement's outcome, according to a concept of what is judged.[19] Kant's answer to the above objections, then, will be to admit that knowledge (of the meanings of words) or experience (which develops my taste) may indeed be useful or required. But what we call 'enabling' knowledge or experience will never constitute knowledge of what kinds of properties make things beautiful (cf. §§32, 45–51). That is why Kant insists that pleasure and pain are the only mental 'presentations' that cannot be made into a concept (for example, §3). In other words, the beautiful *does not and can never* rest upon an objective concept of the beautiful, or any other such concept, inclination or value, which exists *in advance*. Thus Kant says the aesthetic judgement is not itself a 'cognitive judgement', i.e. is not knowledge (§5). Saying therefore that 'I like beautiful things' is not a pre-judgement – it is virtually a tautology (something like 'Pleasurable feelings are pleasurable') which thus pre-determines nothing. It follows that there is no determining concept of the beautiful. This is an extremely important idea, of which we already caught a glimpse when discussing universality. We will explore it in more depth when we discuss the third moment in Chapter 2.

It may be that what we have called enabling knowledge can be brought to bear on an object in different ways. In my judging of a Medieval painting, for example, I may look for various standard iconographic symbols. You, however, may judge it in terms of the artist's technique and materials. We are both looking at the same painting, but are *forming different pre-sentations* of it. Thus, if two people disagree in their aesthetic judgement, it *may* be because of an interest in the object. But it may also be because they are interpreting the object differently and thus in effect judging *different objects*. Kant only rarely touches on this issue (for example, at the end of §16). We will return to this problem in Chapter 4.

This disinterestedness, strictly speaking, may be very difficult to achieve. However, Kant can at least hold it up as an ideal, something to strive towards, just as he did with universality. Moreover, it is not necessary that we have no interest in fact – which may be impossible for even the most saintly or dispassionate of people – only that the interest is not determining our judgement (and it is thus 'free'). Analogously, we might be happy to admit that no officer of the law or judge in a court of law (who are only human) can be *entirely* without prejudice – but we do insist that in the carrying out of their duties they put any prejudice out of action. It is the judgement that is disinterested, not us.

SUMMARY: The notion of 'interest' turns out to be a complex test of aesthetic judgements. There are two main types of interest: from *agreeable* sensations, or concepts of the *good*. Only aesthetic judgement is free or pure of such interests. Interest is defined as a link to desire, or a determining connection to the existence of the object. Kant accordingly claims that the aesthetic judgement must concern itself only with form, not content. He also wishes to describe the mental activity involved in the judgement as 'contemplation', that is, as what we called 'self-contained'. To understand this, we distinguished enabling from determining knowledge or experience. Kant summarises this section (at §5, Definition) writing, '*Taste* is the faculty of estimating an object or a mode of presentation by means of a liking or aversion which is *apart from any interest*. The object of such a liking is called *beautiful*.'

Necessity and Common Sense (Fourth Moment)

The fourth moment begins to take us beyond a mere definition of aesthetic judgement, to the ground of such judgements. Kant is now claiming that such judgements presuppose what he calls 'common sense' [*Gemeinsinn*], and even argues that all four moments of the beautiful are summed up in this notion (§22).

Kant distinguishes this 'common sense' from the everyday meaning of the term.[20] Today, common sense is attributed to someone who tends to make decisions that most other people would find intelligent and pragmatic. We might also say that they are 'sensible' or 'level-headed'. Such a 'common sense', however, is still an intelligence, reliant upon concepts. What Kant means here is more literal: the usage of 'sense' is akin to 'sense organs' such as sight or touch. In general, a sense is a particular mode of becoming aware of something. By 'common sense', then, Kant means that we all actually have a kind of sense in common (see also §40). The sense in question is that through which we become aware of the beautiful, that is, through the feeling for certain states of our own mind (aesthetic pleasure) (§20). Really, we should call it common or public *feeling*. The possession of common sense, Kant hopes to prove, is an *a priori* condition of aesthetic judgement, and is thus clearly related to the idea of universal communicability.

However, in most of §20, Kant does not say exactly this; rather he talks of common sense as an *a priori* but subjective 'principle' of taste.[21] This would be the principle or rule with which judgement, in the particular case of aesthetic taste, legislates for our mental faculty of feeling. So, we seem to have three different meanings for common sense: first, an *a priori* faculty of a feeling for the beautiful; secondly, a common or public aspect of that feeling, thus its universal communicability; and thirdly, a subjective principle for judgement. What exactly is their relationship?

Kant begins his argument by asking in what way the aesthetic judgement could be said to be *necessary*. By 'necessity' he means that a thing or situation could not have been otherwise. Here, the concept of necessity refers to judgement. If the circumstances for forming the judgement are all present and properly attended to, then the judgement will necessarily follow, and could not have been otherwise. This seems like another way of looking at universality. When I say that my judgement is universal, I am asserting that this judgement has been and will be true, everywhere and always. 'Universality' suggests all other *actual* people, places and times in which the judgement takes place.[22]

When I say that some judgement is necessary, however, I am no longer focusing on the judgement itself, but on the conditions of the judgement. Thus Kant writes in the *Critique of Pure Reason*, 'That is *necessary* (exists necessarily) whose connection with the actual is determined according to universal conditions of experience'.[23] By 'universal conditions of experience', Kant means our cognitive faculties, as we discussed on pp. 12–14 (folios 23–28). Necessity is thus a 'modal' concept: it refers to the *manner* in which I make a judgement, rather than to the content of it. 'Necessity' suggests all other possible circumstances. For example, if I say that the assertion 'These two apples and another two make four apples' is necessary, I mean that it is true regardless of what kinds of things I might have been adding up. Thus, the paradigm for necessity is what can be proved to be the case from first principles (in the case of this example, the basic principles of mathematical addition), which are themselves true and valid prior to any particular circumstances. Necessity refers (in Kant's analyses) to the grounds of whatever it is that happens.

Most necessary judgements, however, have a quite different character from aesthetic judgements, because there is no concept for the beautiful.[24] So how can Kant now say the aesthetic judgement is necessary? First, he asserts that the necessity can only be singular and 'exemplary'. That is to say, because the judgement neither rests upon, nor produces a concept, it functions only 'as if' it were following (or was an example of) 'a universal rule that we are unable to state'. Each judgement stands alone but is necessary as if an instance of some principle that itself cannot be formulated.

Both universality and necessity function under this 'as if'. Universality means that the judgement functioned as if it were a description of an actual property of an object; necessity means that the judgement functioned as if conditioned by an *a priori* principle. The exemplary nature of the necessity of the aesthetic judgement means that the content and the process of my judgement concerning, for example, *this* beautiful mountain scene *tell me nothing definite* about the 'principle' that grounds the judgement, and thus also tell me nothing I could apply to my judgement concerning the beauty of some other thing.

Kant continues by arguing that the exemplary necessity of the aesthetic judgement is also a *conditioned necessity* (§18–19). What does this mean? We discussed the idea of a 'condition' in the Introduction to this book. A judgement is conditioned if something else must be the case prior to and in order for the judgement to be properly formed. Kant claims that any judgement made in accordance with a fixed *logical* rule ('A bachelor is unmarried'), or that is based upon the 'universal conditions of experience' understood as the conditions for any intelligence whatsoever is necessary *unconditionally*. These conditions are so wide as to not really be conditions at all.

In contrast, the judgement that something is beautiful is necessary, but rests on a condition: namely, the subjective *a priori* principle of the faculty of taste, which Kant calls common sense. The judgement borrows its necessity from this principle; but because it is subjective (judging by feeling, §20), that necessity is only exemplary. This principle performs the function of the hidden law mentioned in §18; its hiddenness is again its subjectivity, for an objective principle could be 'exhibited' or described. That is to say, everything happens *as if* there were a determining principle which functioned in the reflective judgement like a concept of the understanding functions in a determinate judgement. However, as before, the 'as if' is all important. It also follows that Kant is saying that beauty may not be the same for all intelligent creatures or machines, but only those (like humans) which have this common sense. Thus he writes that the aesthetic judgement will be 'valid for everyone who is so constituted as to judge by means of understanding and the senses in combination (in other words, for all human beings)' (§9).[25]

But what exactly is meant by the 'public' aspect of the phenomenon of common sense? What kinds of things can be communicated? Clearly, any truly objective property of the object, such as its size, mass, temperature, or duration. These can be communicated if only because we can point them (or their direct effects) out to others in our common world, and build concepts of them together. But we have already suggested that beauty is not a *natural* property like this. More importantly, then, than *what* can be communicated is *why* something can be guaranteed to be communicable.

Here we must take for granted the basic epistemological results of the *Critique of Pure Reason*. As the condition of all our experience, we must assume the operation of the higher cognitive faculties, especially the understanding, according to principles. The transcendental function of the cognitive faculties guarantees the objectivity and communicability of our knowledge – that is, it makes possible for humans a *common world* about which to think and speak. By 'communicability' [*Mitteilbarkeit*], Kant does not mean that every other human will *already* know what I have in mind, or even strictly speaking that there necessarily exist other humans at all. Rather, the communicability of something (a thought, a feeling) means that, in principle, other humans could think what I think, feel what I feel, and so on. That is, there is nothing *necessarily* particular to me standing in the way of such communicability; all humans must have the conditions for such thoughts or feelings.

One might think that the guaranteed universal communicability of such cognition occurs precisely because of that common world, and the objects in it. Even if that world must be understood as in some way constituted by us (idealism), nevertheless it is *about that world that we communicate*. Thus, communicability can be understood from two perspectives: first, as the sharing of a real world and its real properties and laws, about which we have knowledge; or, secondly, as the sharing of the same faculties of cognition which operate to transcendentally constitute or make possible our experience (and thus knowledge) of that world. As we discussed in the Introduction to this book, Kant's basic philosophical point is that these two are equivalent. But the way they are equivalent for theoretical cognition (the second being the transcendental ground of the *objectivity* of the first, according to determinate principles) is lacking in aesthetic judgement. This leaves us with a puzzle: how does aesthetic judgement (and the feeling of pleasure linked to it) relate to cognition, so as to be transcendentally constituted by it and thus universally communicable, but without being objective?

By contrast, it seems to make sense to assert that, with respect to the colours we see, the tastes we taste, and the pleasures we feel, everyone *could* be seeing, tasting and feeling differently. The common words we use for these things would be arrived at by the observation of situations and behaviour. And how would we ever know? Does it even make sense to ask how something *actually* felt? (In fact, it makes so little difference to anything that such a hypothesis is on the borderline of being absurd, although it retains an intuitive plausibility.) Now, we may think that such a difference among people between how we actually see or feel is unlikely. This is an inference we make from the science of perception – an experimental or empirical inference

– and thus the argument has a certain famous circularity about it. Nevertheless, if I say to you 'That car is red', it seems reasonable to conclude that I am not actually communicating a sensation. I am communicating a relationship of association between that sensation and external patterns of behaviour, such as the use of the word 'red', or coming to a halt at a traffic light. Kant is arguing a similar point at the beginning of §39.

But Kant's point about the feeling of pleasure which is my apprehension of the beautiful is stronger. Because of common sense, I *know* that my experience of the beautiful is the same as everyone else's – conditional only on their possession of common sense. The claim of universality requires this. Above, we compared the meaning of 'sense' in 'common sense' to its meaning in 'sense organs'. We can now see why this comparison was only half right. We have only experimental evidence for our sense organs really being common; we could be wrong, and there could be, at least in some cases, another explanation, such as mere commonness of behaviour. In the case of common sense, however, the commonness is built in to the very notion of an aesthetic judgement. Thus, to the precise extent that we claim universality for our judgements about the beautiful, we must also claim that everyone knows exactly what I mean and how I *feel*. Thus Kant writes that here 'we do not have to take our stand on psychological observations' (§21); and that such judgements are not questions of 'private feeling' but of an assumed 'public sense' (§22).

The various dimensions of common sense thus come together. On the side of the individual subject forming a judgement, common sense refers to an ability to feel pleasure in the beautiful. This ability could only exhibit the *a priori* necessity Kant claims it does if it contains within itself a subjective but *a priori* principle. On the public, inter-subjective side, however, common sense refers to the universal communicability of this feeling. But the public side, not surprisingly, seems ultimately to be grounded in a claim about each human's faculties, or their *transcendental subjectivity*.

This is where Kant takes a new step. What does the subjective principle rest on or consist of? And what is universal to everyone's subjectivity? Above we saw that the conditions of cognition are also the conditions of objectivity, and thus universality. Kant now wants to claim that there are certain presentations which bring the cognitive faculties into 'agreement' *in general* without agreeing to any of the particular concepts or principles of the understanding, or any particular thing presented in space and time (by sensibility). This, it is claimed, would be the mental state in the aesthetic judgement when contemplating the beautiful. It is this agreement that Kant is trying to describe with ideas like the 'free play' or 'harmony' of the cognitive faculties in §9 or 21. This 'agreement in general' is not a feature of me as a particular being, but is a universal feature of subjectivity – indeed, it is grounded in basically the same feature that makes possible any knowledge or experience at all. Thus, it is both universally communicable, and functions as a subjective principle giving the judgements that result the characteristic of necessity.

As yet, this explanation is unsatisfactory, for at least two reasons. We have not seen Kant even attempt to prove the existence of, or validity of, common sense. All we know of such a proof is that it will probably involve the idea of a harmony between the cognitive faculties. Moreover, we have little detail concerning what this 'harmony' might be. A sketch of the proof shows up in §9, and in §21 Kant will add a touch more detail (though agonisingly little) to an argument which he believe proves and explains all of this. Later in the book, in the Deduction, the proof is repeated with still more detail, but with variations.

SUMMARY: The fourth moment attempts to show that aesthetic judgements must pass the test of being 'necessary'. But this necessity is of a peculiar sort: it is 'exemplary' and 'conditioned'. With the notion of condition, Kant reaches the core of the matter. Kant calls the condition 'common sense', by which he means the *a priori* principle of our taste, our feeling for the beautiful. Kant wants to claim that in the aesthetic judgement, the universal communicability (the assumed public aspect of feeling), the exemplary necessity (based on a subjective principle), and a subjective faculty (of feeling for cognitive harmony) are all different ways of understanding common sense. He also suggests that common sense in turn depends upon, or is identical with, *the same faculties as ordinary cognition*, that is as those features of human beings which make possible any experience whatsoever.

CHAPTER SUMMARY: For Kant, the aesthetic judgement, or judge-ment of taste, consists of the ability to connect pleasure with the experience of a beautiful thing. This 'thing' could be a natural, or an artificial, object. Kant's four moments of the beautiful can be seen as a set of tests for ascertaining when pleasure is a properly aesthetic feeling, that is, when this notion of 'mere experience' is satisfied.

One of these moments (in Kant's order, the second) discusses *universality*, by which Kant means that the aesthetic judgement always implicitly makes a claim on the judgements of others, and that such judgements 'tend toward' universality. However, they do so without having a determining concept of the beautiful, which means that our knowledge of the object may inform, but cannot determine our judgement of it. Universality of the judgement also entails the universal communicability of the feeling which arises from contemplation of the beautiful. Another of the moments (Kant's first) discusses *disinterestedness*. Interest in the agreeable and in the good are not the same as the aesthetic, which is free of interest. Interest here means a relation of desire with respect to the real existence of the object. Kant claims that it follows that a disinterested judgement would judge on the mere form of the object, rather than its content. The judgement is described as 'contemplation' which we might understand as being mentally 'self-contained'.

The final moment we looked at (Kant's fourth) is a study of its necessity. The judgement is said to be necessary only in an exemplary fashion – as if the object were an example of a law that 'remains hidden'. Accordingly, the judgement is also conditioned by a subjective but *a priori* principle, which Kant calls common sense. This subjective principle is understood as equivalent to the universal communicability of aesthetic feeling, and thus universal validity of the judgement. As far as aesthetic judgement of the beautiful is concerned, the remaining problem is to discover the inner workings of this principle, that is, how aesthetic judgements happen.

2

Purposiveness and Harmony in Judgements

The third moment of the beautiful, which occupies the first half of this chapter, takes us still further beyond the simple description of aesthetic judgements 'from the outside'. On p. 74 we will return to the transcendental argument concerning common sense which concluded the fourth moment and related passages. The aim of these arguments is to justify, at last, the possibility of universally valid aesthetic judgements.

The Form of Purposiveness

In the Introduction, we discussed the notion of purpose (or 'end') and purposiveness (or 'finality'). A 'purpose' is an object the cause of which is a concept of it. A cup of coffee is my purpose – meaning I form a concept of the coffee and act so as to realise that concept. 'Purposiveness' is the object's property of having or appearing to have (or to belong to the realisation of) a purpose (compare Introduction IV and §10).[1] Turning on the kettle is purposive because it belongs to the chain of events co-ordinated by a purpose. In the third moment of the beautiful, Kant wants to make two major claims about the aesthetic judgement. The first of these, we have seen before: the judgement of the beautiful object happens in the absence of any particular concept, including a concept of the object's purpose. The second claim is that, despite the absence of a determinate purpose, the object is judged to be purposive. Thus, Kant's famous notion of 'purposiveness without a purpose' (or 'finality without end').

Consider the following set of analogies. Similar versions of these arguments are to be found throughout the literature on Kant and intention, and are ultimately based on Kant's own illustrations (for example, the note at the end of §17, or §42).

I am walking through the jungle, surrounded by natural shapes and colours, some of them familiar but many of them exotic to me. These natural things do not appear to me to have been produced by human action according to intentions.[2] However, after a while, I come across an old typewriter. It is clear to me that this object does not belong here; it is not a natural form. I know this object has been manmade, for a purpose – it is a machine or a tool. I know it has an 'objective' or 'determinate' purpose (§§11, 15) – namely, typing things on paper – and is therefore final or has purposiveness.

It will be useful to make a distinction between the object itself as the fulfilment of an 'internal' concept of a purpose ('perfection'), and the 'external' concept of a purpose which the object is there to serve (that is, its 'utility', §15). Whenever something is produced, there must be an intermediate intention just to make it or finish it off. This is an answer to the question 'How?' Suppose I am putting together some bookshelves. As I work, my internal intention is simply to finish the assembly process, and I need not look beyond that stage. The bookshelves *themselves*, once finished, are the fulfilment of a intention. Internal intentions have the property of fully accounting for all the properties of the object. Why do I drill a hole of just that size and depth in exactly that location? Because the instructions tell me to. That 'fully accounts' for the drilling, but is hardly a satisfying explanation.

Being bookshelves, they *also* have the external intention of holding books in rows; that is, they have utility beyond just being what they are. This is an answer to the question 'Why?' This external intention may be plural: they may also have been chosen to look good in a certain room, or to hide an imperfection in the plaster of a wall. The *explanation* of the internal purpose takes us to external intentions. The hole is drilled there to make the shelves level and of maximum strength to hold books. Unfortunately, these external intentions have the property of always leading to further external purposes. (One of the great philosophical questions, since ancient Greece, has been: Is there a *final purpose* to this sequence of 'whys'? See below and Chapter 5.)

What do we mean by 'objective purpose'? Certainly, Kant means an internal purpose; but he must also mean an external purpose, at least insofar as that is taken to be connected to the object, rather than thrust upon it. The bookshelves, as objects, probably *are* meant to hold books, and probably *not* meant to hide shoddy plasterwork. It does not matter if the concept behind the object's production cannot be fully determined empirically, or if the object accumulates more uses as time goes on, because Kant is focusing on a case in which no concept of a purpose is available *in principle*. Most, if not all, human productions fall into the category of objective purposes.

I leave the typewriter behind and walk on through the jungle. Soon I come upon another unusual object, but this time I do not recognise it. Let us say it is a stick of wood which appears to have been carved. Immediately it is clear to me that the stick does not belong here, is not natural to the jungle, and yet I do not know anything about what the stick may have been made for. It has an internal purpose, since I could carve a duplicate, but I don't know *why*? Is it a simple machine, a cultural or religious artefact, a musical instrument? Indeed, I am prepared to admit that, just perhaps, it was formed naturally after all by a freak occurrence. Yet it appears to me designed, *as if* it has a purpose. The feature of beauty we are discussing – purposiveness without an external purpose – is similar to this notion. Usually, I would judge something purposive starting from a concept of its purpose: I know what it is to drive in a nail, and I deal with the hammer as purposive on that basis. But in this case, the purposiveness appears first, before the purpose.

However, we are not quite there yet. The stick I found may be mysterious to me, its purposiveness may appear first to me, and I may never expect to discover its purpose, yet *the purpose is there to be found.*[3] It was made to dig with perhaps, or as an idol for worship, or as a toy. It is only *here and now* that the object presents a puzzle: the object *has*, I feel, a objective external purpose, I am just in ignorance of it. The absence of an external purpose for the *beautiful qua beautiful* (that is, the beautiful object considered merely as beautiful) is not an accidental feature, Kant asserts, but an *essential* feature. Thus, the mysterious stick is not yet a perfect analogy. In the case of natural beautiful objects, like a flower, for example, we might also claim that there are purposes, which can be known. The flower is for attracting insects, perhaps even a certain species of insect, and for effecting reproduction through pollination. This may explain certain features of the flower, but *does not explain its beauty*. If I know the external purpose of the flower, I must ignore it in my aesthetic judgement (§16).

If indeed the stick was made by a human being, then it will have been made for a purpose. Works of fine art [*schöne Kunst*], however, are indeed made by humans, but have no objective purpose which *accounts for their beauty*. Certainly, art works will have *internal* purposes – concepts that the sculptor forms of what the piece will look like, or concepts that the musician has of what a passage in an opera will sound like. Even if many of the details of the finished work only emerge in the creative process itself, prior to the addition of those details, or at least at the same time, there will be a concept of them.[4] However, what we already know from the second moment is that this internal purpose is not sufficient to the object as beautiful. In addition, Kant claims, fine art *qua* beautiful does not have external purposes either, and thus no objective purpose. Certainly, a painting may have been made to have a particular emotional effect upon a viewer; or as a commission; or it may have been made to commemorate, celebrate, communicate or protest against some person, event or belief; or it may have been made simply because the artist enjoys painting. But none of these reasons is adequate to the thing as art – they do not *make* the thing art.[5] Art, insofar as it is art, is not made for any objective purpose.[6] If I know these external purposes, I must look past them in forming the aesthetic judgement. This recalls our discussion of what we called 'enabling knowledge' in the previous chapter on pp. 53–4.

The beautiful ought to be pure of any dependence upon concepts at all. If so, the beauty is called 'free'. If not, beauty may still be possible, but is merely 'dependent' (also translated as 'accessory'). Dependent beauty, Kant argues, is possible only in two cases (compare §§16, 17): first, that of *perfection*, and second, that of the *ideal* of beauty.

By 'perfection' Kant means an exact realisation of a concept of an internal purpose together with closely defined concepts of external purposes. If in building my bookcases and achieving the purpose, I stand back and claim 'Perfect' then what I mean is that the actual bookcase is an exact realisation of the conception (concept of the internal purpose) I had. Of course, beauty cannot rely upon a concept; thus perfection cannot be the *reason* why something is beautiful (this is discussed at length in §15). But it can co-exist, as it were, with the beautiful. This is the subject of §16.

Kant gives several examples, among them a church. A church can be judged freely and thus purely, as it would be by someone who did not know what a church was, or by someone who can 'abstract' from the concept church. But then we would be entitled to say only 'It is beautiful' and not 'It is a beautiful *church*'.[7] The latter is only possible if the judgement is in some way dependent upon a concept of what a 'good' church is. Kant never fully explains how perfection relates to dependent beauty. Perhaps we can say this: a beautiful church is one that is as beautiful as it can be within the constraints of the concept of church, and achieves this limited beauty by way of but nevertheless not because of a perfect realisation of the concept of a good church. That is, beauty puts the constraints of the concept to good use. The formal constraints on a sixteenth-century sonnet might be another example. In such cases, dependent beauty results from a 'matching' of the constraint of conceptual form to the otherwise free beauty (which, Kant elsewhere suggests, can be *too* free; see §50) that is so constrained.[8] But there can be, and are, many examples of perfect sonnets that are bad poems.

By 'ideal' Kant means the realisation of an absolute maximum of the beauty of a type of thing (§16). But what things, he asks, and how does this happen? Clearly, the type of thing will have to have an objective concept of a purpose. So ideal beauty in nature is impossible, Kant argues, because such beauty is free and thus pure. Similarly, as we pointed out above, the external purposes of things are at best approximate. Because of this, while objective purposes can perhaps be pinned down for particular things, they cannot for *types* of things. Ordinary things do not have a definite enough concept to form an ideal. Only one type of thing in the whole world has a sufficient concept, Kant claims, and that thing is a human being.

The ideal is the existence of something as adequate, not to an ordinary concept, but to an *idea of reason*, in particular the idea of the moral law, as a law governing the highest or final purpose of man. The ideal, Kant says, is the human being living in complete accord with the moral law. As we discussed in the Introduction, the adequacy of something to an idea is, strictly speaking, impossible. How can a spatial or temporal object (like a person) 'realise' an idea of reason when the latter is precisely what lies *beyond* space and time? But just as the ideas of reason are regulative, so the ideal of beauty is regulative. We strive to achieve this impossible ideal. Only human beings have *within themselves* an idea (that of morality through freedom) that they can attempt to realise in their appearance, worldly selves and manner of behaviour.[9] This extraordinary and far-reaching claim – a profound image of the nature and even purpose of our lives – helps us to see what is meant when Kant claims that practical reason is the highest of the faculties, and all other faculties ultimately exist to serve it. Similar claims occupy Kant at the end of his book.

Another interesting and influential consequence of the section on the 'ideal' is that human beings – either in themselves and their behaviour, or in the society and history within which they live but also help to form and grow – act very much *like art works*. Humans strive to realise the ideal, to create themselves as fully or legitimately human. The general problem of some kind of 'realisation' of an idea of reason is not an isolated problem. It is one that Kant also struggles with throughout his text: we will return to it, for example, in our discussion of the sublime, and in Kant's account of fine art. Finally, we should again note that this whole issue relates to Kant's basic problem for the *Critique of Judgement*. Judgement was supposed to provide a link between the practical realm (moral laws) and the theoretical realm (of people and things in nature). The problem of the realisation of the moral ideal in one's body and behaviour is thus a version of this general problem.

SUMMARY: The third moment of the beautiful introduces the pro-blem of purpose (or 'end') and purposiveness (or 'finality'). Kant claims that the beautiful has to be understood as purposive but without an objective or determinate purpose. This notion has some similarity with an artificial object of unknown function. This analogy is insufficient because we assume that there is a purpose to be found. Beauty in nature will appear (for our cognitive faculties) as purposive, but its beauty will have no purpose. Fine art is more complicated. Although such works may have had purposes behind their production, nevertheless, these cannot be sufficient for the object to be beautiful. Any such knowledge we do have must be abstracted away to form the aesthetic judgement properly. Kant discusses here a number of ways in which concepts or ideas might relate to beauty, and introduces notions such as free beauty, dependent beauty, perfection and the ideal of beauty. Still, we are left with the problem of understanding how a thing can be purposive, without having a objective purpose.

Purposiveness and Intention

So far we have discussed the issue of purposiveness in negative terms. But can we get any closer to understanding what purposiveness without purpose means positively?

Suppose I walk out of the jungle and on to a beach. As I stroll by the seaside, a wave washes over the sand and then recedes. Behind it, on the drying sand, a pattern remains. It is a message; in fact, it appears to be a few lines of poetry. It could be a few familiar lines of Shakespeare, or it could be a combination of words which has never before been seen. There could be many explanations: a communication by some intelligent sea-creature; a trick played on me by some clever practical joker; the god of the sea; a submarine in the bay with some new machine for controlling the waves; or it could be a marvellous accident, produced by the random action of the waves. It is difficult to assess immediately which of these is most likely, and which is least likely.

Basically, there are three possibilities. First, I find out that some person or some intelligent thing has produced these lines deliberately and with the intent to either make or reproduce poetry. Secondly, I am never able to find out how the lines are produced. Thirdly, I eliminate all intelligent agents, and am left with the random wave-action. The question to ask, for each of these, is how ought the few lines to be taken – are they really poetry? In the first case, there is no problem. Although the message and its presence on the beach may have other important implications (for example, that there really is a poetry-loving god of the sea), we feel perfectly comfortable interpreting the lines as poetry. The second case still presents no problem. Though we do not know who the author is, or even if there is an author, we *can* treat the poem like one of the many anonymous verses in existence.

But the third case is more troubling. It is troubling because in treating the impressions upon the beach as *language*, we seem to be forced into assuming someone or something who writes or speaks. Does it make sense to talk about a poem that was literally never written? Instead, we might want to argue that the waves have produced a pattern in the sand; this pattern *resembles* the pattern that might have been made by someone writing a message in the sand; however, the pattern was produced by random wave-action and not by someone writing a message; therefore, the pattern is not a message or a poem, but just looks remarkably like one. Is this a satisfactory way of thinking this through?

The deciding criterion has been the possibility of an intention (concept of a purpose). If the pattern in the sand definitely had an author, or even *may* have had an author, then at least there may have been a concept of a purpose. If the pattern had no author, then it had no purposiveness, and therefore is not a poem, is not even language at all; it just *resembles* language and poetry.

However, we only know the purpose from the product. That is, we only know that someone has a thought when they actually say something. What happens 'behind the scenes' can be disregarded. Why, then, could someone not argue as follows? The pattern resembles in every way what could have been produced by an intelligent, purposive author; but being an intelligent, purposive author just means producing messages such as that which this pattern resembles; the random wave-action produced this message, and is therefore an author, and the pattern is a poem.

We have two arguments now, and each one looks plausible. To take the issue further would require long detours through the philosophies of language and mind. However, one interesting aspect has been overlooked. We said the message was (or resembled) a *poem*. Does this matter? What if it had been an ordinary message, like 'LOOK OUT, BEHIND YOU!' If we consider again the third case, where we are sure the pattern merely results from random wave-action, the first argument made above (the pattern merely resembles language-use) would be strengthened. 'LOOK OUT, BEHIND YOU!' merely *resembles* a message, and is not one. To be a message, it must in some manner *intentionally refer* to the world, and not just closely resemble the behaviour of someone who has such an intention. Even if there was, in fact, something behind me, for example a tiger coming out of the sea, the pattern still would not be a message. Such a coincidence would make the whole phenomenon more extraordinary and unlikely, but would not alter the fact that there was no purpose behind the 'warning'.

But if the pattern resembled a poem, and especially if it resembled what we judge to be a *good* poem (in Kant's language, beautiful or, more particularly, *fine art*), then it seems more likely that it would be treated as in fact a poem, regardless of where we decided it came from. The poem seems to *stand on its own* in a strange way. (Accordingly, my judgement of it is 'self-contained' in the manner we have already begun to consider.) It would, of course, be a poem entirely separated from the life and times of any author – thus interpreting and even reading the poem might present some unusual difficulties. But does this separation necessarily prevent it from being a thing of beauty and of artistic meaning? Presumably not, any more than a natural landscape cannot be beautiful just because it was *not* designed by Capability Brown. Thus, Kant follows a similar line of argument with respect to all natural beauty. If the poem is considered 'beautiful' in some broad sense, then we do not need a definite author or purpose behind it in order to treat it as purposive, and thus something more than a random pattern. Let us say the poem comes first, implying an author, rather than the author coming first and writing the poem. The poem is purposive without a definite purpose: that is, it exhibits some kind of order within itself, without any possible explanation of exactly what or how that order is.

Having walked past typewriters, sticks and finally messages in the sand, we have finally arrived at something like what Kant means by 'purposiveness without purpose'. The poem in the sand exhibits purposiveness without a definite purpose, while the mere 'message' in the sand only resembles something that has purpose. Purposiveness without purpose has a number of important implications for how we understand aesthetic judgements and the presentations they judge. The judgement, it follows, is singular, dealing with the object as an absolute particular. This is to say that no question of the 'type' of object relevant to its beauty enters into or emerges from the judgement. It follows as well that the object, considered aesthetically, has a certain *holism*. By this is meant that the object cannot be understood as a mere concatenation of parts, but must be understood from the point of view of the whole form. It is this notion that the over-used expression 'the whole is greater than the sum of its parts' has in mind. Not all things are such wholes, certainly: a clock *is just* the sum of its parts and nothing more. That is to say, its function can be perfectly understood by 'adding up' the operation of each part. In general, anything for which there is a determining concept of a purpose is just the sum of its parts. This follows from the basic function of concepts in our mental life, according to Kant: concepts function precisely by being the rule of a synthesis, of a putting-together or adding-up. But the beauty of a flower is not a question of adding up its petals and stamens; and the beauty of a poem is not the sum of the meaning of its individual words. That which is purposive without purpose – or again which pleases universally without a concept – has to be apprehended as a *whole form*.[10]

Our bizarre example of the 'poem' in the sand – a kind of halfway house between an artefact (any produced thing) and nature – would, however, just be an explicit example of what Kant claims is the essence of my experience of *any* beautiful object. It is as if we are so used to applying simple concepts of 'nature' or 'artefact' that it takes an apparent paradox to make us see that the situation of beauty was not that simple to begin with. This account of fine art (the poem) is in fact extended from a general account of natural beauty. Unless we are strict creationists, believing in God as the sole 'author' of the world and everything in it, at the beginning and for all time, we do not normally treat natural objects as *actually* designed or final. Kant claims, however, that to the extent that a natural object is seen as beautiful, then it is being seen *as if* designed. *How* made, and for *what reason* we can never know – even the creationist can not comprehend the mind of God. Nor does the fact that some things appear designed, as has often been supposed, prove the existence of a creator (see Chapter 5). Nevertheless, this purposiveness of nature can be a profound experience, and is certainly a pleasing one.

Unqualified purposiveness alone is not what is required by beauty. There must be a purposiveness without an objective or determinate purpose. For if a definite purpose could be discovered (even if only in principle), the beautiful object becomes just another manufactured good, like the typewriter, and can be *fully explained* with a finite set of quite ordinary concepts. In this case, it would no longer be the work itself we judge, but its origin and explanation. Thus, in Chapter 1, the absence of a concept for the beautiful is not an accident, but is essential. The situation is thus also related to Kant's rejection of any *external*, determining interest in the beautiful, on the basis of, for example, some moral idea of what is good or just. It is important that it is the presentation of the object – our 'mere experience' of the object as a whole – and *that alone* which is the occasion for our aesthetic judgement and aesthetic pleasure. In the case of, for example, a painting, we know it was made (probably also by whom, when and where), and we assume the artist had in mind a number of ideas or wider purposes when making it. It may even be important to know these when judging a work of art, in much the same way as one must know English to judge a poem, play or novel written in English. Kant's claim is that these intentions on their own are never enough to determine the outcome of the aesthetic judgement. Fine art exceeds or goes beyond any of these intentions: it has a 'life of its own'. Judgement requires that we abstract from any known or suspected concepts of purposes.

> SUMMARY: The example of the poem in the sand on the beach allows us to explore the idea of purposiveness without purpose. Here, the problem is that of *intention*. Is merely the observable behaviour (the poem) a sufficient notion of intention? Or is intention something real, in someone's mind, 'behind' the object? The difference between a message appearing in the sand, and the poem, suggests that works of art have a self-sufficiency. The poem can be experienced as purposive even if we *know* there was no purpose or intention. This is related to the notion that there can be no concept of the beautiful.

Purposiveness and Pleasure

The judgement of taste results in or involves pleasure. Kant usually makes a stronger claim still (for example in §12): the judgement seems to 'consist of' a 'feeling'. This may seem strange. The judgements given by engineers or court judges are not 'feelings'. We might be more comfortable in saying that an aesthetic 'judgement' is something which asserts 'X is beautiful', that is, something which attaches the predicate 'is beautiful' to some object. Kant would argue that, if you analysed the situation, all of the important 'work' of judging has been done in the attainment of the feeling. What happens on the basis of that feeling – explicitly attaching the predicate 'is beautiful' – adds nothing to it. Feeling, Kant asserts (for example in §9), is the way (and the *only* way) the mental state of contemplating beauty makes itself known to itself.

Still, the question is why do we feel pleasure in the beautiful? This question may seem odd: the beautiful is a nice thing, of course one should feel pleasure in contemplating it. But we can still ask what is beauty *qua* purposiveness without a purpose such that it is a 'nice thing', that is, such that pleasure is necessarily present in the contemplation of it?

In the Introduction, we defined what pleasure means for Kant.[11] There we said that pleasure is a feeling of the actual or, at least, possible attainment of a purpose. However, in the beautiful, no purpose is attained, by definition. In an ordinary cognitive *reflective* judgement, the discovery of a new idea and of its application to some previously unsolved problem is, Kant claims, the most basic kind of mental pleasure. It is *as if* the problem had been 'made' all along to be solved by just this new idea, or as if the new idea fulfils the destiny of some puzzling phenomenon. Thus there is a link between purposiveness and pleasure.

In the fourth moment, we discovered that a beautiful presentation is purposive for cognition in general. That is, the presentation exists as if it had been designed to suit our cognitive faculties. Although there is and can be no definite concept of a purpose, the beautiful nevertheless *satisfies* cognition. Further, the beautiful agrees not just with this or that concept, but with cognition in general – with the whole function of objective though. It furthers the interests of life; it 'quickens' [*beleben*] (or 'enlivens') our cognitive faculties (see, for example, §12). This is felt as pleasure, which is both an awareness of this satisfaction, and an incentive to continue in the activity of contemplating the beautiful. Kant writes, 'we *linger* in our contemplation of the beautiful, because this contemplation reinforces and reproduces itself' (§12).

Section 12 is also intended to show that, although the judgement of taste is based upon *a priori* factors in the subject (namely, common sense), one cannot *demonstrate* (or prove) *a priori* the connection between the representation of an object and the aesthetic feeling of pleasure. There are three reasons for this. First, if that were the case, then we would have to have a concept of the beautiful. Secondly, such a connection would be a cause and effect relation between a presentation and the feeling; and if the demonstration were *a priori*, then the cause and effect relation would have to be determined *a priori* also. Although as we saw in the Introduction to this book, cause and effect must be one of the *a priori* rules of the understanding, we also saw that the rule is necessarily quite empty. So the fact that a given presentation (of a sunset, say) causes the aesthetic feeling is an empirical or *a posteriori* matter.

Thirdly and finally, it is strictly speaking incorrect to say that the pleasure is *caused by* the presentation of the object (and thus somehow distinguishable from it as an effect), which then *causes* one to 'linger' on the presentation.[12] The one mental state or activity (contemplation) does not cause another (pleasure); they are the same, considered as mental states. The 'quickening' of the cognitive faculties is the same metaphor (if it *is* a metaphor) as calling pleasure itself the 'feeling of life' (§1).[13] Since for these reasons, we cannot conceive of the contemplation in terms of an ordinary cause and effect relation, in which cause and effect can be separated as discrete entities, therefore one cannot demonstrate *a priori* the connection between a particular presentation and aesthetic pleasure. Instead, there is a causality wherein the effect and the cause are the same.[14]

Claiming that one cannot demonstrate *a priori* this connection is equivalent to saying that there is no concept determining the 'enlivening'. At the moment, then, this thesis that there can be no *a priori* demonstration just seems like another subtle way of making those points we have seen Kant make before, especially the lack of a determinate concept for the beautiful. However, that there is no *a priori* demonstration of the aesthetic judgement entails, from the point of view of theoretical cognition, that the judgement is contingent, not necessary. And yet, from the point of view of reflective judgement itself, the necessity is given as an *a priori* principle. This dilemma turns out to have significant consequences, both in the Antinomy of the 'Critique of Aesthetic Judgement' and in the 'Critique of Teleological Judgement'.

SUMMARY: Why do we feel pleasure in the beautiful at all? Pleasure seems to be the result of some attainment of a purpose, but the beautiful has no purpose. Rather, Kant says, it is the mere purposiveness of the beautiful for cognition *in general* that serves as if it were a purpose. The exact role of 'cognition in general' and of what we have called the 'self-containedness' of the mental activity in aesthetic judgement is not yet clear. So, our task now is to try to understand what is going on in this peculiar mental act.

Overview

Before going on to consider the role of 'cognition in general' and the 'self-containedness' of the mental activity in aesthetic judgement, let us pause for a moment to summarise the conclusions Kant has reached. The aesthetic judgement has four moments. The first two seem relatively straightforward descriptions of how such judgements behave: they are disinterested, pleasures that claim to be universal. The next two moments are more clearly asking about the nature of such judgements themselves. Kant concludes the fourth moment by saying that such judgements are necessary (in an exemplary and conditioned fashion), based upon what he calls 'common sense'. Common sense functions as an *a priori* but subjective principle of aesthetic judgements (judgement's legislation for the faculty of feeling). By 'common sense' is also meant a faculty of responding with feeling to the beautiful that all humans possess, and thus that this feeling is public or communicable. Common sense also refers to our feeling of our cognitive faculties in accord *in general*, rather than always in particular, determinate judgements. Above we summarised key aspects of these points by defining aesthetic judgements as related to the 'mere experience' of a thing. Similarly, we called the judgement 'self-contained' (without concept or interest) but still subjectively valid (universal and necessary, as if based upon a principle). Kant's term is 'autonomy': that which is free, but gives a law to itself.[15]

The third moment is the one we have been discussing in this chapter. Here, Kant argues that the object of the aesthetic judgement is always seen to be purposive without any definite purpose. This last description is intended to begin explaining what happens in 'common sense', that is, how the beautiful can conform to the cognitive faculties *in general*. For the rest of this chapter, we will explore this strange notion of 'conformity' or 'harmony' more closely. As with the other *Critiques*, the explanation, if it is going to succeed as an explanation, must turn out to be *transcendental* in nature – that is, to give the *a priori* conditions under which such judgements are possible.

On the basis of the four moments of the beautiful, and Kant's extensive running commentary upon them, let us summarise Kant's discoveries thus far in the following full definition of an aesthetic judgement. *The aesthetic judgement consists of my consciousness that a feeling of pleasure, independent of any interest, lies within the 'self-contained' contemplation of the mere form of a presentation of an object, which is thus called 'beautiful';[16] this feeling (and thus judgement) presents itself as universally communicable and necessary, because founded upon 'common sense' as a subjective a priori* principle, despite being determined apart from any objective concept. Pleasure is felt because the presentation of the beautiful is experienced as subjectively purposive, though without a definite purpose, with respect to the harmony of the cognitive faculties.[17]

The idea of harmony between or among the faculties of cognition is the key idea. What does Kant think is going on in such 'harmony', or in common sense for that matter, and does he have any arguments which make these ideas more than mere metaphors for beauty? At the end of Chapter 1 we had no such argument. At best, common sense was plausible as a possible explanation of the tendency to universality observed in aesthetic judgements (as Kant admits in §17). Such a demand for universality could be accounted for nicely if we assumed a faculty for taste, which might also explain the idea of universal communicability and, if it had an *a priori* principle, the exemplary necessity of aesthetic judgements. This, however, is rather weak. Kant believes he has an ingenious route to proving the case with much greater certainty.

Throughout the four moments of the beautiful, Kant has dropped many important clues as to the transcendental account of the possibility of aesthetic judgement: in particular, we have talked about communicability, common sense and the harmony of the cognitive faculties. Kant then veers off to the sublime, representing a different problem within aesthetic judgement. He returns to beauty in §30, which forms the transition to the passages tantalisingly called the Deduction. Sections 35–40 are directly relevant to the problem of common sense and harmony, returning to the type of argument begun in §§9 and 21, which we have not yet fully discussed.

The Arguments of the Deduction

The argument for universal common sense (or an equivalent) comes in two versions which emphasise different notions. The first is in a highly compressed passage in §21 (with the addition of related material in §9); the second is in the Deduction (§§30–40, but especially §§35–40). We shall take them in turn, but try by the end to combine them so as to form as complete a version as possible. It will be necessary to dwell on this material for some time and in some detail. This is because these arguments appear to be climactic moments in Kant. Moreover, it would be plausible to claim that Kant's whole account of aesthetic judgements stands or falls through these arguments.

The First Version: Common Sense

We discussed the context of the first version of Kant's arguments at the end of the previous chapter. Kant is working out the particular nature of the necessity attached to aesthetic judgements. The necessity in question is *exemplary* because the judgement is based upon a *subjective* condition. This condition Kant names as common sense, which we can briefly define as the *a priori* subjective principle of the faculty of taste, which (if there is indeed such a principle) would also assure the universality of the human response to the beautiful.[18] Section 21 is entitled 'Have we reason for presupposing common sense?' Kant's argument looks something like this:

1. In objective cognition, whether entirely theoretical or empirical – that is, the thinking of natural objects so as to obtain knowledge of them – all of the elements at work in cognition (imaginings, concepts), and the judgement which results (along with the 'conviction' in that judgement), must be communicable. For this communicability is virtually equivalent to objectivity (what Kant here calls 'a harmony with the object'), as we discussed at the end of Chapter 1.

2. However, on the purely subjective side of such cognition, the 'mental state' [*Gemütszustand*] of 'attunement' (or 'accordance') [*Stimmung*][19] or 'proportion' [*Proportion*] of the cognitive faculties (imagination with understanding) must be equally communicable. For if these subjective conditions are unique and necessary conditions of cognition, such that knowledge could not happen without them, then they will be just as universally shared as the objective presentations in step 1 above. Such proportion is assumed to be shared, then, not as itself a presentation of an object in a common world, but as a mental state necessarily tied to such presentations.[20]

3. In real circumstances, this proportion will be different for different objects. Let us try one way of understanding what this idea of proportion might mean. If I am doing mental work that is strictly subject to rules, like adding two numbers together, then the understanding (in supplying the concepts of number and addition) is doing most of the work. The imagination is solely responsible for the mere intuition of a quantity – it is not 'playing' or 'free' at all. If, on the other hand, I am trying to solve a brain-teaser, then the imagination may have to work hard: filling in missing bits of information, trying out many possible solutions, seeking variations on the data given or their arrangement. The understanding, comparatively, only has to provide a concept such that I can recognise the solution when it pops up. So, the 'proportion' of these faculties might be the various ways in which they have to work, depending upon the mental task undertaken. Such a proportion will also vary according to quite contingent subjective factors, such as how quick I am at mathematics, or whether I have come across the same or a similar puzzle before. There may also be more than one way to reach a solution. In other words, even given the same object, not everyone will use the same proportion of imagination and understanding in the cognition of it. As a condition, it is not unique. Thus, this is just a psychological observation, rather than an *a priori* transcendental claim. And indeed nowhere does Kant insist that such a *variable* proportion must be universally communicable. So, when he talks about the communicability of the proportion, what does he mean?

4. Despite this variability in particular instances, it must be the case that there will be one unique proportion that is most suitable for cognition

generally, and that this initiates the 'mutual quickening' [*Belebung*] or 'harmonious accord' (as Kant puts it in Introduction, IX) of the cognitive faculties. This is the proportion which is found in the attempt to think the beautiful presentation. However, here Kant seems to be asserting that the existence of this general proportion is necessary, not just for the beautiful, but also (subjectively) for all (even ordinary) cognition.

Confusingly, Kant also sometimes says that the beautiful has a 'harmony' [*-stimmung*] with or for cognition generally (see, for example, Introduction VIII, §38, and the General Remark after §22). Thus he will claim that the beautiful is purposive for cognition. The former way of using 'harmony' (harmony among faculties) indicates the way in which the purposiveness is realised or grasped within thought, the latter (beauty in harmony with cognition) indicates that purposiveness itself. Thus here, where Kant is concerned with the validity of judgements concerning such purposiveness, the former way is more fundamental. However, later when he is analysing the implications of aesthetic judgements, he returns to the dramatic importance of saying the beautiful in nature is judged to have purposiveness (compare Chapters 4 and 5).

5. This unique proportion (perhaps precisely because it is, so to speak, 'between' faculties) cannot be apprehended through any concept, but is rather *felt*.[21] Normally, feeling is entirely subjective and without universality, but here it must be communicable and thus universally necessary. The principle according to which this feeling is asserted to be universally necessary is common sense. In the particular case of the beautiful, that means the ideal commonness in the feeling of aesthetic pleasure.

6. Common sense is necessary for ordinary cognition and thus any knowledge, or else the mental state involved in cognition will not be communicable, as it must be. However, since this same common sense is also precisely the basis of aesthetic judgements, Kant answers the question of his own title: we have good transcendental justification for the assumption of the existence of common sense. And this common sense in turn legitimates the universality and necessity claimed by aesthetic judgement.

A fascinating argument, but there are at least three holes in it as it stands. First, why should we believe that the aesthetic judgement consists of the harmony of the cognitive faculties? Or, more generally, why should we assume that aesthetic judgements have anything to do with cognition? The above argument simply assumes this. Why, in particular, should we accept that our aesthetic response is related to *cognitive* judgements as Kant must assert? The answer is purposiveness. Suppose that we accept that purposiveness without determinate purpose is a feature of the beautiful, in both nature and art. It also seems reasonable to accept that purposiveness *without* determinate purpose is related to ordinary purposiveness *with a purpose* (for example, ordinary judgements about made or used objects). That is, purposiveness means the same thing and therefore is dealt with by the same mental functions. But ordinary purposiveness is clearly a cognitive matter: it has to do with particulars and concepts, and grasping the concept as the cause of the object. It would seem to follow, then, that purposiveness without determinate purpose must also be related to cognition, although in a different and special way. In other words, *the experience of the beautiful as purposive is the clue* that allows Kant to assert that aesthetic judgements are indeed judgements, and thus have some relation to the cognitive faculties. (That is why all the peculiar material about the possibility of scientific systems in the Introduction is so important.)

The second hole is the issue of why we should believe that ordinary cognition also depends upon this unique proportion, and upon common sense. And the third is the issue of why we should believe that there exists this one unique proportion of the cognitive faculties at all, rather than the variable proportions Kant also mentions? It has to be admitted that Kant does not address the last two problems in any detail at all. However, in the 'General Remark' which follows §22, Kant makes some useful comments.

Everything hinges on there being cognitive faculties *at all*, rather than a mere subjective play of the faculties of presentation 'as scepticism would have it' (§21). Imagination and understanding are not notions of mental abilities which are derived from empirical psychological observation of just any mental acts. What makes imagination (or more generally, sensibility) and understanding proper faculties in the Kantian sense is that their operation is constituted *a priori*. It was just this that the first half of the *Critique of Pure Reason* aimed to prove. Thus, the imagination is not just any presentation of sense which does not actually come immediately from our sense organs, and which is subject only to empirical and subjective 'laws of association'. The imagination is an activity governed and constituted by the *a priori* principles of all intuition: space and time as *a priori* pure forms of intuition. So in aesthetic judgement, the imagination in its 'higher' form consists of the production 'at will' of 'forms of possible intuition' (§22, General Comment, translation modified). That is, imagination is set 'free' and is 'spontaneous' so as to be hindered in the first instance by nothing but the forms of possible intuition, which are the pure intuitions of space and time, as the *a priori* principles of all sensibility. The freed imagination thus more closely corresponds with the *a priori* outer limits of the imaginable.[22]

Similarly, the understanding, considered as a faculty of theoretical cognition is not just the source of this or that concept, but is that which is governed *a priori* by the pure principles of understanding. We might say that in aesthetic judgement the understanding too is freed (compare §39). It is freed from supplying particular and determining concepts in order to be the source of lawfulness in general. Imagination and understanding, thus, are present in aesthetic judgement *in their essence* as faculties. They are doing in the most general possible way what they always do in particular ways.[23] However, cognition only results, and judgements are only accomplished, when these two faculties work mutually. In ordinary cognition, the understanding tends to rule over the imagination; in aesthetic judgement, it is the reverse (§22, General Remark). But never one without the other – that would be a form of madness (compare §50). This may have gone some way towards explaining what is meant by there being unique proportion for cognition in general, rather than always variable proportions.

It may also help to explain why such a proportion, and indeed also common sense, is required for ordinary cognition. There was an ambiguity in the above argument. Was Kant saying that the feeling of thought for itself was required *actually* in the course of ordinary cognition, such that no determinate judgement could find completion without such feeling? It is possible to interpret §21 in this way, but Kant never makes such a claim elsewhere, and indeed states unambiguously on several occasions that ordinary cognitive judgements are 'intellectual' rather than felt (§§9, 40).[24]

Another way of reading the argument in §21 is that feeling is rather a red herring, and the real stress is on cognitive harmony or proportion itself. In addition to this passage, Kant claims on many occasions that the proportion of the cognitive faculties is required for both aesthetic judgement and ordinary, objective cognition (§§9, 35, 39). For example, Kant writes at §35, not about aesthetic judgements alone but about all judgements:

> The subjective condition of all judgements is our very ability to judge, i.e., the faculty of judgement. When we use this faculty of judgement in regard to a presentation by which an object is given, then it requires that there be a harmony [*Zusammenstimmung*] between two presentational faculties.

We could interpret this as the 'fit' between intuition (or imagination, productive of intuitions) and concept. Certainly, it is not hard to see how this fit could vary in different judgements on different objects. In the case of determinate judgements, it is validated by the concept itself (intellectually). Where there is no concept (that is, in reflective judgement), the fit is both different in nature (a free or spontaneous harmony, rather than a determined one), and so is its mode of calling attention to itself, through the feeling of pleasure at a purpose attained, rather than intellectually. For every judgement, there will be such a harmony. However, it is still difficult to see the sense in saying that this harmonious accordance could ever be the *unique condition* for the cognitive faculties in general, as is required by Kant's argument.

Now, we might just say that ordinary determinate cognition requires this unique proportion in the sense that ordinary cognition simply requires the *a priori* principles of sensibility (intuition or imagination) and understanding. But, again, this would not serve Kant's argument as given above. The argument clearly hinges on the proportion between the cognitive faculties being required *in the same sense* by both determinate cognition and aesthetic judgement. That way, the possibility of the former can be a proof of the possibility of the latter. Unless Kant can fill this gap, the argument is sadly incomplete. Before we attempt to fill the gap, let us see whether a solution might arise in the second version of Kant's Deduction.

The Second Version: Universal Validity

Those sections called the 'Deduction' seem to provide much more detail regarding Kant's meaning. However, the Deduction itself (§38) is short, giving us interpretative problems similar to those above. In §37, what Kant claims to be proving is the universal validity of pleasure in the beautiful. The aesthetic judgement is not just the connection of pleasure to the presentation of an object, but the connection of such pleasure as universally valid. This is not a distinct kind of pleasure but a distinct way of that pleasure belonging to a mental state. However, he characterises this as a 'rule' or 'principle' of judgement – that is, the connection of pleasure to the presentation according to an *a priori* principle – which is precisely how common sense was introduced in §20. So this second argument, at least, is pulling at the same oar as the first.

Our reconstruction of the argument in §38 begins as a kind of compressed statement of the four moments of the beautiful:

1. Consider a judgement which gives an 'estimate' [*Beurteilung*]²⁵ of an object, which does not proceed on the basis of any sensation of the object, and is not influenced therefore by corporeal *interests* which arise because of those sensations.
2. Consider further that this judgement does not proceed on the basis of any concept of an object – neither a theoretical concept (what it is, was, or could be in the natural realm) for a practical concept (concerning whether something ought to be, according to a conception of the good).
3. Steps 1 and 2 exclude all 'matter' for such a judgement – anything which makes the judgement inseparable from, and thus dependent upon, the real existence of an object (see the discussion on disinterestedness starting on p. 50). The judgement can be formal only, and thus also a type of reflective judgement.

So far, this is familiar territory. But the argument now takes a slightly new turn:

4. In saying it is formal and free of 'matter' in the above sense, we mean that although the judgement is a judgement of the presentation of a particular (singular) object, no *particular* determination of either sensation, or understanding forms a *necessary* part of the judgement. For if it did, there would be either a relation to the real existence of the object (through sensation or a concept of the good), or at least the possibility of determinate cognition (through a theoretical concept). We might understand Kant's point in the following way: in the aesthetic judgement, my thought can range widely and still be 'within' the proper judgement of the object. For example, suppose I am judging a painting aesthetically, and paying attention to its colours and colour-relationships. I may ignore or perhaps even imaginatively exaggerate or alter (in order to better exhibit to myself the form) the colour sensations that I actually receive.[26] That is, as Kant says, I am not 'confined' to (also translated here as 'restricted' by) that particular mode of sensibility given to me. Similarly with the concepts of any particular represented objects in the painting (a horse, a king), should others occur to me in the course of my properly aesthetic contemplation (the horse suggests country life, or other animals; the king, authority, great wealth and so on). In ordinary cognition of the world, this lack of restriction would be entirely out of place, and indeed would be a sign of an unbalanced mind.

5. However, considered *in general* (that is, in their essence as faculties), the cognitive faculties of imagination and understanding are *likewise* not restricted to any presentation or kind of sense, or any concept. Such a judgement as the aesthetic judgement described above is possible only by reference to these subjective conditions of any judgement. This is because first there is no other way remaining to explain how such judgements could happen, all other possibilities having been eliminated by the previous steps; yet, secondly, all judgements *must* involve the cognitive faculties. That is, if we assume that aesthetic judgements are indeed judgements, then they will have some relation to the faculty of judgement which in turn must involve the cognitive faculties. Every judgement is the placing of a particular under a universal (Kant's Introduction, IV); judgement's job is to coordinate these other faculties. Thus, there must be a source of a particular (sensibility; but here as productive imagination in its freedom, rather than in any particular presentation it comes up with) and a universal (here the understanding in its conformity to law, rather than as the source of any one concept).[27] Given this, the four moments (compare, for example, §§5, 9, 12) then systematically go about eliminating the possible variations on

this particular/universal scenario. This elimination is repeated and extended in steps 1–4.

6. Because such faculties in general are required for all theoretical cognition, regardless of its object (as Kant claims to have proven in the first *Critique*), they can be assumed present *a priori* in the same form and in the same way, in all human beings.

7. The presence of the cognitive faculties in their various relations is equivalent to the notion of the universal communicability of any mental state in which these faculties are involved *a priori*. This is the same proposition as the first step in the previous version of the argument.

8. Therefore, such a judgement can be presumed universally valid for all humans.

This argument has two notable differences from the first, which help us to understand them both. First of all, it makes no mention of feeling as a mode of access to cognitive harmony, and thus no explicit mention of common sense as an *a priori* principle of feeling. In §40, however, Kant discusses common sense again in the former terms. Thus, whether feeling with its particular non-cognitive and non-objective qualities is here required (as it was in the first version – it was these qualities which demanded the introduction of common sense and the principle of universal communicability) is an open question as yet.

Secondly, this new version of the argument seems to solve the above problem of exactly how this principle of universal validity for aesthetic judgement is supposed to be related to ordinary determinate cognition. Namely, the mere existence of the cognitive faculties in 'relation' is sufficient as the transcendental guarantee of both. Formerly, Kant had it that the additional notion of proportion was the common link. And that led us to the above problem of how proportionality (in a strict sense) was supposed to be also the condition of ordinary objective cognition. In other words, so long as Kant can demonstrate that aesthetic judgement relies upon the cognitive faculties and upon nothing else which might be merely contingent or subjective, the task of the Deduction (to show universal validity) is complete. The notion of proportion (or 'harmony', as is seen again already in §38 'Comment') is part of the *explanation* of exactly how such judgements take place. An explanation (in this sense) is a different issue from the Deduction of validity. However, in the very next section (§39), the notion of proportion returns in the old way, and Kant writes:

This pleasure must of necessity rest on the same conditions in everyone . . . [and] the proportion between these cognitive faculties that is required for taste is also required for the sound and common understanding . . .

In other words, although it looked briefly as though we might have taken a step forward, Kant has landed us back with the same problem. It is not just the cognitive faculties in relation in general which are the link between the possibility of aesthetic judgement and the possibility of 'ordinary sound understanding', but just as before, the unique proportionality.

However, precisely by *not* mentioning the harmony of the faculties as such, this second argument has suggested a useful distinction, which is compatible with what Kant says throughout the *Critique* (with the exception of a very few places such as the passage from §35 quoted above). Above, we distinguished between the mere possession of the cognitive faculties, and there being a unique proportion between them. We might also distinguish between this proportion [*Proportion*] as an *a priori* feature of the relation between the faculties, and the harmony[28] of those faculties as a real feature of their activity in aesthetic contemplation. What Kant has called the 'proportion' or just 'relation' between these faculties is now seen as the *a priori* standing *potential* for the free harmonising activity of these faculties in and through the presence of the beautiful presentation. This potential is the *condition* for ordinary cognition in the sense we suggested (but at the time discarded) in our discussion of the first version: namely it is identical to the faculties considered in their essence as transcendental activities.

The problem then becomes one of showing that the free harmony of the cognitive faculties is both possible, and nothing but those faculties, once freed and on the occasion of the beautiful. This task we have begun above in suggesting that imagination and understanding are present in aesthetic judgement *in their essence* as faculties. This then allows us to make sense of other sections of §35 wherein Kant writes:

> [T]aste, as a subjective faculty of judgement, contains a principle of subsumption; however, this subsumption is not one of intuitions under *concepts*, but rather one of the *faculty* of intuitions or exhibitions (the imagination) under the *faculty* of concepts (the understanding), insofar as the imagination *in its freedom* harmonises with the understanding *in its lawfulness* [*Gesetzmässigkeit*].

The qualifying expressions ('in its freedom' or 'in its lawfulness') do not indicate one feature among others of these faculties, nor a distinct and special feature which can show up under certain conditions, but the essence of these faculties in general considered in relation to one another, and in any activity whatsoever. This essence is most perfectly exhibited in the particular activity which is the contemplation of the beautiful and thus the formation of the aesthetic judgement. But it is also required for ordinary cognition.

What does Kant's argument now look like? In each of the above two arguments, the key move can be expressed like this: whatever conditions are necessary for the possibility of ordinary cognition must be assumed to exist universally. If aesthetic judgement can be proven to rest on these same conditions, necessarily and uniquely, then the universal communicability of the claims or the content of such judgements will have been demonstrated. Our problems above boiled down to whether the conditions were indeed the same. If they were, then the argument works, but it became difficult to see how aesthetic judgements were supposed to be different from ordinary objective cognition. If they were not, then the argument fails.

We can now see a light at the end of the tunnel. As we now understand the situation, the conditions (that is, the cognitive faculties) are indeed the same faculties considered as essential potentials to provide or accomplish certain presentations or activities, and (when in relation) to provide for cognition in general. But within particular activities, this potential is only realised in part in determinate cognition, because, first, a concept puts a halt to the mental activity of judging; secondly, the sensibility is likewise restricted, both by the sensed or imagined object itself, and by the concept; and thirdly, the presentation of the object is not such as to give the faculties the freedom to realise their full potential with respect to one another (it does not appear purposive). Only in the case of the beautiful is there nothing to halt the activity, and a presentation 'suitable' for freeing the faculties to the full mutual expression of their essence. Perhaps, then, we have at last discovered the true hinge of Kant's Deduction of the validity of aesthetic judgements.

It follows that the aesthetic judgement is not just one type of judgement among others, but is the highest type, insofar as it is the instantiation of the essence of judging. That would fully explain why Kant, in a critique of the faculty of judgement in general, should focus on aesthetic judgements, and also why he should consider them so important vis à vis the moral 'vocation' of human beings (see Chapters 4 and 5).

But what has happened to feeling and common sense? Where do they now fit into Kant's argument, and his overall account of aesthetic judgement?

In the first version of the argument, it was the universal common sense for the feeling of the proportion between the cognitive faculties that provided the hinge of the argument. Kant's second argument makes no mention of feeling, and yet as we have seen, the sections leading up to it claim that its purpose is precisely to validate the universality of the feeling of pleasure in the beautiful. Furthermore, shortly after the brief Deduction, Kant is back to talking about common sense.

However, now that we have reached some clarification about notions like proportion and harmony, even the first version of the argument does not seem to require common sense. Instead, we find ourselves speaking merely of the *a priori* potential of the cognitive faculties for harmony. We are left with the problem of interpreting how the notion of common sense fits back into the overall proof.

Above, we tried one way, which was to assume the distinction between the conditions of the judgement, and the explanation of its actual course. This meant that pleasure and common sense were a kind of psychological account of how aesthetic judgements happened, and in particular of how we 'become aware' of the harmonisation of the faculties. This 'psychological' account would have nothing to do with the validity of such judgements. But the contingency of such an interpretation might imply that there could be *another way* for such judgements to happen, or for us to become aware of cognitive harmony. This Kant would never allow – it goes against the whole task and flavour of the third *Critique*. Thus, we have to find a way for notions like feeling and common sense to be integral to the properly transcendental account of the possibility of aesthetic judgements.

In an important sense, we have already answered this question. Previously, we have made much of what we called the 'self-contained' quality of the mental activity in such judgements. This meant two things: first, that the mental activity did not depend for its determination on anything exterior to it, such as the actual existence of the object, or ideas of the good; secondly, that the conscious mental activity (the contemplation) does not properly speaking produce but is identical to the pleasure (§12). The feeling of pleasure is an incentive to continue in a certain state: if I like it, I want to keep doing it; and to want to keep doing it is to like it. But the harmonising activity of the cognitive faculties in and through the presentation of the beautiful involves an internal 'causality', it 'reinforces and reproduces itself' – it thus *is* the pleasure. The phenomenon of aesthetic pleasure is thus not something external to, and caused by, the harmonising relation of the faculties that we have been talking about. And, as we have seen on several occasions, common sense can be construed as an *a priori* ability to feel aesthetic pleasure. Thus, there is no problem of 'reintroducing' the issue of the feeling of pleasure or common sense back into Kant's argument. Common sense as the subjective *a priori* principle of taste just is the proportion, or potential for harmony, of the cognitive faculties which, when it actually takes place, manifests itself as the feeling of aesthetic pleasure. Pleasure, in turn, is an aspect of the internal 'causality', or the lingering of contemplation, which is how the judgement realises itself as an *real activity* of the cognitive faculties.[29] It is subjective precisely because, considered as an ability to feel a pleasure associated with a purposive cognitive activity without purpose, it cannot be neatly tied up in determinate concepts.

Thus, talking about a 'principle' of common sense is itself a shorthand way of designating the *a priori* potential for harmonising activity between the cognitive faculties as the condition of aesthetic judgements. This acts like such a principle (it is 'regarded as' such a principle, §18) insofar as it is unique, *a priori*, necessary, and universally valid. Thus Kant says that common sense functions as if there were a 'public feeling' or 'public sense'

(§§22, 40), as if everyone shared literally the *same sense*, and could therefore communicate about it. Thus we finally have established the link between three key ideas: universal validity and communicability, common sense as principle of taste, and the harmony of the faculties. Kant's unfortunate habit of using these ideas nearly interchangeably, and slipping back and forth between them, has left many readers of the book baffled and frustrated. Hopefully we have accounted for Kant's justification for this slipping.

Although from the point of view of analysing the subjective conditions of aesthetic judgement it appears to be derivative, Kant wants to emphasise universal communicability. This is because it is the public, 'visible' face of the universal validity of taste, and thus has implications for the public or communal aspects of taste. That is, it suggests how the beautiful operates in societies, and leads Kant to talk about issues such as the nature of criticism, of influence, or of culture. He writes (at §40): 'We could even define taste as the ability to judge something that makes our feeling in a given presentation *universally communicable* without mediation by a concept.'

We have now arrived at an important point in Kant's thought: we have been able to demonstrate the *a priori* validity of the principle of taste. This means that Kant's analysis of how aesthetic judgements 'behave' (the Four Moments) is no longer either merely descriptive or speculative; it has been established as a real possibility of human cognition. Having done this work, Kant can now go onto other things, although the *Critique of Judgement* does not in fact exactly follow this order:

1. He can turn his attention to the other main category of aesthetic experience: the sublime (§§23–9). We will discuss Kant's account of the sublime in Chapter 3.
2. He can explore several special cases of the beautiful, for example, the 'Ideal' of the beautiful (§17, see p. 65, and discuss at greater length the whole problem of beauty in fine art (as opposed to natural beauty) (§§43–54). We will look at the latter in Chapter 4.
3. He can return to the general problem of the book, which is the manner in which judgement might serve as an all-important mediator between the theoretical and practical realms (see, for example, §§58–9). We will discuss this notion at the end of Chapter 4.
4. Kant can now turn to the other main form of judgement that interests him: teleological judgement (§61 onwards). This will be the subject of Chapter 5.

SUMMARY: The Deduction appears in at least two versions in Kant's texts. Both attempt to demonstrate explicitly the universal communicability, and thus inter-subjective validity, of judgements of taste. The key move for both is to claim that the aesthetic judgement rests upon the *same unique conditions* as ordinary cognition, and thus that the former must have the same universal validity/communicability as the latter. The first version runs into problems because, among other reasons, it seems to require a feeling of proportion between the cognitive faculties as a condition of any cognition whatsoever. That thesis Kant himself contradicts elsewhere in the text. The second version only seems to avoid this problem if taken out of context. These appear to be two solutions. The first seems to lie in describing the proportion as the standing *a priori* possibility of the faculties being freed to mutually enact their essence. Thus the key move becomes possible without our assuming that, empirically, the two different kinds of judgement share the same mental activities (such as feeling or harmony). The second solution appears to lie in reaffirming the mental state of the judgement as self-contained, such that common sense as the subjective principle of taste is not exterior to the judgement itself, and thus does not have to be accounted for separately. So, the potential of harmony turns out to be equivalent to asserting the universal existence of common sense, as the principle of a feeling for the beautiful.

CHAPTER SUMMARY: This chapter began with Kant's third moment of the beautiful, the last of the four Moments in our discussion. Here Kant claims that in the aesthetic judgement, beauty (in both nature and art) is seen as purposive without purpose (final without end). In other words, the beautiful would be the kind of thing which appears to be designed or made for some purpose, but with the actual concept of that purpose necessarily unavailable. In the case of art, there will be purposes of some type involved in its production, but they will be insufficient to account for its beauty; that is, knowledge of the purposes will not determine it to be beautiful. The problem of purposiveness without purpose is closely related to the problem of intention. Does the purposiveness of the work of art necessarily lead us to posit a determined intention in the mind of the artist or author? It turns out to be plausible to suppose that works of art have a 'self-sufficiency', which relates to the idea of self-containedness we introduced in Chapter 1. Furthermore, purposiveness becomes the explanation of the fundamental feeling of pleasure in aesthetic judgements. The fulfilment of purposes is pleasurable, Kant argues. In the absence of a purpose, it must be the purposiveness itself (of the beautiful, and for 'cognition in general', Kant says) serving *as if* it were an purpose. The apprehension of this purposiveness is thus pleasurable.

It remains for Kant to demonstrate that something which appears purposive without a purpose, and which thus is contemplated with pleasure, will appear and be pleasurable universally. Or equivalently, that the aesthetic judgement can be said to be grounded *a priori* upon a principle. There are two versions of such an argument in the text, and several other fragments of argumentation. In all versions, however, the key move involves a demonstration that the aesthetic judgement rests upon the same unique *a priori* conditions as ordinary cognition, and thus that the former must have the same universal communicability as the latter. In the process we understood the notion of harmony among the cognitive faculties (imagination and understanding in this case) as the most free and most perfect realisation in activity of the *a priori* essence or 'vocation' of those faculties in relation or proportion.

3

The Sublime

From the Beautiful to the Sublime

Early in this book, we noted that the beautiful was only one of the types of aesthetic experiences Kant would discuss. Because the beautiful and the sublime parallel each other in many ways, it was useful initially to limit our discussion to the former, as Kant himself does. The sublime stands at its most general for anything which makes us experience *awe*: this could be a piece of architecture, a canyon, a passage in an epic poem, or even a human action (heroism, for example). Among natural things, the example most writers come up with is that of a violent storm, in particular huge, dark churning clouds, howling winds, sudden magnificent flashes of lightning, and so forth. Such things tend to inspire awe in us, we marvel at their size and sudden, arbitrary force. Among manmade things, Kant comes up with the examples of the Great Pyramids in Egypt, or the huge cathedrals of European cities. For the moment, let us define the sublime as 'the feeling of, or associated with, the *overwhelmingness* of an object'.

Neither the idea of the beautiful nor the idea of the sublime is Kant's invention. The distinction between the beautiful and the sublime had already been made, on similar if not identical grounds, in ancient philosophy. However, for many hundreds of years, aesthetics had been dominated by the question of the beautiful. It was only around Kant's time that the sublime had become a topic of interest again; although this time it was the sublime in *nature* primarily. Perhaps this was because in the seventeenth and eighteenth centuries, physics was able to describe things that were both of awesome size, and yet governed by the same laws as ordinary sized objects on earth. It is this strange combination of familiarity and unfamiliarity which is characteristic of the aesthetic experience of the sublime in nature.[1]

However, that does not explain why Kant should be interested in the sublime in his *Critique of Judgement*. The beautiful is only discussed because it is an aesthetic judgement, and aesthetic judgements in turn are only discussed because Kant's overall purpose is to understand how judgement in general works. We need provisional answers to at least two questions: why the sublime is *aesthetic*, thus presenting similar philosophical problems to the beautiful; and how it differs from the beautiful? Kant never proves or even discusses whether the beautiful and sublime are the *only* two aesthetic experiences (leaving out the tragic, picturesque, comic, and so on).

Kant begins his discussion by comparing the beautiful and the sublime. He gives us three relationships of identity. First, both the beautiful and the sublime are pleasing on their own account – that is, apart from any interest. For example, if I am *frightened* by the storm, I feel an immediate interest in saving my skin, and I am then in no fit state to experience sublimity. It is only if I can fully experience the storm, but just on the edge of safety, that its sublimity is revealed to me. Secondly, the sublime too is a reflective judgement – for Kant this follows directly from the notion of overwhelm-ingness. For that which is overwhelming is in excess to our ability to fix it or pin it down with ordinary sensible cognition. Thirdly, both please uni-versally (or *claim* to do so). Again, as in the case of the beautiful, there is a strong implicit claim of the normativity of my judgements about the sublime. This is a common enough experience: it is often difficult to understand why someone is not impressed by something that you find sublime. Since these were some of the key characteristics of aesthetic judgements in general, as discussed in the four moments, Kant claims that the sublime is also such a judgement.

Kant then states three relationships of difference. First, he states that while beauty dealt principally with the form of its objects (for example, the shape and arrangement of objects in a painting), the sublime is possible even in the case of something that is literally *formless*. That is, something that is either random in its appearance (like the storm, or the raging ocean), or *may* have some overall form to it, but is too vast (or too small fast, slow, and so forth) for us to take in its form adequately or completely (Kant's example is an Egyptian pyramid which, he claims, cannot be appreciated *simultaneously* in terms of its form, its size, and its detail).[2] Secondly, he argues that though beauty is not *reducible* to the notion of 'charm' it is nevertheless *compatible* with such charm (for example, in the inclusion of ornamental features in a beautiful building). The sublime, however, has no relation with the charming or ornamental at all. The sublime Kant says, is more 'serious', partly because it involves negative feelings akin to pain. Thirdly, he argues that the beautiful in nature (and analogously in fine art) consists in a recognition of the 'pre-adaptation' (thus 'purposiveness') of natural objects for our ability to judge them. Indeed, it is only for this reason that pleasure arises from the judge-ment. In the sublime, on the contrary, the initial experience involves the *ill-adaptation* of the object for, or even an '*outrage*' against, our sensible judgement. Our faculty of cognition always sets out to look for form in its objects, or some feature that is in some other way *manageable* by that faculty; the sublime generally resists all this. The universe will appear in the first instance, and almost uniquely in our experience, as a *counter-purposive* and uncomfortably 'alien' or 'uncanny' place for us (but in a way quite different from my *fear* of the storm). And yet somehow the experience concludes in pleasure.

It is already clear that the sublime will present Kant with a quite curious philosophical knot to untie. The *a priori* principle of judgement in general is the purposiveness of judgement with respect to cognition, and yet here is an experience which straightforwardly seems to deny this principle. Understood in this way, the sublime seems to constitute a threat to Kant's whole account of judgement.

Kant then says something very confusing: nothing in nature, properly speaking, is sublime. This does *not* mean that only artificial objects are sublime: as with the beautiful, nature is Kant's constant emphasis. Recall, however, our discussions of the beautiful: we said the judgement had to be considered *subjective* (although no less valid for that) which meant that there was something strange in calling an object *itself* beautiful. Rather, the 'presentation' of the object to our sense is felt to be beautiful. However, saying that in the judgement of the beautiful, nature is only subjectively purposive, means neither that this purposiveness is unimportant, nor that it lacks implications for how we must judge nature, or ourselves. The beautiful at least says something about the *form* of the object. But the sublime is still more radically subjective. Kant will argue that what is properly called sublime is a feeling *completely* internal to the subject, not the object which is merely the *occasion* of that feeling happening. Why might Kant suspect this to be the case?

The sublime, we have already established, characteristically proceeds not by conforming to the faculties of sensibility or imagination but by 'outraging' them. Such an outrage is precisely painful. According to the definition given in Kant's introduction, pleasure is the feeling of a purpose or end having been achieved. The sublime object as overwhelmingness refuses to allow the purpose of cognition to be achieved. And yet the *whole* experience is nonetheless pleasurable. We enjoy encountering the sublime. Why? This relates to an old question – at least as old as Aristotle – as to why one feels something like pleasure in watching, for example, tragedy in which terrible things happen to people. Certainly, there is no direct pleasure in observing pain (even a stage presentation of pain). Something else must be happening other than the mere object and its apprehension, something that leaves the object behind, so to speak. Thus, Kant is arguing that if this 'something else' were not the case, the experience would be impossible because it would mean feeling pleasure *immediately and because of* pain, which is self contradictory. There is a commonsense manner in which one can feel pleasure because of pain, but only *mediately*, by way of something else. For example, a good workout in the gym may be painful in itself, but gives me pleasure because it is thereby serving the purpose of making me healthier or stronger. We will be discussing what this 'something else' which happens in the experience of the sublime, transforming pain into pleasure, later in this chapter. For the moment, emphasising this *transformation*, we will just call the sublime a two-stage process.

SUMMARY: The sublime is the second of two types of aesthetic experience discussed by Kant. Traditionally, sublimity was the experience of objects or events that inspire awe or are otherwise overwhelming. It too, Kant claims, involves reflective judgement, and thus shares many of the features and conditions with the judgement on the beautiful. The key puzzles of the sublime experience are, first, how any judgement could be formed on the basis of counter-purposiveness; and second, how an overwhelming experience, which should be experienced as frightening or otherwise displeasurable, can instead be experienced as a pleasure. Kant proposes that we must think of the sublime experience as having two stages, the first involving counter-purposiveness and displeasure, the second overcoming that in some way and thus being pleasurable.

The Mathematical and Dynamical Sublime

Kant distinguishes between two types of sublime. The *mathematical sublime* is characterised by the overwhelmingness of the experience being because of its spatial or temporal enormity (its size). The *dynamical sublime* is characterised by the overwhelmingness of the experience being because of the hugeness of its power.[3] The former 'outrages' our *imagination* because we cannot 'take it all in' at once. The latter 'outrages' our *will* because we know that, as sensibly conditioned beings, we are helpless before it.

Let us discuss the mathematical case first. Sections 25–6 carry a famous argument which concerns the possibility of *measurement*. Kant argues that all objective measurement of things (the very cornerstone of natural science) requires a standard of measure (an inch, a mile, a second, and so on). Once a standard (a unit of measure) has been found and presented, then measurement of anything is an essentially mathematical process of multiplying the standard (ten inches, sixty seconds, and so on). But where does the standard unit come from? This cannot itself be a merely mathematical entity, Kant argues, it must ultimately depend upon a subjective intuitive grasp of the measurement unit (where, again, 'subjective' does not mean 'personal'). The essence of measurement in space and time is not, therefore, *number* or *numbering*, but a type of sensing, a grasping of a unit which subsequently can be numbered and counted.

With respect to the aesthetic category of the mathematical sublime, this yields a definition of the sublime as that which is greater than any imaginable unit of measurement multiplied in the imagination any number of times (Kant says it 'surpasses' any standard, §25). The qualification 'imaginable' and 'in the imagination' are all important. For there is no object anywhere in the universe which is not made small by some mathematical accumulation of units of measurement. The sun's diameter is big, but much smaller than 50 million kilometres. The galaxy is big too, but much smaller than 50 million light years, and so on. The mathematical sublime does not depend upon mathematics (for which nothing is 'big' save infinity itself), but upon the intuitive condition of all mathematics: the ability to present for oneself a unit of measurement. How does this work? Kant is not very clear on this point – and there has long been a temptation simply to ignore these sections as not being either coherent or valuable – but we can at least propose an answer using his ideas.

First of all, it is clear from Kant's definition of the sublime that the imagination is involved twice: once to present (or rather, in the sublime, fail to present) the unit, and once again to (fail) to present the multiplication of the unit which would form an adequate presentation of some object. Either of these two failures is sufficient for the faculty of cognition to stumble, and thus the mathematical sublime has to be considered as itself divided into two forms.

My faculties of sense are intimately bound up with my body. This is obvious, but Kant singularly fails to remind us often enough, mainly because he is concerned to emphasise those dimensions of the sublime which are *a priori*. The body is both that through which and that with which I sense, and also, equally importantly, that which senses; that is, the sensible aspect of me. It is hardly surprising, then, that our experiences of the sublime should most naturally be determined by a relation to bodily size, by the kinds of things I am familiar with on an immediate, bodily level. This is, let us say, a first-order sublime experience, and obviously has more to do with the first failure of the imagination (a failure to present a *unit*), for the body itself determines what units of measure are most naturally and immediately available to me (for example the length of an arm, how far I can walk in an afternoon, the time of a heartbeat, or of my waking/sleeping cycle). If there is an object that seems to require measurement in units in excess of these 'natural' units, then our ability to measure intuitively stumbles. Kant might be able to agree with all of this, but it is certainly not an experience founded in my *a priori* subjectivity.

A more complex, second order experience is involved in feeling the sublime. Here it is less a question of the unit of measurement itself than the possibility of adequately applying the unit. My aesthetic judgement of the sublime can demand agreement from others, but not necessarily as a first-order sublime experience. This is because what is *a priori* here, and perhaps even a proper subject for transcendental philosophy, is not my particular body itself (which is contingent), but *the fact that I exist as a sensible and embodied being*, and this includes an aesthetic and ultimately felt relation to spatial magnitude. Let us explore this second-order sublime experience more closely.

If I try to construct an intuition of a whole object, this requires sense, memory and imagination. Take a cat, for example. Suppose for simplicity I start viewing the cat at the back and slowly move my gaze towards the head, from tail to hind legs to belly and so on. Kant calls this process of the focus of intuitive attention moving from element to element 'apprehension' (§26). It is because the construction of the presentation of the object must 'go through' this apprehension that we can say it is a presentation of that particular cat. Memory is required because I must hold in reserve all the bits of the object that I have already seen (the tail) while I go onto see other bits (chest, forelegs, neck, head). Imagination is required because I must unify and present all these bits into one whole intuition, according to a concept of the object – perhaps forming something like an 'image' of the whole cat. Kant calls this 'comprehension' (§26). It is because of such comprehension that the presentation is *of a cat*, rather than of a fragment of something undetermined. But both memory and imagination have limits as to how many bits they can deal with before 'giving up'. If there is an object that is big enough, then memory and imagination will give out before reaching the end. I have no intuition of its *magnitude*. Such an object is literally unintuitable *as a whole*.

But surely I can just back off a bit and get the whole cat in one view? Yes, but then I cannot distinguish all the smallest parts of the object, with the result that it just looks like a vague blur, or at least not like the particular thing that it is, and I *again* can form no sense of its real magnitude. But what defines what the appropriate size of the parts are? Is not the tail of the cat made up of many bones, and still more hairs, and still more skin cells, and so forth? Similarly with its hind legs. There will always be a different level of resolution which will either diminish or increase the number of parts. So, considered as an object of a total science of biology, say, the cat is sublime, as is an ant.[4] Because of the extra levels of mediation through technology (the microscope), this experience is perhaps rarely felt.[5]

Returning to the more immediate, ordinary scenario, one could still ask how I could think the Pyramid of Cheops is sublime when it is several hundred times smaller than Monat Everest. But, at *any one* level of 'magnification', there will *always* be a limit to memory and imagination, and so

Kant takes it to be proven that these limits are more to do with the universal essence of these faculties, than with contingent and personal factors like how good my eyes are or where I am standing, or what my past experience has been. Obviously, however, these factors will have some influence. If so, then it is *contingently* the case that all humans happen to have similar abilities of perception and memory, and similar habitual exposures to units of measurement. In what sense, then, does the sublime experience have *a priori* necessity? It is not at all yet clear how Kant might deal with this problem.

Combining this account of the breakdown of the attempt to form a whole intuition, with the former argument about the intuitive nature of the unit of measurement, we can say what Kant never quite gets around to saying. This second-order type of mathematical sublime occurs when in the imagination I find it impossible to provide a level of detail (thus the notion of a unit of measurement) sufficient to respect the *particularity* of the object as being a unique object (the sensible demand that comprehension *proceed through apprehension*), and yet to provide a whole intuition of it (the sensible demand that apprehension *completes itself* in comprehension). Briefly expressed, in the sublime there is a failure of the task of adequate cognition, which is to both present the object in its *haeccity* (as this particular, or 'thisness') and its *quiddity* (as the kind of thing it is, or 'whatness').

The solution we just proposed runs into trouble insofar as it seems directly to contravene Kant's statement about purity just before the partition in §26. A pure sublime experience would be one that does not proceed by way of a concept. Does the above reconstruction of Kant's argument require a *pre-existing* concept of a cat or pyramid, for example, such that a unit of measurement appropriate to such an object could be found? Certainly, we are not arguing that I have a determinate concept of the object (because then the sublime would be what Kant calls the 'colossal', §26) but rather that an 'appropriate' level of resolution is that which would suffice to *eventually* form a fully determining concept for that particular object. If I think of a mountain as just a geometrical cone, then either a mountain range is no more sublime than an ice-cream stand, or its sublimity is of the first-order type. But if I recognise that what is needed to distinguish one mountain from another (to respect its particularity) is to see it as a unique collection of ravines, cliff faces and boulder fields, then a mountain is sublime because I am then unable to grasp it both at that level of detail and all at once. Its *haeccity* escapes me. Arguably, for Kant this would still be the 'impure sublime'.

In the 'General Comment' following §29, Kant returns to the issue of purity. The starry sky is not experienced as sublime, properly speaking, if we think of it as a myriad of suns, possibly with planets orbiting them and other rational beings on some of those. This is far too bound up with concepts. It must rather be apprehended just 'how we see it'. Similarly with the ocean, which must be seen as 'poets do', perhaps 'like an abyss threatening to engulf everything'. On these grounds, Kant thus rules out both human productions (despite his own examples of pyramids and cathedrals) and animals of a determinate species from being sublime at all because of the clear teleological or taxonomic concepts involved. However, all this is disingenuous on Kant's part. For, as we know, he spent many hundreds of pages in the *Critique of Pure Reason* trying to demonstrate that experience could never be entirely unrelated to conceptual synthesis. There are certainly concepts involved in seeing the ocean as an abyss threatening to engulf us! As we said with respect to aesthetic judgements of the beautiful, the problem is not that aesthetic judgements might involve some concepts – for that is inevitable – but whether those concepts function as *determinate* for the judgement, and thus whether they can be abstracted from in order to form a properly aesthetic judgement. 'Purity' in Kant's sense is unattainable as such, but that does not mean that there are not interesting distinctions to be made about types or degrees of impurity.

The first-order sublime might be accounted more 'pure' in Kant's sense than the second-order. Kant instead seems to give the status of the pure sublime to that which is sublime through having no clear set of features – a rapidly changing storm or a vast seascape – and for which therefore no concept could be fully determining (although again, concepts are involved in the judgement: not least, the concept of a storm). Such chaotic, natural appearances he labels 'crude nature' (§26). Here, one *could* still talk about levels of resolution and parts (like a weather forecaster). But certainly, that is not how the storm is actually experienced. In other words, the storm is not experienced as a set of parts which need to be unified. The storm 'outrages' my imaginative ability to present it precisely by the chaos of its form: it is formless, and thus also without discrete parts. However, the case of the storm is already bordering on the non-mathematical type of the sublime, the dynamical.

In the mathematical sublime, we have detected at least three variations: (1) the first-order sublime with respect to one's contingently conditioned and embodied imagination; (2) the second-order sublime in which the problem is in both grasping the object as a whole and in its particularity; this too seems to involve a degree of contingency in its grounds; and (3) the pure sublime, which defies form *per se*. In all of these cases, Kant wants to claim, an object that exceeds such limits (regardless of its mathematical size) will be presented as 'absolutely large' (§25). (It is, in fact, not completely clear how this notion of the 'absolutely large' applies to the third variation.) This 'concept' of the absolutely large, because it has to do with the sensible, cannot arise from either understanding or reason; and yet, because it is also strictly speaking unpresentable, it cannot arise from the faculty of sensibility either. Moreover, the absolutely large object is presented only in *feeling*, initially, the feeling of displeasure at the breakdown of sensible cognition; feeling is the legislative realm of judgement. 'Absolutely large' must be, Kant claims, a unique *a priori* concept of judgement. Accordingly, the subjective principle of judgement which allows that concept to be discerned reflectively in our experience[6] is thus the version particular to the mathematical sublime of the principle of common sense: namely, the ground of the universality and necessity of aesthetic judgements.

The above three way distinction of first-order, second-order and pure sublime is one explanation of what is going on in these dense passages; but it is not without problems. Kant starts to give another account in the last paragraph of §26, where the sublime is accounted for in terms of the infinite regression of ever larger units of measure. It is not clear if this is meant to cover all cases of the mathematical sublime, and certainly not clear that it could. Perhaps the only *object* that appears sublime on truly *a priori* grounds is the 'starry heavens above me' (as Kant famously suggests in the conclusion to the *Critique of Practical Reason*).[7]

Recall, however, that the sublime must be a two-stage process. In the first stage, there is an *displeasurable* 'outrage' against (in the case of the mathematical sublime) sensible cognition which essentially involves imagination. The second stage somehow arranges it such that the overall experience is pleasurable. Before we turn to Kant's understanding of what this second stage must be, let us look briefly at the other major type of the sublime, the dynamical, which presents a slightly different first stage to the process.

The dynamical sublime is certainly analogous to the mathematical, and can thus be dealt with more briefly. In this case, a 'might' or power is observed in nature which is irresistible with respect to our embodied and sensible will – that is, with respect to our ability to determine and execute action in an ordinary sense. Through an act of imagination presumably akin to the one described above for the mathematical sublime (Kant gives us few details to go on), we become aware of a deficit in our ordinary will with respect to a power apprehended in nature. One of Kant's clearest examples is the ocean, with its cliff-like wave fronts, and vast, hidden currents. With the exception of its occasional and uncanny moments of calm, we are indeed helpless with respect to the ocean. Our will is frustrated and displeased by the spectacle of that which so obviously dwarfs it, and upon which it can make no perceptible mark. As with the mathematical sublime, the displeasure is linked to the idea of the experience being counter-purposive. The world is not experienced as something that could accord with our will, which is to say, something with respect to which the will could do its proper job – to act, and by acting to achieve things. Such an object is 'fearful' to be sure, but (because we remain disinterested) is not in fact an object of fear. Again, were we to actually experience fear, then the possibility of an aesthetic experience is *ipso facto* ruled out. It should now be clear why the pure mathematical sublime Kant discusses ('crude nature') is moving towards the dynamical sublime.

Such chaotic objects are usually also centres of force; indeed, it is their inner power that tears apart their apparent form.

At the beginning of §28, Kant defines the dynamical sublime as 'a might that has no dominance over us'. We might be inclined to think that this lack of dominance is a reference to the absence of fear, and certainly that is partly the case. But while the absence of fear is necessary for the aesthetic judgement, it is factually only contingent – a little bit closer to that river and we would be carried away. Because of this contingency, it is unlikely that the absence of fear is what Kant has in mind. Instead, he is probably referring to what we have been calling the second stage of the sublime experience. Further, 'might essentially without dominance' is the object of a certain feeling (initially, the negation of the will), and thus also (subjectively) a description of the principle of the capacity for such feelings, which must be a universal feature of human nature. As with the 'absolutely large', 'might essentially without dominance' is contradictory at the level of the sensible will; and as nevertheless a *sensible* presentation, is alien to pure reason too. Thus, although Kant does not make this claim, the notion of such a might *essentially* without dominance, together with the rule of its discernment in experience, must be the *a priori* subjective principle for the possibility of the reflective judgement of the dynamical sublime – just as the notion of the 'absolutely large' was for the mathematical sublime.

SUMMARY: The first stage of the sublime experience has two varieties: mathematical (having to do with magnitude) and dynamical (having to do with power). Kant's account of the former includes an account of the fundamental basis of all measurement: the aesthetic grasp of a unit of measurement. For a given object of experience, if either the appropriate unit of measurement is itself beyond our aesthetic grasp, or the number of instances of a unit is too great for our imagination, then our ability to 'comprehend' the object in one intuition breaks down. In the dynamical sublime, the object presents itself as powerful beyond the ability of my embodied will to offer any resistance. In both cases, the result is a displeasure, because the fundamental purposes of, respectively, my cognitive faculties and my will are rendered impossible.

The Second Stage of the Sublime

For the most part, the second-stage sublime is treated separately by Kant for the mathematical and the dynamical sublime. But he also claims that the second stage for each happens 'in the same way' (§28). The second stage must answer a series of questions which Kant has raised: (1) Why is the sublime experience greeted with pleasure (which always has something to do with purposiveness) when it seems to involve displeasure (that is, when it is 'counter-purposive')? (2) How is a judgement made on the basis of a counter-purposive experience at all? (3) Why does Kant write that there can be no sublime object in nature? (4) What exactly is meant, in the account of the mathematical sublime, by the 'absolutely large' and, in the account of the dynamical sublime, by a 'might that has no dominance'? For thus far we have only defined these concepts of judgement negatively, by saying what they are *not*.

Essentially, Kant will answer these questions by claiming that we are misspeaking when we represent the sublime as a property of a natural object or form.[3] What is sublime is the 'supernatural' mind that contemplates. In each case – the mathematical and the dynamical – the mind is led to discover within itself something that transcends even the apparently 'sublime' object in nature. For the mathematical sublime, it is the rational idea – and corresponding demand to cognition – of *totality*; for the dynamical sublime, it is the rational idea of *freedom*, and again the corresponding demand for that freedom to be realised in acts of will.[9]

We will need to recall a few key ideas discussed in the Introduction to this book. Reason does not mean just our ability to reason (that is, to deal logically with arguments and justifications). Rather, for Kant, reason refers above all to two other employments, not reducible to (though he suggests subtly related to) the above. First, theoretical reason, the independent, spontaneous formation of and *demand for the realisation of* the ideas of reason, which are one version or another of the *totality of conditions*. Cognition is thus compelled to pursue the impossible task of thinking totality in and beyond the natural. Second, practical reason gives the form of the moral law to free will: it takes the idea of freedom as both making possible and entailing moral obligation.

With respect to sensible cognition, 'nature' means: all those things and events which behave according to the laws of experience (natural laws, which take the form of cause and effect). There is no imaginable end to our experience of nature: behind everything we perceive must be something else. This endlessness is, of course, closely linked to Kant's analysis of the first stage of the mathematical sublime. But this endlessness of experience is different from the idea of the *totality of all nature*. Nature is exceeded by the rational demand for totality in cognition. This is because to think nature as a whole in a way adequate to reason would include, Kant argues, asking about the *ground* of this totality, otherwise the totality itself remains contingent and unthought. It would include, therefore, the issue of the supersensible or noumenal ground of nature.

In the mathematical sublime, therefore, what is properly speaking sublime is not the empirical object, no matter how excessive to our sensible cognition; rather, what is sublime is our *faculty of reason and its idea of totality*, which must necessarily be 'absolutely large' with respect to any sensible object.[10] This solves the above problems about the contingency in the basis of the first stage of the sublime. These contingencies become irrelevant, since however good our imaginations or memories, they *necessarily* will experience the totality demanded by reason as 'absolutely large'. The universal validity and principled necessity of the sublime judgement is established at the second, not the first, stage. This second stage is pleasurable because it reveals an unexpected purposiveness in the very failure of sensible cognition to present the object in the first stage. Nature is thus not *directly* purposive, as in the beautiful, but the failed act of presentation is put to a purposive use. That failure serves to 'negatively' exhibit the idea of totality and the whole 'higher' faculty of reason ('General Comment' following §29).

For the dynamical sublime, there is a similar relation to 'freedom' as there was above to 'totality'. Freedom does not lie at the level of the ordinary, sensible will; that is, it does not just mean 'doing what I like or want'. This is because what I like or want is, according to Kant, straightforwardly caused (at least in part) by my psychology or physiology, all of which is clearly at the level of the empirical, sensible self. Such apparently 'free' action remains a part of nature. 'Doing what I like' would be an illusory freedom. True freedom is nothing but a transcendence of or autonomy from *natural law* so that there can be rational conformity to moral law. Both rational demands, notice, are formulated negatively: absolute totality means totality *without natural limits*; freedom means *activity without natural determination*.

With respect to the dynamical sublime, therefore, Kant writes that such objects as the powerful ocean 'raise the soul's fortitude above its usual middle range and allow us to discover in ourselves an ability to resist which is of a quite different kind . . .' (§28). In particular, nature is (mistakenly) called 'sublime merely because it elevates the imagination to the exhibition of those cases wherein the mind can be made to feel [*sich fühlbar machen*] the sublimity, even above nature, that is proper to its vocation' (§28, translation modified). In particular, the sublimity belongs to *human freedom* which is, by definition, unassailable to the forces of nature. Because of our transcendent freedom, the might of nature has no dominance over us.[11] The role of reason here is not as that which supplies an idea of absolute totality (as in the mathematical sublime), but as that which is essentially supersensible, transcendent to (that is, free from) all determinations of nature, inner and outer. But this has huge implications, since it is precisely the same point Kant made in talking about *practical reason* – the possibility of morality. The dynamical sublime is closely related to morality without which the dynamical sublime would be impossible (see below). The dynamical sublime is the revelation of our moral nature, as that which transcends our sensible selves. The demand of reason for self transcendence of will is thus related to demand of reason to obey moral law. Through it, we are shown to belong to a transcendent 'community' of supersensible beings, created in the very image of God.

In both mathematical and dynamical sublime the initial displeasure is, so to speak, redeemed. For it brings to mind the transcendent aspect of our humanity, our reason, which is capable of thinking and demanding totality above and beyond any merely sensible object, and which is capable of thinking a freedom which transcends any merely natural law. The result is a strange relation of discord or strife *within us*, as reason (for example, in the mathematical sublime) demands an impossible totality of sensible cognition, and cognition in turn pleads unconscionable limitations to reason. This conflict is nevertheless a kind of harmony or purposiveness and thus is felt as a kind of pleasure, Kant claims, for two reasons. First, the very failure of the imagination serves as a symbol – or rather, a *negative exhibition*, marking by way of a lack or an absence – of the transcendence of reason. In a certain way, then, sensible cognition and will do succeed in their native purposes where they seemed doomed to failure. Secondly, it appears that reason's demands are, in this instance, in 'resistance' to the inner interests of sense, or indeed that this even involves 'sacrifices' ('General Comment', after §29). Yet, Kant conceives of this as, in fact, a revelation of sensible cognition or sensible will's true 'vocation': 'to [obey] a law, namely, to make itself adequate to that [rational] idea' (§27). In other words, these sensible faculties – although they certainly have their own functions – belong to human beings and are thus *also* properly a means for the higher faculty of reason. They are coordinated with respect to moral vocation.

However, the sublime experience is subject to a kind of forgetting, which Kant calls 'subreption', meaning a hidden theft. In this, the respect due to the laws of reason is illegitimately transferred to the external object of sense. Thus, we say the mountain itself, or at least the sensible experience of it, is sublime. We thus *feel* the result of the second stage of the sublime experience, but only notice the occurrence of the first stage. The revelation of human transcendence is forgotten. This 'subreption' is Kant's explanation for why, in the common usage of the term, 'sublime' refers to objects outside us.

The dynamical sublime involves the recognition of the force of reason's idea of freedom, which is the ground of the possibility of moral action. This connection to morality (for the sublime in general) becomes even more explicit in Kant's discussion of what he calls 'moral culture' (§29). The context of this discussion is to ask about the modality of judgements on the sublime – that is, are they necessary, and do they have the same implicit demand on the necessary assent of others that judgements on the beautiful have?

Kant's answer is that there is an empirical factor required for the sublime: not the contingency of the limits of imagination, but rather a 'moral culture' such that the mind of the experiencer is 'receptive' to rational ideas. This can only happen if the faculties have been so cultivated as to *already* understand (indeed, *feel*) morality to be a function of freedom. Or, more generally, so cultivated as to conceive of human beings as having a dimension which in some way transcends nature. By 'culture' or 'cultivation' [*Kultur*] is meant both a particular training that our faculties of understanding and judgement undergo as these faculties attain maturity, and also the context within which this happens: civilisation as a set of practices, institutions, traditions, and paradigms that are the means by which this training is achieved. A *moral* culture is not one that just demands moral behaviour – that is, which regulates in some manner its members. For this could happen by way of the threat of punishment or a promise of reward (either natural or super-natural); or simply a respect for external authority (again, natural or super-natural). Rather, a moral culture is one that has developed the capacity for understanding and feeling the fount of moral action in man's freedom for moral law. It thus sees the moral as the proper expression and 'maturity' of human beings in their freedom. But for most human beings, the real possibility of this coming home to one's self, so to speak, is that culture in the first sense be mediated through what above we called 'civilisation' (culture in the second sense): education, religion, philosophy, and so on. Thus, moral culture is the highest possible stage of civilisation, towards which all humans strive, according to Kant.

SUMMARY: Formerly, we focused on the object in nature (the mountain, or the storm). Kant now argues that this was merely a catalyst, and that nothing in nature is properly speaking sublime. Instead, in the second stage we see that it is our own faculty of reason, and the laws it demands of us, that is sublime. In particular, the rational demand for totality in cognition for the mathematical sublime; for freedom of the will for the dynamical sublime. The presence of these rational laws is felt precisely because ordinary cognition or will breaks down. This second stage thus redeems the displeasure of the first by showing that the first stage was indeed purposive.

Although the *a priori* conditions for the sublime experience are to be found universally in human beings, it is not the case that all human beings can experience the sublime. The reason is culture. Our cognitive faculties, and the mental faculty of feeling, must be subjected to a kind of training. Such training results in the ability to feel the demand of reason, and to understand human existence as involving a super-sensible, free aspect. Moral culture, according to which we can explicitly experience ourselves as the moral beings we have always been, is required for, and in turn reinforced by, the sublime experience.

Conclusions to the Analytic

By way of drawing this chapter to a close, several broad observations concerning Kant's account of the sublime and the beautiful suggest themselves.

First of all, Kant's treatment of the sublime is quite clearly at the top of a pyramid of philosophical ideas: it assumes as a background that we agree with virtually all of the major notions in Kant's previous work. This was also the case for the beautiful, to be sure, but it stands out in the sublime. For example, in order to be able to agree with the details of Kant's account of the mathematical sublime, we need the account of epistemology, and especially the role of imagination and synthesis, from the first half of the *Critique of Pure Reason*. Similarly, in order to appreciate the treatment Kant gives of the second stage, we need the account of the nature and role of reason, with its strange accompanying ontology of the sensible and supersensible. With respect to the dynamical sublime, furthermore, we need Kant's understanding of will, freedom and the moral law as developed in the practical philosophy especially from the 1780s. Were one to quibble with any of these ideas, Kant's account of the sublime would have to suffer. Of course, the same was true of the account of the beautiful, and will continue to be true when we look at fine art and teleology.

We *could* see this as a problem: the Kantian philosophical system as a fragile house of cards. However, Kant and many of his contemporaries saw it differently: the elements of the system mutually reinforcing one another. In other words, the fact that Kant is able to give a remarkable and powerful account of the sublime retroactively provides additional evidence for the truth of his starting point. The fact that the cornerstones of his philosophy could account for so much, in such a rich and thought provoking way – could in other words *make sense* of such widely varying elements to our human experience – all made it seem as if philosophy had reached the pinnacle of its achievement. Part of both the philosophical interest, and the subjective pleasure, in dealing with Kant is to come to terms with this vast system.

The second observation is that for the beautiful we had a deduction, in several versions, which purported to demonstrate that the subjective principle of the beautiful was necessary *a priori*, and legislating with respect to the faculty of feeling. Kant argues that the sublime does not require a *deduction* in the same way that aesthetic judgements of the beautiful do

(§30). His reasoning is that the beautiful, while involving a subjective harmony of the faculties and the feeling of his harmony, nevertheless makes claims about the form of the object which is called 'beautiful'. That is, it makes claims akin to objective judgements about the world. It is necessary, therefore, to validate the right to make such claims. With the sublime, however, the subjectivity of the judgement is complete, thus involving no claims about any objects.

This seems rather unfortunate for Kant. Throughout the 'Analytic of the Sublime', there is often rich description but rather scant argument that would demonstrate that these descriptions must be accurate. The closest he gets to a justification is one that is already familiar: at the end of the previous 'General Comment', arguing against Burke's equally famous treatment of both the sublime and beautiful, he claims that any treatment of aesthetic judgements which remains in the realm of mere psychology could not, in principle, account for all the features of such experiences (in particular the peculiar claim to the assent of other in such judgements). The treatment of the sublime thus has a kind of philosophical arbitrariness about it. However, Kant could reply that the sublime is simply a connection between faculties he has already studied. He argues that the exposition of the two mental activities involved in the sublime is at the same time its deduction: first, the activity of the comprehension of nature; and secondly, the activity of the sensible self with respect to the demands of reason. Since these are well understood (Kant feels), the sublime requires no special additional justification. Still, that would not take into account the role of reflective judgement, and of its special principles. In other words, although the sublime makes no claims about the purposiveness nature, it does make claims about the possible purposiveness of the failures of our cognitive faculties with respect to our feeling for rational ideas. And these claims have not been subject to a deduction.

Our third observation is that the points Kant makes about moral culture and civilisation could easily be taken as prime examples of the pernicious habits many philosophers have of taking their own historical, geographical, racial or sexual situation as the universal model. Similar worries have been raised concerning the various examples and asides Kant provides in the analytic of the beautiful, in his discussion of genius and fine art, and in the whole conception of the relation between aesthetic judgement, morality and politics. Kant clearly claims that the way he (and his contemporaries) understands and experiences, for example, freedom and thus also the sublime is uniquely correct and also should be the goal for all others. Of course, few philosophers in history are not guilty of the same crime, and contemporary thinkers will no doubt be held up in the future as equally biased. If we are going to be rigorously historical about such matters, it is at least important that we properly understand Kant here, and this involves three issues.

First, to his own mind he is hardly holding up a contingent fact as a prescriptive universal. On the contrary, insofar as his philosophy is critical and transcendental, he believes himself to have looked 'behind' all contingencies for the essential and indeed transcendental features of all human experience. Where he has clearly failed to do this, we still have to ask whether the fault lies with Kant (and is thus contingent) or with his conception of philosophy (and is thus necessary, and far more worrying). Moreover, Kant feels understandably grateful to, and thus celebrates, his historical situation for being that which has made it possible for his philosophical vision to be so sharpened. Secondly, Kant is in fact an extraordinarily liberal thinker on many of these points (partly this is due to the influence of political thinkers such as Rousseau). In his mind, there is no essential difference in the constitution of the faculties between the 'savage' and the most cultured citizen of Königsberg. There is only a difference, precisely, of certain forms of culture, both in the sense of the training of the faculties and in the sense of the wider, social dimension that makes possible or provides that training. And an aspect of a culture can *only* be accounted 'superior' if it in some way involves the training of our faculties taking the lines that belong essentially to those faculties. But it is by no means impossible (indeed, it is very likely) that there can be innumerable modes in which this encouragement can be embodied. Nothing in Kant makes his contingent 'historical, geographical, racial or sexual' situation uniquely essential to this process. If Kant sometimes claims the opposite, then *there* must lie the error. Thirdly, it follows that a more interesting objection by far would be an analysis of Kant's thinking which shows an *intrinsic* bias on national, gender or racial issues on the part of certain concepts, analyses, methodologies, or critical philosophy as a whole.

Our final observation relating to Kant's account of the sublime and the beautiful is that the claims about moral culture show that, for Kant, aesthetics in general is not an isolated problem for philosophy but intimately linked to metaphysical and moral questions. We will shortly see similar issues raised with respect to the beautiful. This is one more reason why it is important not to assume (as too often happens) that even the 'Critique of Aesthetic Judgement' is a book merely about beauty and sublimity. As important as it is for the history of aesthetics narrowly conceived, it is always equally important to understand Kant's claims in a wider framework. Moreover, this 'link' has an even greater significance for Kant: it shows reflective judgement 'in action' as a mediating faculty, relating together theoretical cognition and reason, for this was the grand problem he raised in his Introduction.

CHAPTER SUMMARY: The sublime is the second of two types of aesthetic experience discussed by Kant. It too involves reflective judgement, and thus shares many of the features and conditions with the judgement on the beautiful. Traditionally, sublimity was the experience of objects or events that inspire awe or are otherwise overwhelming. But in what way are objects and events 'overwhelming'? And why is the overwhelming experienced as pleasurable, instead of painful? The answer to the first question involves distinguishing between the mathematical sublime and the dynamical sublime. In the former case, the object is distinguished by its vastness, such that it exceeds the grasp of the imagination, and thus also of sensible cognition. In the latter case, the object is characterised by great power, such that it exceeds the ability of the sensible will to resist it. In both cases, however, Kant argues that the experience is an ultimately displeasurable one, since the purposes of these faculties (sensible cognition and will) are annulled. Where then does the pleasure come from?

In each case, there is a second stage of the sublime. In the mathematical sublime, the annulment of the purpose of cognition is the trigger for our feeling the demand of the rational idea of totality, which nevertheless insists upon the metaphysical total cognition of the object. With respect to this idea, then, everything sensible is minuscule. The initial shock of the overwhelming turns out to be purposeful (and thus pleasurable) with respect to revealing the higher, rational side of our nature. In the dynamical sublime, the failure of the sensible will is again the trigger for feeling the demand of the rational idea of free will, a will that can be dominated by no sensible power, no matter how great. Again, the initial stage is in fact purposeful in revealing through feeling our freedom.

It can be universally expected of all human beings that they 'contain' the transcendental conditions of this sublime feeling, but it is not necessary that everyone is factually aware of this feeling. The relevant faculties must be trained, and this involves what Kant calls 'moral culture'. Through such culture, human beings become able to feel the demands of reason within themselves, and are thus able also to experience the sublime.

4

Art, Genius and Morality

From Nature to Art, and from Art to Fine Art

Starting in §43, Kant addresses himself particularly to fine art for the first time. He is moving from a discussion primarily aimed at the beautiful or the sublime apprehended in *nature*, to artificial productions. Since the nineteenth century, the discussion of aesthetics has revolved almost exclusively around fine art. Natural beauty, if treated at all, tends to attract only secondary consideration. Kant is therefore 'old-fashioned' on this point, participating in an important tradition unbroken since the Renaissance (and significant too in the ancient world) for which beauty in nature is the ultimate model of beauty in art. However, it is worth pointing out that, because he gave a new and influential account of artistic genius, Kant is in fact partly responsible for the change that followed. Moreover, Kant's treatment of nature has to be understood as not just a historical contingency, that is, merely determined by eighteenth-century attitudes. Rather, his approach also fits in perfectly with his grand, general thesis about the mediating role of judgement. In other words, Kant has reasons far beyond aesthetics for apparently following a conventional approach, and beginning from nature.

Thus, fine art seems to 'borrow' its beauty or sublimity from nature, in the sense that beauty here is both the same concept as beauty in nature, and is even parasitical upon natural beauty. Kant says that, despite a few differences, we judge aesthetic objects in nature and in fine art in basically the same way, and he entitles §45 'Fine Art is an Art Insofar as It Seems at the Same Time to Be Nature'. The important difference is that while the question of a 'maker' for nature remains open, in the case of fine art we can investigate the production of objects (who made them, why, and when), not just the mind that judges them. The account of this production culminates in Kant's hugely important treatment of genius. Fine art *qua* beautiful, however, appears to be a secondary concept with respect to nature, and Kant has done all the real philosophical work prior to the discussion of fine art.

On the other hand, in being judged aesthetically nature is seen 'as if' purposeful, designed, or a product of an intelligence. But these latter concepts are borrowed from the realm of human action, from 'making' in general. Since reflective judgement requires us to view nature as purposive, the notion of natural beauty itself can be seen as secondary with respect to the notion of *making*, that is to say, art understood broadly. Thus, the relation between nature and art is much more complex than it seems at first, and clarifying this relation must be Kant's first priority. He therefore sets out on a long, taxonomic study of art, at each level indicating its specific difference from that which is not art (see Table 2).

He begins by distinguishing 'Doing' (*Tun*) from natural happening. 'Doing' is a general term for the activity of causing something to be, according to a preceding notion of what it is; that is, a purposive action that has as its result a product or work. The English word 'making' is perhaps closer to Kant's meaning. Knitting a sweater, cooking a quiche, or writing *Great Expectations* are all examples of doing or making in this widest sense. Kant seems to be excluding, from the start, any activity that does not have a concrete product as its outcome: a goalkeeper saving a penalty shot, a wink, or my *reading* Dickens' *Great Expectations*. Certainly, the product is the guarantee of the social aspect of the activity, for it has a certain duration, and can be shared and examined. Nevertheless, it is difficult to see any other reason why Kant should have to exclude such 'non-productive' actions, and in fact there are several good reasons for thinking otherwise. For example, as we shall see, Kant will go on to claim that fine art, strictly speaking, has no interest in the real existence of its product. Furthermore, it could be argued that several types of fine art have no such concrete product or, if there is a product, it is a mere *record* of the activity itself, for example dance, or musical improvisation.

If I make a chair, I must have some notion in advance of what I am making. We thus distinguish making from nature (here, nature is not the object of an aesthetic judgement) because we know there is no prior notion behind the activity of a flower opening. The flower does not have an idea of opening prior to opening – it doesn't have a mind or a will to have or execute ideas with. The situation is more difficult in the case of slightly more complex organisms (Kant discusses bees, for example).[1] But because he is heading for an understanding of fine art, he limits his investigation to human beings.

Kant now sets about narrowing this broad notion of making, in order to focus on the concept first of art, then of fine art (see Table 2). Making includes both 'art' and 'science'. Art (*Kunst*) means something different from science – as Kant says a *skill* distinguished from a type of *knowledge*. Art involves some kind of practical ability which is distinct from a mere comprehension of something (how to solve a differential equation, what is the chemical composition of quartz, and so on). The latter can be fully taught; the former, although subject to training and perhaps even including 'enabling' knowledge, relies at bottom upon native talent. Thus, Kant will later claim, there can be no such thing as a scientific genius, because a scientific mind can never be *radically* original, which would mean that the 'rule' of its scientific accomplishments could not be taught (§46). All scientific achievements result in 'products' that are intrinsically conceptual and thus learnable.

Table 2   *The Definition of Fine Art*

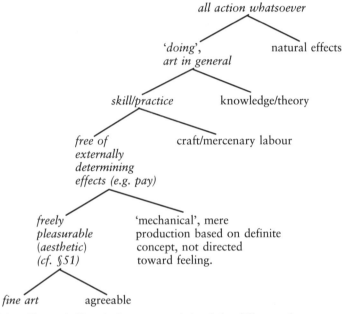

In defining 'fine art', Kant indicates at each level the difference between art and that which is not art. He then narrows his definition to distinguish between fine art and that which is agreeable.

Art, then, is not science. Furthermore, art is distinguished from *labour* [*Arbeit*] or *craft* [*Handwerk*], the latter being something satisfying only for the pay-off that results and not for the mere activity of making itself. In art (not surprisingly, like beauty), the focus is on the purposeful activity itself, and is thus *free* from any interest in the existence of the product.[2] Art, then, is defined as a free, skilful making. It is now necessary for Kant to narrow this down further to the notion of fine art, in opposition to any other type.

Arts are subdivided into mechanical and aesthetic. The former are those which are controlled by some definite concept of a purpose to be produced and are fixed upon the making of a thing, not upon the feeling of pleasure to be had through the thing independently of concepts. Kant does not give any example here, nor does he explain what could motivate such a making, without either pleasure or other pay-off. However, we should not let Kant's well-known thirst for naming and fine distinctions distract us from the key point, which is that aesthetic arts are those wherein the 'motivation' is merely pleasure itself. There may be pleasure in the activity itself, at least by anticipation, but above all there must be pleasure through the thing made. Finally, Kant distinguishes between agreeable and fine art. This especially is familiar from the early sections of the book: the former produces pleasure through sensation alone, the latter through taste proper.

This sequence of differentiations defines the problem that Kant wishes to address. The above definition is, however, only a mirror image of the four moments of the beautiful. Kant is taking many of the properties of the reflective judgement of a presentation considered as an *object*, and projecting them onto the side of the *production* of that object. Thus, for example, we have an experience of disinterested pleasure, as well as purposiveness, but without a fully adequate concept as its purpose (that is, neither science, nor mechanical production). Art, even fine art, 'always presupposes a purpose in the cause (and its causality)' (§48). But this concept is in some way exceeded, perhaps only by taste, or perhaps (as we shall see) by genius.

We feel reasonably secure that we know how it is possible for clockmakers to make clocks, or glass-blowers to blow glass. This does not mean that *we* can make clocks or blow glass, but that as a kind of activity it does not seem (to Kant) to present *philosophical* problems. We have also investigated how someone *contemplating* a work of fine art (or the beautiful/sublime in nature) is able to judge it. But it is not yet clear how, on the side of production, fine art is made. It is clearly not just a matter of applying good taste, otherwise all art critics would be artists, all musicians composers and so forth. (It is also possible for a critic to have better taste than the artist, but not on that account to be an artist.) Here, taste – although still important – is no longer a sufficient account of the possibility of fine art. Kant has focused on the problem so that he can now raise the key question: in what, in addition to aesthetic taste, does the talent of the fine artist consist? However, he answers this question in a rather circuitous manner.

In the accounts of the beautiful and the sublime, Kant proceeded by analysing an apparently simple experience until he reached a paradox, and then claiming that only a transcendental analysis could solve the problem. Thus (among other such paradoxes), the beautiful was subjective, but claimed universality; and the sublime was painful, but pleasurable. Now, there are two similar paradoxes for fine art. The first of these is easy to state: fine art is a type of purposeful production, because it is made; art in general is production according to a concept of an object. After all, one is working with materials and there is a *science* of materials. Thus, in order to paint successfully, you need at least concepts of the properties of various types of paint, the mixing of colours, the techniques of brushing and layering, and the qualities of various types of canvas. Further, if your painting is at all figurative, you must have a concept of the object being represented; or if it is not figurative, then some concept of the effect to be achieved. But the concept of a purpose involved in fine art has to be exceeded, as we noted above, or else any judgement on it will fail one of the key criteria of all aesthetic judgements: purposiveness *without a purpose*. Fine art therefore must both be, and not be, an art in general.

The second paradox is not so easy to see. Kant starts by noticing that we have a problem with the *overwrought* – that which draws attention to itself precisely as an artificial object or event. 'Over-the-top' acting is a good example. Literature also can be too precious – not necessarily in the sense of sentimentality but in being too literary. Examples in the visual arts are harder to think of, because self-consciousness of process seems much more common there, but often inferior works can be distinguished to the extent that they follow the rules of fashion rather too slavishly, and become instant clichés. Contemporary works of art commonly draw attention to their own artificiality (this is a characteristic of post-modernism), and yet this too can be done in a 'natural' manner, or just crassly. Kant expresses this point by saying that, in viewing a work of art we must be aware of it as art, but it must nevertheless appear *natural*. Here, 'natural' stands for the appearance of freedom from conventional rules of artifice – 'nature', therefore, in the sense of that which stands opposed to all products of civilisation.[3] Kant will in a moment radicalise this point by claiming that works of fine art must have the characteristic of *originality*. This entails a freedom not just from 'conventional' and well-known rules of production, but freedom from the determining (as opposed to enabling) influence of any rules whatsoever. The paradox is that art (the non-natural) must appear to be natural.

Kant must overcome these paradoxes and explain how fine art can be produced at all, and he does so by way of the notion of 'genius'. Indeed, in §46, the first step toward a solution is taken when Kant, in initially defining what he means by 'genius', explicitly addresses himself to the relation to nature. He writes (at §46),

> *Genius* is the talent (natural endowment) that gives the rule to art. Since talent is an innate productive ability of the artist and as such belongs itself to nature, we could also put it this way: *Genius* is the innate mental predisposition (*ingenium*) through which nature gives the rule to art.

In other words, that which makes it possible to produce (fine art) is not itself produced – neither by the individual genius, nor (we should add) through his or her culture, history or education. But here, 'nature' has still another meaning which Kant seems to be conflating with the one discussed

above. The new concept of nature here is that which is essential or fundamental in something – much as one might say 'It is in a cat's *nature* to catch
mice.' But, when it comes to the nature of the subjectivity of a human being
we know that, for Kant, part of this nature (in this new sense) will not be *in
nature* (in the sense of the objects legislated for by the faculty of the
understanding). Part of the nature of human beings is 'super-natural', such
as the spontaneity of the higher cognitive faculties;[4] thus the idea of 'natural
endowment' above. However, this human nature might have some overlap
with the Rousseau-influenced first conception of nature above, especially
where the latter is interpreted in terms of freedom from imposed rules of
production. That would make Kant's conflation more than just a sleight of
hand, and gives us no less than three conceptions of 'nature' operative in
Kant here: first, nature as the law-governed object of cognition; second,
nature as the essence or basic features of something; third, nature as opposed
to civilisation.

But what is meant, in the quotation on p. 110, by a 'rule'? At the end of
§47, Kant distinguishes between supplying 'material' for fine art (supplying
what Kant will later call the aesthetic idea that lies behind the production of
the work) and elaborating the 'form' (the production of a formally beautiful
object). The rule supplied by genius is more (although not exclusively) a rule
governing *what* is produced, rather than *how*. Thus, while all fine art is a
beautiful 'presentation' of an object (§48), this partly obscures the fact that
genius is involved in the original creation of that which is to be presented.[5]
The rule then, is a rule of production which both *encompasses* the (quite
ordinary) concept of the purpose to be produced and, as we put it above,
exceeds that concept in such a way that the result is aesthetic.

The 'how' (the 'form') is usually heavily influenced by training and
technique, and is governed predominately by mere taste (§47), which allows
the production of a formally beautiful but rather 'empty' object. Taste, Kant
claims, is an evaluative faculty, not really a productive one (§48). If fine art
were merely a matter of taste, then the concept of a purpose that makes the
production possible as art would be exceeded, but not encompassed. The
beauty and the purpose would be irrelevant to each other. Kant therefore
writes (§48),

> If the product has been given a likeable form, then this form is only the
> vehicle of communication, and, as it were, a manner [adopted] in dis-
> playing the product, so that one still retains a certain measure of freedom
> in this display even though it is otherwise tied to a determinate purpose.

Thus, the *real* production of genius takes place in ideal independence to the
'mechanical' production of the work itself. The rule of its production (that
total set of intentions governing the what and how of its production) which

allows the genius to actually make some specific thing is *radically original*.
Similarly, fine art must have the 'look of nature' (§45), where 'nature' is
understood in the third sense above, in that it lies outside the cycle of
imitative rule-following within which all other arts in general are caught up.
This leads Kant to make some suggestive, but never fully worked-out,
comments about artistic influences and schools, and the role of culture, of
technique and education and so on (see, for example, §§49–50).[6] This means
also that fine art is never an *imitation* even of previous fine art, though it may
'follow' or be 'inspired by' previous art (§47).

SUMMARY: With fine art, Kant seems to turn from nature as the
primary focus of beauty. In order to distinguish fine art from any other
kind of purposive activity, Kant provides a series of specific differences
starting from any 'doing'. This clarification in part duplicates the
results of the four moments of the beautiful, for example disinterestedness or the concern with mere form. However, any doing or making
requires the existence of a concept of a purpose – of what it is that is
going to be made. The key difference between beauty in art and in
nature is the existence in the former of a concept of a purpose. How a
concept could be involved, and the result still be aesthetic, is a key
problem. To solve it, Kant introduces the notion of genius. Genius,
then, is a talent that is founded ultimately on the *a priori* faculties of the
human being, and thus founded in nature (in the sense of 'the nature of
the human being'). This talent creates the utterly original material for
fine art (which for this reason appears natural in the sense of not
drawing attention to its artificiality), which exceeds and encompasses
its purpose, and then (as a slightly secondary occupation), 'expresses'
this material into a beautiful form.

Genius and Aesthetic Ideas

Genius provides the material for fine art. So, what distinguishes one 'material' from another, such that genius might be required? What genius does
above all, Kant says, is to provide 'spirit' or 'soul' [*Geist*] to what would
otherwise be uninspired (§49). This peculiar idea seems to be used in a sense
analogous to saying that someone 'has soul', meaning to have nobility or a
deep and exemplary moral character, as opposed to being shallow or even in
a sense animal-like; but Kant also, following the Aristotelian tradition, means
that which makes something alive rather than mere matter. There can be an

uninspired fine art, but it is not very interesting (pure beauty, mentioned above, may be an example). There can also, Kant warns, be inspired nonsense, which is also not very interesting. Genius inspires art works – gives them spirit – and does so by linking the work of fine art to what Kant will call *aesthetic ideas*.

Such ideas are defined in the third paragraph of §49. Kant claims that the faculty of (productive) imagination can work itself free from nature in the first and third senses above, and

> create, as it were, another nature out of the material that actual nature gives it. [Though in doing so we] follow principles which reside higher up, namely, in reason (and which are just as natural to us as those which the understanding follows in apprehending empirical nature).

The aesthetic idea is a presentation of the imagination to which no thought is adequate. Such ideas are 'counterparts' – let us say, mirror images – to rational ideas (which we encountered in the Introduction, and in Chapter 3 on the sublime). The latter are thoughts to which nothing sensible or imagined can be adequate; rational ideas are 'transcendent' to sensibility.

Because the situation Kant is describing is complex, let us try to define the roles each of these notions is playing in the production of fine art. As with all art, there is a concept of a purpose ('what kind of thing the object is meant to be', §48) involved. Although not a perfect match, we can identify this with the idea of *genre*. There are at least four justifications for this. First, Kant is happy to speak in generic or related terms about the varieties of fine art in §§51–3, and often elsewhere. Secondly, the notion of genre captures the difference Kant suggests between a *perfect* instance, and a properly aesthetic instance (§48, and compare §15).[7] For example, a perfect example of a detective novel is not necessarily a good detective novel. Thirdly, it also captures Kant's idea of the concept being, from the point of view of judgement, both the preliminary grasp of 'what kind of thing the object is meant to be', *and* what it is meant to do, since genre-concepts often carry expectations as to the impact they are meant to have on the viewer/reader. Fourthly, the notion of genre fits in well with Kant's discussion of rules and 'academic correctness' (§47).

Aesthetic ideas are 'counterparts' to rational – or as we shall see perfect – ideas. We can say that these rational ideas are the thinkable content of the work of art, its 'theme'. Kant does not use this notion, nor make it explicitly distinct from what we called genre above, but arguably it is present and required.[8] Like 'genre', such a 'theme' is *in itself* another dimension of conceptual purpose: it is the (fictional or ideal) object referred to by the work itself. Thus we might say that the work is 'about' the idea of benevolence, for example. The 'theme' is, in itself, probably quite banal from an aesthetic point of view, although it may have intellectual interest.

Aesthetic ideas seem to be 'straining' after the intuitive presentation of such rational or perfect ideas. They are imaginative presentations that are transcendent to (are 'unexpoundable' in terms of) any concept – in particular, to any concept of a purpose of a work of art (§49 and §57 Comment I). They are the 'spirit' of the work, that which makes it stand out as a work of art. Kant writes that the aesthetic idea 'is a presentation that makes us add to a concept [of an object] the thoughts of much that is ineffable, but the feeling of which quickens our cognitive faculties'(§49).

To understand this, we can distinguish between a number of different possible types of objects based on their relation to the above notions of 'taste' (the achievement of merely beautiful form), 'genre' (concept of the work as purpose), 'theme' (the rational idea as thinkable content), and 'spirit' (aesthetic idea).

First, consider a 'pot-boiler' – a more or less perfect example of a particular genre, with little else to recommend it. Secondly, consider an artless attempt to state a 'theme' or 'message': perhaps a book of philosophy. It may be well-written, or poorly written, but is not beautiful. It has a genre, certainly (meditation, treatise, dialogue, and so on), but that is irrelevant. Thirdly, consider a merely beautiful form. Here, as Kant asserted above, the beauty is a 'vehicle' for some 'genre', which may in itself be excellently carried out. It may also be a vehicle for some 'theme', for some intellectual idea or other which, although perhaps interesting from a philosophical point of view, remains without 'spirit' – imagine a work of art that is indeed tasteful, but rather dull. Rightly or wrongly, a so-called 'novelist of ideas', or a technically excellent but overly-intellectual sculptor, is often accused of such a partial failure.[9] Kant accordingly argues (at §49):

> Of certain products that are expected to reveal themselves at least in part to be fine art, we say that they have no *spirit*, even though we find nothing to censure in them as far as taste is concerned. A poem may be quite nice and elegant and yet have no spirit. A story may be precise and orderly and yet have no spirit. An oration may be both thorough and graceful and yet have no spirit.

Fourthly, consider a mad, chaotic work full of imagination and partial conceptions, but going nowhere, so to speak – the work, perhaps (but who can tell?) of a genius without discipline (the 'inspired nonsense' we mentioned above). Similarly, Kant writes 'shallow minds believe that the best way to show that they are geniuses in first bloom is by renouncing all rules of academic constraint, believing that they will cut a better figure on the back of an ill-tempered than of a training-horse'.[10]

Finally, consider a formally beautiful entity that itself is the expression of something higher but which *cannot in any other way be expressed*. There must still be a genre and a theme (both different aspects of the concept of the purpose), but now both are encompassed and exceeded. Kant explains (at §49),

> Now if a concept [of a purpose] is provided with a presentation of the imagination [an aesthetic idea] such that, even though this presentation belongs to the exhibition of the concept, yet it prompts, even by itself, so much thought as can never be comprehended within a determinate concept.

In this last case, the theme is still perfectly thinkable as such, but now the artist's imagination has created an aesthetic idea which directs thought to pursue it. Kant is suggesting that only an aesthetic idea can be such as both to pursue the ideas of reason (and thus quicken the whole faculty of reason), and at the same time to belong 'to the exhibition of the concept' – the quite ordinary concept of the *sensible* purpose of the productive activity. By way of the aesthetic idea, the genius thus places a hint of the supersensible object of rational ideas into the sensible object. The 'spirit', the beautiful form, and the purpose are inseparable, to the extent that were they to be separated the work 'evaporates'.[11] Inspired fine art is beautiful, but *in its very beautiful form*, it is also a communication of the state of mind which is generated by an aesthetic idea.

There is no fully developed argument here but Kant's line of thought must be this: suppose fine art were *not* inspired by aesthetic ideas 'produced' through natural genius. Then, either the concept of a purpose according to which the artist produced the work is quite determinate for the object as a whole, in which case the result cannot be beautiful. (This would be the first or second cases above.) Or, the object is beautiful, but this must be quite irrelevant to either the genre or theme. (This is the third case above.) The notion of an aesthetic idea, then, is the only hypothesis that can account for the *integration* of the sensible, aesthetic and intellectual elements in the work of fine art. That the aesthetic idea is a product of the free imagination, and is thus independent of any conventional rules for the production of art objects, and is even grounded in an entirely *a priori* manner in the nature of the human faculties, all follow quite obviously for Kant.

None of the above, however, provides an adequate explanation of how an aesthetic idea is supposed to accomplish this integration. The relevant passages in §49 are both confused and compressed. Although we introduced the aesthetic idea as the 'counterpart' to a rational idea, in fact Kant seems to suggest two different manners in which aesthetic ideas can be the *spirit* of fine art. First, the aesthetic idea is a presentation of a rational idea (one of Kant's examples is the moral idea of 'cosmopolitan' benevolence; he also speaks of 'invisible beings, the realm of the blessed, the realm of hell, eternity, creation, and so on'). Of course, we know that there is no such adequate presentation. On Kant's description, the aesthetic idea seems to function by prompting a surplus of thoughts that are purposively coordinated together in precisely the same way as thoughts engendered by the presentation of a naturally beautiful form are purposive. In this first case, this purposiveness is explicitly directed *towards* the 'presentation' of rational ideas, thus immediately arousing the *interest* of reason.[12] Kant writes, '[the presentation by the imagination] prompts, even by itself, so much thought as can never be comprehended within a determinate concept'.[13]

Secondly, the aesthetic idea can be an impossibly perfect or complete presentation of an empirical experience and its concept (death, envy, love, and fame are Kant's examples). We can have a sensible experience of envy, but not perfect, archetypal envy. Here the aesthetic idea is not presenting a particular rational idea so much as a general function of reason, the striving for a maximum, a totality or the end of a series. And again, the effect is a purposive 'expansion' of the concept beyond its ordinary determinate bounds.

The aesthetic idea is not merely a presentation (or 'counterpart') of some other (otherwise unpresentable) concept, which we called its *theme*. Nor is it simply an unthinkable presentation that expands the given sensible concept of an object (genre) so as to entreat cognition to 'so much thought as can never be comprehended within a determinate concept'. It is *also* one that will set the imagination and understanding into a harmony, creating a similar kind of self-sustaining and self-contained purposive activity as the beautiful. Thus, Kant writes that 'spirit' 'imparts to the mental faculties a purposive momentum, i.e., imparts to them a play which is such that it sustains itself on its own and even strengthens the faculties for such play' (§49).

The aesthetic idea does for thought what the presentation of the naturally beautiful did. So pleased is Kant with his notion of aesthetic ideas that he generalises it for all beauty, writing 'we may in general call beauty (whether natural or artistic) the *expression* of aesthetic ideas . . .' (§51). As we said above, genius places a 'hint' of the supersensible into the sensible – which is exactly how purposive nature is experienced in the beautiful. We shall return to this notion below.

But the task of the genius is not yet complete: he or she still must 'hit upon' suitable particular images (such as the 'attributes' discussed above) generated in this lively harmony. (Thus, contrary to Kant's earlier claims, it is not merely taste that is responsible for the form of the product.) In practice, this will often involve a set of what Kant calls 'aesthetic attributes', more ordinary, intermediate images: 'Thus Jupiter's eagle with the lightning in its claws is an attribute of the mighty king of heaven' (§49). In themselves, these images may be merely conventional (or, if original, they are potentially conventional). However, it is the selection and organisation of these attributes that creates the aesthetic form of the work of art. These images, well chosen and fixed into the work as product, will not immediately communicate the idea itself to the reader of the poem or the viewer of the painting; that would be impossible for an aesthetic idea. Rather, Kant argues, the art work will 'communicate' the particular mental state of harmonious purposive excitation which blossoms up around the idea in the mind of the genius. For what is communicated is the 'mental attunement' engendered by the aesthetic idea (§49). Only in that way is the idea 'expressed'. So significant is this distinction between direct communication and indirect communication through expression, that Kant classifies all the fine arts on the analogy of the qualities of expression in speech. 'Word, gesture and tone' become the arts of speech (especially poetry), the visual arts, and music (§51).

Kant is concerned that the ideas of the genius are in some way communicated. For genius as absolute originality is somewhat at odds with taste, with its concern for orderly communication. Kant argues that when push comes to shove, it is the former that has to give, because 'if the imagination is left in lawless freedom, all its riches produce nothing but nonsense'.[14] Nevertheless, precisely because in poetry the imagination reaches a maximum of freedom, Kant categorises it as the highest of the art forms. He writes, and this is a remarkable compression of much of his theory of fine art:

Poetry fortifies the mind: for it lets the mind feel its ability – free, spontaneous, and independent of natural determination – to contemplate and judge phenomenal nature in the light of aspects that nature does not on its own offer in experience either to sense or to the understanding, and hence poetry lets the mind feel its ability to use nature on behalf of and, as it were, as a schema of the supersensible.

(§53, translation modified)

Kant's theory of genius, though remarkably vague at times, has been enormously influential, especially for much of nineteenth-century thought. Particularly influential were the radical separation of the aesthetic genius from the scientific mind; the emphasis on the near-miraculous expression of the ineffable, excited state of mind; the link of fine art to a 'metaphysical' content; the requirement of radical originality; the tight integration of aesthetic forms, intellectual ideas and sensible purposes; and the elevation of poetry to the head of all arts. All these claims (though not all of them unique to Kant) were intellectual commonplaces for well over a century. Indeed, when avant-garde modernists protested (often paradoxically) against the concept of the artist by using the techniques of 'automatic writing' or 'found objects', they were reacting, for the most part, against this concept of the artist-genius.

SUMMARY: The particular contribution of genius to fine art is what Kant calls 'spirit'. A mere product can be in agreement with taste, but incidentally, without a spirit that animates and integrates the whole object. In particular, the spirit is the presence of an aesthetic idea, a presentation of the free imagination which is 'unexpoundable' in any determinate concept. The aesthetic idea is linked to both a rational idea, which it strives to present, and to the sensible concept of the object's purpose – it thus integrates the work's intellectual and sensible dimensions. The aesthetic idea is purposive for the faculties of thought much as the beautiful natural presentation was. The genius expresses this purposive mental activity in the work.

The Problem of the Supersensible

The remainder of this chapter will draw together some disparate but very important threads of argument that Kant left slightly underdeveloped in his 'Critique of Aesthetic Judgement'. These arguments concern three notions above all: first, the role of the notion of the supersensible in this part of the book; secondly, the relationship between aesthetic judgement and morality; thirdly, the implications of the ideas of communicability and common sense. We will see that these notions coalesce into at least a skeleton of an account of the general importance (both metaphysical and moral/political) of aesthetic judgements. Also, these notions will make possible a smoother transition to the second half of Kant's book, 'The Critique of Teleological Judgement'.

The proper place to begin is with §55, which forms the beginning of the 'Dialectic of Aesthetic Judgement'. As we saw in the Introduction, by 'dialectic' Kant means the paradoxes or other types of nonsense that a cognitive faculty falls into when it begins to 'reason' – to form and assert universal propositions – beyond the critical limits proper to it. Kant thus claims that 'dialectic' is a natural consequence of a faculty that has not been thoroughly and continuously subjected to critique. Although individual aesthetic judgements claim universal validity, they are certainly not universal *laws* because they lack any determinate concept. So, Kant claims, it is the critical account of the possibility of taste that runs into dialectical difficulties. Our understanding of aesthetic judgement in particular finds itself on the horns of a dilemma, or an 'antinomy' (two contradictory propositions that both seem to be inescapably true). Kant writes (§56):

> Hence the following antinomy emerges concerning the principle of taste:
> (1) *Thesis*: A judgement of taste is not based on concepts; for otherwise one could dispute about it (decide by means of proofs).
> (2) *Antithesis*: A judgement of taste is based on concepts; for otherwise, regardless of the variation among [such judgements], one could not even so much as quarrel about them (lay claim to people's necessary assent to one's judgement).

If the first of these (taste is not based on concepts) were not true, then one would be able to prove one's aesthetic judgements, just as one can prove the Pythagorean Theorem, or that steel is harder than wood. But the assumption throughout the discussion of beauty has been that such proof is impossible. If the second (taste is based on concepts) were not true, then it would make no sense for me to be able to place a claim upon the agreement of another. Everyone's taste would be *absolutely* subjective. But, again, all along we have assumed that it makes sense for one to say 'But you *must* find this scenery beautiful!'

By this point in his book, however, Kant's reader will know exactly how to solve this problem. According to the principle of all reflective judgements, beauty exhibits a purposiveness (here without definite purpose) with respect to the harmony of our cognitive faculties. By showing that such a harmony among the cognitive faculties is universally possible, Kant has shown us a basis for judgement which is both universal in its applicability, but indeterminate in its application. That is to say, it makes possible judgements that behave *as if* based on a universal concept of some purpose (because they demand universal assent). This concept has a validity guaranteed by an *a priori* principle (and is therefore necessary), but judgements are not in fact based upon determinate concepts of the understanding (and thus not subject to the analysis or demonstration of concepts, or proof). The dialectical illusion that stands behind the above antinomy is a too-narrow grasp of how conceptuality can happen so that objects can be subject to judgement. It is solved, then, by enlarging our assumptions about what can perform concept-like functions.

So far, the ground is familiar. But how is this supposed to be a different argument from the deduction of aesthetic judgement in §38? Kant suddenly introduces what looks like, from the point of view of how we have discussed the deduction of taste, a whole new issue.[15] In order to exhibit this issue, we need to rethink what the above antinomy means.

It could be the case that nature as the object of scientific laws ('nature', as Kant is fond of saying, according to the 'immanent' principles of the understanding), is somehow itself responsible for the beautiful forms in nature. Kant speaks at length in §58 of the formation of mineral crystals as an example of purely formal beauties in nature being quite patently produced as a result of ordinary laws of nature. This possibility demonstrates, for critical philosophy, the *idealism* of the principle of purposiveness. Kant thus states, 'we receive nature with favour, [it is] not nature that favours us' (§58). He writes (§58),

> Just as we must assume that objects of sense as appearances are ideal if we are to explain how we can determine their forms *a priori*, so we must presuppose an idealistic interpretation of purposiveness in judging the beautiful in nature and in art.[16]

In other words, when we consider matters from the wider point of view that is the system of transcendental philosophy, aesthetic judgement does not concern itself directly with purposes in nature, but merely with the subjective relation that presentations of nature have to our cognitive faculties in general. Such an idealism gives us a negative result: it excludes us from saying that 'subjective purposiveness is an actual (intentional) purpose that nature (or art) pursues, namely, harmony with our faculty of judgement' (§58). Any given object in nature must be subject to the necessary laws of nature; that which we apprehend as beautiful form is no exception. However, Kant writes of reflective judgement in general,

> So this transcendental principle must be one that reflective judgement gives as a law, but *only to itself*; it cannot take it from somewhere else (since judgement would then be determinate); nor can it prescribe it to nature.
>
> (Introduction IV, emphasis added)

Judgement's principle of the purposiveness of nature is valid only for judgement's own activity; it is not valid for cognition of nature (theoretical philosophy), nor for the faculty of desire (practical philosophy). But from the point of view of the activity of aesthetic judgement itself, such beauty is actually purposive, and thus connected to pleasure. After his Introduction, Kant just assumes this, for it belongs to the structure of the faculties (judgement as legislative for feeling). Indeed, sometimes he even slips up, using phrases of the type 'beauty in nature', rather than 'beautiful presentations of nature' (see, for example, the 'Comment' following §38). The critical question was always less 'What is the principled assumption of judgement?' than 'Is there a transcendental validity to that assumption?'

So, as we saw above, the actual form of an object can be accounted for on the basis of natural laws (such as the chemistry of crystal formation); what those laws cannot account for is judgement's claim that the form is purposive. The real antinomy here, then, is between the claims *immanent* to our judging activity (there are indeterminate purposive forms in nature, which we now know to be universally valid for all judges) and the claims *exterior* to that activity (nature has to be understood as legislated for only by the understanding, and thus as subject to its laws alone). And this is exactly how (although in a quite different context) Kant states the upshot of the antinomy in §59, writing: 'contradictions, would continually arise from the contrast between the nature of these faculties and the claims that taste makes.' At which point Kant moves on to discuss again judgement's giving a law from and to itself, reinforcing our above discussion of judgement's 'point of view'.

In the deduction of aesthetic judgements, Kant demonstrates for such judgements the universal validity of the subjective principle of common sense. That apparently took care of things on the side of the subject. Immanent to judgement, this principle assumes the purposiveness of nature, and does so necessarily and universally. But when judgement begins to 'reason', and that principle is taken to be universal *beyond the faculty of judgement*, then an antinomy arises. The critical limits proper to judgement are not respected. Not surprisingly, the above antinomy, as we reinterpreted it, turns out to be close to how Kant conceives of the antinomy of teleological judgement in the second half of his book (see Chapter 5). Our transformation of the terms of the antinomy of aesthetic judgement has begun to show how the two halves of Kant's book might be struggling with exactly the same issues, at bottom.

So, how is this antinomy to be solved? What every antinomy requires is a new point of view from which the paradox is no longer *necessarily* binding. In all of Kant's previous antinomies, the new point of view is always the critical distinction between appearances and things-in-themselves; and so it is here. If we are asking for a concept that accounts for this purposiveness without also contradicting the necessity of laws immanent to nature, it must be a concept of what Kant calls the realm of the 'supersensible' 'underlying' all nature and all humanity. By 'supersensible' Kant means that which exists in itself, but which only shows itself in the manner that we, as finite human beings, are capable of experiencing it. As we know, no other concept is adequate to grasping the beautiful object as beautiful. So judgement is forced to assume (for its own purposes, and not as an object of knowledge) the indeterminate *rational* concept of a supersensible realm underlying all purposive forms in nature, and all purposive activity in the subject. This seems to result from a treatment (for the purposes of understanding *communication*) of the standing potential for the harmony of the cognitive faculties as if it were a concept of something. The supersensible is then the ultimate basis of the universality of the claims of aesthetic judgements. This assumption *could* have been made explicit by Kant much earlier – in the Deduction, for example[17] – except that he was there focusing on the *a priori* grounds of aesthetic judgement simply in the subject's faculties.

The supersensible as ground is by no means a determining concept for the cognition of nature – it plays no role at all – but it is certainly *compatible* with that cognition. Thus, while judgement has to assume such a ground, the cognition of nature in general only admits it as a possibility. That mere possibility, however, completely blunts the edge of the antinomy.[18] Thus Kant writes (at §57), emphasising as we have done the deep similarity between the antinomies in all three critiques,

> [T]he antinomies compel us against our will to look beyond the sensible to the supersensible as the point [where] all our *a priori* faculties are reconciled, since that is the only alternative left to us for bringing reason into harmony with itself.

In this way, through the aesthetic judgement, purposive nature gives us a 'hint' of the supersensible. As we shall see below on pp. 134–41, this inspires an immediate interest in beauty on the part of reason, thus beginning the integration of the supersensible here with the ground of the possibility of the good.

Furthermore, according to the necessary *a priori* principle of judgement, nature in the beautiful is purposive for our human cognition. The cognitive activity of contemplation is itself purposive (see, for example, §12); this being purposeful toward itself is an aspect of its self-containedness.[19] Thus, from the point of view of judgement, there is a corresponding assumption of a supersensible ground for the subject at the basis of *this* purposiveness, while, again, for theoretical cognition, this is an invalid assumption, but at least possible. In the sections on the antinomy of taste itself, Kant claims (at §57) that the concept involved in judgements of taste

> is reason's pure concept of the supersensible underlying the object (as well as underlying the judging subject) as an object of sense and hence as appearance. For unless we assumed that a judgement of taste relies upon some concept or other, we could not save its claim to universal validity.

On one hand, then, we have as a result of our critique of aesthetic judgement a transcendental idealism. This asserts merely that beauty in nature can be experienced in no other way than as purposive, because that purposiveness is the subjective condition on which the experience is possible at all. But it cannot disprove the possibility of a real, but theoretically unknowable, supersensible ground. On the other hand, we have the actual practice of aesthetic judgement which has to take a more 'realist' line. Taking beauty as 'in' nature, it assumes the validity of the rational concept of a supersensible ground both of that natural purposiveness, and of the purposive activity of the judging subject. This peculiar situation becomes still more so in the 'Critique of Teleological Judgement'.

SUMMARY: There is an 'antinomy' natural to aesthetic judgements. An antinomy arises when a faculty begins to make illegitimate universal propositions outside its field of critical competence. The antinomy of taste concerns whether or not such judgements must involve concepts in order to be, in the relevant way, communicable. But the real problem is the relationship between judgement's immanent assumption of purposiveness in nature, and the claims the understanding makes as the faculty legislative for nature. The solution lies in the possibility of a supersensible foundation which unifies the disparate claims of the faculties. A similar, but more detailed, relation to the supersensible is argued in the 'Critique of Teleological Judgement'.

Morality, Culture and Related Issues

Culture and Common Sense as Real, Social Notions

At the end of Chapter 2, having discussed at length the 'Deduction', we claimed that Kant had solved (at least to his own satisfaction) the foundation in common sense of aesthetic judgements on the beautiful. This meant that the various features of such judgements as subjective mental acts (universality, disinterestedness, and so on) had been given a transcendental explanation. (As we have just seen in the previous section, the features on the side of the object – namely, purposiveness in nature from the point of view of judgement – remain to be fully understood.) However, Kant seems to want to claim that there is one feature left over. He writes (§40):

If we could assume that the mere universal communicability as such of our feeling must already carry with it an interest for us (something we are, however, not justified in inferring from the character of a merely reflective power of judgement), then we could explain how it is that we require from everyone as a duty, as it were, the feeling [contained] in a judgement of taste.

A duty is an unconditionally necessary action which is a law for everyone – it is one of the central concepts of Kant's moral philosophy.

The problem here is that, first of all, we know from the second moment that aesthetic judgements lay claim to a universal validity (though only subjective, that is not a *factual* validity), and thus also lay claim to the agreement of others. Such a notion requires that the judgements be universally communicable. Secondly, we know from the deduction how this universality is grounded in the cognitive faculties understood transcendentally. But in this, Kant is now telling us, such a universality is in practice no different from, for example, scientific judgements, purely objective and determinate judgements. They too operate under the expectation of being universally held, and also communicable; but they contain no incentive to actively seek the agreement of others. What does it matter, I might say, to my judgement 'as such' whether you agree or not? I'm perhaps surprised if you do not, but I do not really care.

But we *do* take an interest in other's judgements. Even in these 'anything goes' times – when it is a *positive* fact of a liberal society and state that judgements of value should disagree – if I feel I have made a valid aesthetic judgement on, say, the new film by my favourite director, then I get bothered when someone else (especially someone I respect) claims that it is rubbish. This could partly be because it makes me question the validity of my original judgement, or partly because it makes me uncomfortable in having to question the taste of the other person. But in either case, it follows that we have an investment in our judgements being properly formed. If I have properly formed an aesthetic evaluation, then others will have failed in their duty if they do not concur. Now, in Chapters 1 and 2 we made much of describing the mental state in aesthetic judgement as 'self-contained'. One of the things this meant was that the feeling of pleasure involved was not tied to the actual, or possibly future, existence of some state of affairs. That is, the judgement was disinterested; no interest either stemming from the sensibly agreeable or from the good was involved in the foundation of the judgement. How, then, could there arise something like a claim on the duty of others to agree?

Scientific and other such judgements have a similar disinterestedness, which is part of what we mean by their absolute objectivity. With respect to scientific judgements, however, one might claim that science (and, for Kant, Enlightenment in general) is not only an *individual* activity (*my* thinking becomes clear and free) but also a *social and collective* activity (we form, for example, scientific societies, and institutions for the delivery of education and the distribution of justice). This was certainly a common feeling in the eighteenth century, with its sense of a Europe-wide scientific adventure, and the associated burgeoning of the scientific publishing industry. Thus, there is a *subsequent* interest in the real agreement of others with my judgements. Without their real agreement, the social and collective aspects of science would not be possible, which is almost tantamount to claiming that science itself is not possible.

Analogously, the aesthetic judgement, once formed, might *subsequently* involve an interest. Kant in particular identifies two types of interest that might be said to *universally* follow on from aesthetic judgements. In §§41–2 he calls these the 'empirical' and the 'intellectual' (the latter will be discussed in the last section of this chapter). Just as in the example of science above, I take an 'empirical' interest in the beautiful because, as universally communicable, it contributes to the possibility of a social existence. The beautiful is one of the things that we can share with others, which can identify us to ourselves and to outsiders as being part of a group (thus, for example, we can talk about the artistic culture of the French seventeenth century). A subsequent interest in sociability therefore attaches, with some universality, to aesthetic judgement.

Kant further claims that aesthetic judgement completes communicability, for while my concepts have always been communicable, the cultivation of my sense of the beautiful allows me to share *even my feelings*. Civilisation reaches its height when communicability 'becomes almost the principle activity of refined inclination' (§41). However, important as this may be to social communities, or to understanding the history of cultures, Kant claims, it is not what he is looking for. For it is only 'empirically' the case that human beings happen to be social creatures through and through.[20] Moreover, the actual existence of a society to be a part of is contingent – Kant talks about a man 'abandoned on some desolate island' not caring either way about beautiful adornments (compare §2). Thus, this interest cannot explain the *a priori* and necessary invocation of the duty of others to agree with my aesthetic judgements.

But perhaps Kant is a touch hasty in dismissing the significance of this 'empirical' interest. For, in the immediately preceding section (§40), he reiterates the conception of 'common sense' (here called *sensus communis*) as being a type of 'shared' sense. He then goes on to explore the meaning of this sharing, writing (§40):

> [W]e must [here] take *sensus communis* to mean the idea of a sense *shared* [by all of us], i.e. a power to judge that in reflecting takes account (*a priori*), in our thought, of everyone else's way of presenting [something], in order *as it were* to compare our own judgement with human reason in general.

This facility judgement has of comparing its own activity with that of others is important, not only for aesthetic judgement, but also for 'sound' thinking in general. In both cases, it is necessary to distinguish, among the conditions and components of a judgement, what is contributed by my individual person (my prejudices or preconceptions; also, the effects of my own body, or my own situation) from what is not so contributed. In that way, one's mind is 'broadened', perhaps to the extent of being able to take a truly 'universal standpoint'. In the history of philosophy, and long before Kant's work, notions such as this 'universal standpoint' have been taken by many (Descartes, for example, or the Humean tradition) to be the key concept in grasping the spirit of truly objective scientific enquiry, and also of morality. Kant is here claiming that the same operation is important for aesthetic judgement (this is also not an entirely new claim). Moreover, as we have seen, the notion of having a 'sense' or feeling is descriptive of one of the ways in which Kant understands the possibility of such judgements. For that reason, he claims, judgements have more right to the name *sensus communis* than ordinary or scientific cognition, which do not involve sense in the same way.

However, it is not yet clear in what way we can 'take account' of others in our judgements. On the one hand, Kant writes that, '. . . we compare our judgement not so much with the actual as rather with the merely possible judgements of others, and [thus] put ourselves in the position of everyone else, merely by abstracting from the limitations that [may] happen to attach to our own judging' (§40). This entails that an actual social existence, in which one might actually compare one's judgements and their processes with those of others, is not necessary. Rather, we *pretend* to do so, as it were, by an inner process of abstracting from subjective conditions. If, in every instance, we did actually compare, then first we would probably accomplish little, and secondly we would be subject to the narrowness of the (probably quite small) group of 'others'. But, on the other hand, one might object that this begs the question of how one acquires the skill of such abstraction, if not through actual communication and comparison with others (for example, in a classroom as children; or later, by subjecting one's views to validation or criticism by others, in publishing, conferences, in the market place, and so on). For, importantly, it is a *skill* that Kant is talking about, one that needs *cultivation*.

Quite clearly, Kant is committed to saying that the *a priori* possibility of such a skill of abstraction separate from others lies in our cognitive faculties, and it's fortunate for us that it is. Once the skill is acquired, it can (ideally at least) be practised in isolation. But, it would seem, cultivating it is a social process. Thus, the empirical interest in sociability and communicability that *followed* aesthetic judgement (§41) is complemented by an interest that *precedes* the judgement, making it (only on an empirical level, of course) possible as an actual skill. 'Culture' or 'cultivation' [*Kultur*] has two meanings in Kant. Most of the time, it clearly means the training of an individual's faculties or other skills – in this case, and most others, the skill in question is aesthetic taste. However, 'culture' sometimes suggests that which is public and shared, and thus indirectly refers to a whole host of institutions, histories, traditions, objects and practices. These embody cultivation by recording and actively passing on 'exemplary' acts of judgement (either of judgement by critics, or of the creation of beautiful objects – thus the existence of critical records, art historical scholarship, museums and collections, and so on); or by institutionalising an understanding of what is involved in such acts (art academies, universities, apprenticeships); or finally, by regulating (and hopefully encouraging) the public disclosure of the activities of judgement so that each might 'take account of' others (here we might include anything from the ancient Greek *agora* to the Internet). Kant summarises a similar set of ideas in the notion of *humaniora* (the 'humanities') in §60. 'Culture' in this second, broader sense has significance (in this context) only insofar as it creates the empirical conditions for cultivation in the first sense. Otherwise, Kant might well claim, it is just fetishism or empty tradition.

In §60, Kant immediately links the problem of culture in both the above senses to a political notion. The basic political problem is directly analogous to both the harmony of the faculties in the aesthetic judgement, and to the relation between free will and the moral law: namely, 'the difficult task of combining freedom (and hence also equality) with some constraint (a constraint based more on respect and submission from duty than on fear)'. This task is begun by permitting and encouraging the free communication of ideas among all sections of society (the most refined and the most simple) and thus 'finding in this way that mean between higher culture and an undemanding nature constituting the right standard (even for taste), unstatable in any universal rules, which is the universal human sense'. The 'common sense', which began as simply a way of understanding the peculiar validity attaching to singular aesthetic judgements, turns out to be linked, even identical to, the ultimate foundations of a harmonious social and political life. Indeed, the model for this vision is nothing other than the relation between the faculties once freed from external constraint.[21]

Kant makes similar claims in a number of other places, such as the essays 'An Answer to the Question: What is Enlightenment?' and 'Perpetual Peace: A Philosophical Sketch'.[22] In the first of these, he famously writes,

Enlightenment is man's emergence from his self-incurred immaturity. Immaturity is the inability to use one's own understanding without the guidance of another. [. . .] For enlightenment of this kind, all that is needed is *freedom*. And the freedom in question is the most innocuous form of all – freedom to make *public use* of one's reason in all matters.
                                                    (*Political Writings*, pp. 54–5)

Even though there may not be a single enlightened individual mind, the public use of reason (by 'taking account of everyone') can become enlightened. This in turn assists the individual to become cultivated in the mature exercise of reason.[23] In Kant's essay, not surprisingly, this 'public use' becomes an explicitly moral and political (in the narrow sense) principle (some of the reasons for such moral implications of aesthetic judgement are explored on pp. 134–41. Kant concludes the essay:

> [O]nce the germ on which nature has lavished most care – man's inclination and vocation to *think freely* – has developed within this hard shell, it gradually reacts upon the mentality of the people, who thus gradually become increasingly able to *act freely*. Eventually, it even influences the principles of governments, which find that they can themselves profit by treating man, who is *more than a machine*, in a manner appropriate to his dignity.
>
> (*Political Writings*, p. 60)

In 'Perpetual Peace: A Philosophical Sketch' Kant takes a formally similar idea and transforms it into a law and test of justice itself. He writes, 'All actions affecting the rights of other human beings are wrong if their maxim is not compatible with their being made public' (p. 126). To be sure, Kant is a remarkably conservative, anti-revolutionary figure, and also perilously optimistic about the progressive evolution of political systems. But there is something compelling about his raising the idea of 'publicness' to such a fundamental role. This role is transcendentally guaranteed by – and indeed modelled on – common sense and the other universally guaranteed principles of our human faculties. But by way of the institutions and practices of publicness, it also reciprocally develops and cultivates those faculties.

SUMMARY: The notion of common sense or *sensus communis* in its role as a public feeling can be further refined. Kant claims it involves, from the point of view of the individual, a kind of testing or rectification of our judgement by comparison with the judgement of others. This happens, Kant claims, as an act of abstraction from the merely subjective conditions of our judgement. But in addition, there is a role for real public communication. Although the transcendental conditions of aesthetic experience can be guaranteed in all humans, the relevant faculties (especially in the case of the sublime) still need to be trained in order to function properly. This raises the notion of cultivation in the sense of a real, social culture: those set of institutions, practices or traditions through which a culture debates or passes on its sense of proper judgement and through which it regulates communication with itself. Kant goes so far as to raise the idea of publicness to a formal principle of justice.

Can We Talk About Beauty?

The Antinomy of Taste, as we saw above, put the following problem very well: we cannot dispute (attempt to prove things) about taste, but we can meaningfully quarrel (disagree). In the end, this follows from the notion of purposiveness without purpose. In the necessary absence of such a purpose, however, how exactly might such a quarrel run? Would it simply be 'That pleases me and should please you,' and the reply 'But it doesn't please me, and shouldn't please you,' and so on? Such a conversation is guaranteed not to get anywhere. In particular, does this mean that it is pointless to talk about art, with friends much less with critics or artists, or to learn about art history, or to read or write art/literary criticism, or even just to read museum catalogues full of background information? That is not Kant's point. If it were, it would be increasingly difficult to understand how cultivation as a *public act* might happen. More generally, it would be difficult to see what universal communication meant.

Certainly, we can discuss the *conditions* under which we are making judgements. I can accuse you of having a certain interest in the object which is swaying your judgement; you can accuse me of having too determinate a concept informing my judgement, of not allowing imagination its freedom. That is to say, we can help teach each other to be properly self-critical and self-reflective on anything that might be illegitimate in our aesthetic judgements. But, can we talk usefully about *individual things* and their supposed aesthetic qualities?

Taste cannot be proven. We can happily move from a description of the make-up and performance of a football team to the conclusion 'That is a good football team'. But none of this, of course, means that aesthetic objects do not have properties. But since there is no (and cannot in principle be any) concept for what is aesthetically pleasing, it is impossible to move logically from a description of a set of properties of an object to the conclusion that it is or should be aesthetically pleasing. On the basis of these properties, one can certainly make statistical generalisations about aesthetic judgements. For example, 'Roses are beautiful flowers' (see §§8, 33), really means 'Those who judge aesthetically tend to find roses beautiful'. Similarly, one could generalise by saying, 'Beautiful objects in nature tend to be symmetrical along at least one line or plane', 'Beautiful objects in nature tend to incorporate certain basic geometrical shapes (circle, triangle, the ancient Greeks' 'golden rectangle')', or 'Beautiful objects in nature tend to be made up of repeated patterns (the petals of a flower, birdsong, scales of a fish)' and so on. Similar generalisations could be made about fine art, at least of certain periods or ethno-geographic groups taken together. Some of the generalisations for nature and art are even roughly the same, because of the 'natural' basis of the production of fine art – but also no doubt because some artists have, in the past, worked in conscious imitation of nature. These are the kinds of empirical rules Kant has in mind in §34 when he writes that *criticism* 'is an art [that] merely takes the physiological (in this case psychological) and hence empirical rules by which taste actually proceeds, and (without thinking about [how] they are possible) seeks to apply them to our judging'.

These are descriptions of beautiful objects *qua* objects, of course, rather than explanations of what makes a presentation of an object appear beautiful. Such rules are the subject of a kind of anthropology of art. If one somehow programmed all of these generalisations into a computer and asked it to assemble a 'beautiful' form, the result *might* be beautiful (by accident, as it were), or (more likely) it would be banal. One cannot even reliably make negative assumptions on the basis of such generalisations: despite *not* being symmetrical, a sunset may be beautiful.

Another way of saying this is to speak of the holism we discussed in Chapter 2. The beautiful form is, so to speak, more than the sum of its parts, which means that any given part, although indispensable to this particular object, is not necessary to the beauty of the object according to the synthesis belonging to some concept of it. But that 'indispensability', however, may mean that opportunities arise for sharpened attention, or for learning. The empirical rules discussed above might well serve in this capacity, turning our attention toward or away from certain salient aspects of the object. In the production of meaningful things, Kant distinguishes between the conceptual 'method' and the aesthetic 'manner' (compare §49 and §60). In fine art, when the manner of the master becomes the method of the student (or inferior talent), then we have the 'ostentatious' and 'stilted' (§49). But the fact that the latter *can* become the former indicates that even the aesthetic manner is subject to *some* objective examination, *some* communicable acts of attention.

Thus, I may be unmoved by a piece of music, until I notice – or someone points out to me – an aspect of the development of the melody, a subtle harmonic shift, a musical quotation from another piece, or the complexity of orchestration. It *might* happen that I then hear a completely different piece of music, and am captivated by it. Certainly, then, there is a role for art history, criticism, and other discussion about art, systematically drawing our attention to possibly salient features of art works. A similar thing can happen with natural objects, for example, insects: we might grow up loathing insects of all kinds as dirty, dangerous or in some other way evil, but the study of insects might reveal to us their rich complexity of structure, or strange and wonderful social behaviour. Suddenly, the world of insects might appear to us to be full of beautiful things.

Or it might not, and this is Kant's point. We can be led by learning and experience to the point where our faculties are appropriately cultivated, and our attention to the object is complete and well-informed, and it is possible for something to 'click' and for our aesthetic judgement to change. Statistically speaking, Kant might argue, there is in fact a convergence; thus the purpose of music or art 'appreciation' courses. But nothing logically can force that change. It is equally possible that, in possession of all the facts, my judgement might still be different from yours. I may understand how the music 'works', but still not like it; I may understand the extraordinary features of the world of insects, but still find them ugly, loathsome things. Kant says this is probably the reason why the ability to form aesthetic judgements is called 'taste' (§33). And it is just like our taste in foods – no one could convince us that kidney tastes good if we do not like kidney.

In the case of fine art, we might suspect that one particular source of information about the work would be, above all, helpful: the artist. The artist (as genius) will be conscious of all the aesthetic attributes in the work, of the aesthetic idea which 'inspired' it, and also of the rational concept that is its theme. Certainly, the artist ought to be able to point out salient properties of the object. Similarly, the artist can tell us the theme – 'the injustice of war', 'the transience of all things human' – but in itself this is likely to be banal. Beyond that? According to Kant's account, the main focus is the aesthetic idea which makes that theme interesting, which makes of those properties a work of fine art. This idea, however – and above all the *procedure* of making in which it plays the central role – is given its rule by 'nature', and not conscious, intentional choice or activity (see §46, but compare §60). A conscious choice would partly be determined by existing rules and interests, and that would compromise the freedom of the imagination, and the indeterminacy of the understanding.[24] The aesthetic idea achieves expression in the work of art itself and in no other way. Thus, in order to fully understand what the genius is telling us about the work, we have to *first* achieve an aesthetic appreciation of the work itself. The artist is no shortcut.

A similar problem arises in considering the notion of *influence*. With some exceptions, the greatest artists have also been influential. They have set in motion styles of art or literature that have lasted for decades or more, they have founded (or have had founded in their name) more or less official 'schools' of artists, they have been held up as exemplary in the institutions of art education, or by 'important' critics, but what could this mean? If by influence we mean a concept of how art is to be 'done', then obviously any such influence is bad news for the possibility of fine art. Only minor artists [non-geniuses] could possibly thrive through mere imitation. Kant thus claims that originality is a key trait of genius: 'genius is the exemplary originality of a subject's natural endowment in the *free* use of his cognitive faculties' (§49). This exemplarity functions in much the same way as the exemplary necessity of the aesthetic judgement (see the end of Chapter 1). That necessity lies not in a rule, but in the free, self-contained, disinterested pleasure arising from the beautiful form. It is exemplary, then, not in forming a rule, but precisely as a well-formed aesthetic judgement, which can then form part of the wider culture that helps 'cultivate' my faculty of aesthetic judgement. Similarly (§49), the genius

> is an example that is meant not to be imitated, but to be followed by another genius. [. . .] The other genius, who follows the example, is aroused by it to a feeling of his own originality, which allows him to exercise in art his freedom from the constraint of rules [and thus perhaps to be] exemplary.

The example in question could be the achievement of the work of art, or it could be some conceptual understanding of some of the practices that lay behind that achievement (for example, using a certain technique, travelling to a certain part of the world, studying some ancient or foreign art, reading and responding to some philosopher or critic). But the imitation of, say, a certain technique is not the end in itself, but a process of freeing oneself from rules, and thus also from imitation (§60). Again, it is a question of the cultivation – by way of the detour of the publicly shared field of objects (exemplars), practices, institutions, traditions – of one's innate talents, even for freedom.

There remains one other possibility for understanding the communicability of taste, although it takes us rather beyond the letter of Kant's text. The aesthetic judgement is not cognitive, in the sense that it not a determined experience of the world or exhibition of a concept, capable of becoming knowledge. But, as we saw throughout Chapter 2, the judgement takes place on the same foundations as all cognition. The harmony of the cognitive faculties is, we said, an *a priori* 'standing possibility', but in the contemplation of the beautiful always a real, concrete activity. In fact, Kant clearly maintains that the actual process of judgement is made up of an endless stream of thoughts which in some way embody the harmony of the cognitive faculties. For example, he writes at §42, that one may turn 'to the beautiful in nature, in order to find there, as it were, a voluptuousness for the mind in a train of thought [*Gedankengange*] that he can never fully unravel'. And, as we have seen, a similar purposive and communicable surplus of thought characterises the mental act of the genius. At least this is the case where the genius is tempered by taste, which here means primarily a concern for the communicability of the mental state (§50).

Just like the properties of the beautiful object, any set of such thoughts is certainly a part of a particular dwelling upon a particular beautiful presentation. But no one portion of such thought is necessary to the judgement,[25] nor adequately expresses either the harmony of the faculties, or the purposiveness of the experience. Rather, it is as a whole and as an activity that such thoughts are the harmony made concrete. An act of mind is purposive without purpose if it generates meanings for itself without concluding, but also without being just random, or entirely subjective. We might say that the thoughts are *recognisably directed towards* the goal of under-standing the beautiful object, but without ever arriving. Suppose then that a critic were to attempt to describe (or even *transcribe*) the process of her thought in the aesthetic contemplation of a particular work of art. This transcription could never be complete, or if it were that would mean that the transcription had transcended being a mere record and had itself become the art of genius, resembling a lyric poem perhaps. Similarly, it could not be a rule for another's judgement. Nevertheless, like priming a pump, such a mere description might well be helpful to another who is trying to begin a proper contemplation.[26]

In any case, the critic has a task beyond that of making bare judgements in order to help the public spend their time and money wisely (for example, 'What play should you go and see in New York')? Similarly, any other discussion of aesthetic judgements also has a task beyond simple agreement or disagreement. This task is to provide assistance to another's aesthetic judgement of the work. We have identified the following overlapping possibilities: (1) providing criticism of extraneous grounds in another's judgement, such as interests, determinate concepts and so on; (2) identifying and drawing our attention to exemplary works, judgements or practices which (despite their singularity) might help cultivate our native faculties of judgement; (3) indicating for attention salient properties of the aesthetic object which go into making up its form; (4) identifying general empirical rules for judgement which might be of assistance in creation or contempla-tion; and (5) describing subjective 'trains of thought' which might form an appropriate starting-point for the aesthetic contemplation of the object. Within the rather tight limitations Kant imposes, beauty can indeed be talked about.

Interestingly, all of these leave out what are by far the two most common forms of criticism today (practices barely in their infancy in the late eight-eenth century): first, the attempt to interpret or demonstrate the *meaning* of a work of art (what is the theme of *Hamlet*; what is the meaning of the *Mona Lisa?*); and second, the attempt to explicate the work as a historical docu-ment, or an instantiation of a set of historically contingent codes or practices (for example, the evidence in *Hamlet* of English conceptions of Northern Europe; *Mona Lisa* as evidence of changing styles of portraiture). Nothing in Kant forms an argument against such approaches, but they are certainly not aesthetic and (at least as generally practised) do not offer the above types of assistance in the cultivation of judgements.[27] It is as if *Hamlet*, for example, can be taken as one of several types of objects, from the point of view of one of several different independently valid types of cognition, and perhaps relying on several different fields of what in Chapter 1 we called 'enabling' knowledge. Kant similarly comments about the same flower being the object of a botanist's study, and of an aesthetic judgement, but not at the same time

(§16). The aesthetic judgement, because it reveals us in our higher 'vocation' as human beings, has to be considered the higher form of judgement (although no doubt less useful in many ways).[28] On this account, however, Kant would have to admit that there could be different approaches to the object *even as an aesthetic object*: in other words, different ways of apprehending its formal beauty, each of which is universally valid and communicable within itself. To take an obvious example, it will clearly make a difference whether I take a Shakespeare play *primarily* as a work of poetry, or as a work of staged drama – the formal qualities of the latter work will be different. Both of these can be aesthetic attitudes, but to effectively different objects.

SUMMARY: We know that we cannot prove aesthetic judgements, but to what extent can we communicate effectively about such judgements, beyond simply helping one another to form judgements in proper accord with the four moments? Certainly we can be informed by others about generalisations concerning what kinds of things tend to be considered beautiful; we can learn how to read symbols so as to properly construe form; and similarly we can have drawn to our attention intricacies of that form. None of this 'enabling knowledge' can determine a judgement, but it can put our reflection onto the appropriate track. Some of the same problems arise in understanding artistic influence. Kant sees influence as an assistance to the feeling of one's 'own originality'. Finally, it might be possible to communicate – in a way not itself tantamount to fine art – aspects of the actual course of mental activity in the contemplation of a work. This could prove useful in, again, setting another's reflection into motion.

The Relation Between Aesthetic Judgements and Morality

At the end of Chapter 3, we noted briefly that for Kant, the experience of the sublime relies upon the moral culture of our faculties. That is, it is necessary that we be sensitised to the feeling of the demands of reason, and above all to respect for the moral law. This further involves an understanding of our real nature as human beings as including a transcendence of nature. 'Culture', as we saw, primarily means training, but also implies the public conditions of that training. Now that we are in a position to get an overview of the entirety of the 'Critique of Aesthetic Judgement', let us return to this topic for both the sublime and the beautiful.

The sublime, properly speaking, is possible only for members of such a moral culture (and, Kant sometimes suggests, may reciprocally contribute to the strengthening of that culture). That which leads in a civilised person to a feeling of the sublime leads, in an uncultured person, to mere terror. Although human beings are essentially susceptible or sensitive to the ideas of reason, it is what Kant calls a moral culture which allows this susceptibility to actualise itself. The 'susceptibility' is a feeling for ourselves as essentially capable of transcending natural law. This culture means both the individual 'cultivation' of our faculties up to the point of their maturity, and the public 'civilisation' that makes the former possible. A moral culture – one which teaches us sensitivity to rational ideas, conceives human beings as capable of higher morality and thus leads us to think of ourselves in terms of transcendence – is required for the sublime. Without this moral culture, reason would never be able to redeem the pain felt in the first stage of the sublime experience. Indeed, subjectively experienced, the practical determination of our will by the moral law is sublime (see 'General Comment' following §29). Such moral experience involves both stages of the sublime: the initial 'sacrifice' of interests of sensible choice and inclination which fail to attain the law; the redemption through the purposiveness of the revelation of a higher 'vocation' as free, supersensible beings.

So, the sublime is in fact subjected to an empirical contingency. However, Kant stresses that this moral culture is not the *ground* of that feeling, but only the contingent condition under which the transcendentally conditioned sublime feeling can be realised in a particular case. That is to say, the sublime is not 'because of' moral culture, but only 'by way of' it. Furthermore, this is no ordinary contingency. Kant claims that we are justified in assuming the universal possession of the *transcendental conditions* for such moral culture, and thus for the sublime, because these conditions are (as in the case of the beautiful) the same as for theoretical and practical thought in general. As we have seen previously, the fact that aesthetic judgements are based upon such necessarily universal features of human thought is precisely that which (on the side of subjective conditions of judgement) justifies the principle of the universality of the aesthetic feeling for cognitive harmony upon which such judgements are based. Like the beautiful, sublime experiences can also contribute to this culture, Kant suggests. Sublimity thus continues the training or 'discipline' of moral culture for an individual, and may also add an exemplary situation to the wider social culture or motivate the creation or preservation of cultural institutions. An obvious example would be the notion of a 'national park' conceived of as under public stewardship.[29]

Importantly, one of Kant's examples here is religion (§28). God is an infinite power manifested (for example, in the Old Testament) in those phenomena conventionally called sublime (storms, floods, and so on). From such phenomena one could hardly feel *physically* safe; and if one did, one would simply have misunderstood the power of God. Does this cause a problem for Kant's conception of the sublime experience only happening in a situation of safety? No, because fear is not the appropriate form of worship in a rational, moral culture. God is certainly 'fearful', but the righteous man is not afraid, knowing that righteousness where justified is in harmony with God's will. This difference between fear and such sublime respect (as characterising different modes of worship) is also the difference, Kant says, between mere superstition and a rational religion. Religion in the former case is based upon the appeasement of fear, almost inevitably involves some anthropomorphism (compare §89n), and consists of nothing but 'ingratiation and fawning'. The idea of a rational religion is a key one for Kant, and we shall see more of it in Chapter 5.

Moreover, as many of Kant's asides indicate, a proper sublime feeling in religion is a political matter, and governments have attempted to regulate religious thought and worship for just this reason (see 'General Comment' following §29). This is because the sublime feeling itself contains truth, it is a revelation of our true 'vocation' – our nature as properly human. This involves a training in *active* attention to freedom and its demands in the moral sphere, certainly, but also as we have seen in religion, and finally in the political. For the latter, to take only the most obvious example, takes a key role (through permitting or forbidding certain practices) in promoting or degrading moral culture itself. To not permit religion its full sublimity is also to not permit this *activity*. Kant believes this happens when religion is made too easy – when ceremonies are so filled with images and stand-ins as to make impossible, or at least unnecessary, an 'experience' of God's proper transcendence. There thus results a training in moral, religious and political *passivity* – something Kant saw as suspiciously in tune with the needs of unenlightened governments. Not surprisingly, such arguments as they keyed into contemporary concerns (debates within Protestantism, and with the Catholic church, and various States' interference in both), brought Kant to several close shaves with the political authorities of his day. But it is also an interesting take on more recent debates concerning the popularisation of religion.

A parallel set of claims is made concerning the aesthetic judgement on the beautiful. Kant notes (§29) that the experience of the beautiful is less dependent than the sublime upon a pre-existing cultivation, resulting in a slightly different characterisation of how such judgements are modally necessary. However, as we saw above in the first section of this chapter, he contradicts this point elsewhere. More significantly, Kant claims that the beautiful is also purposive with respect to moral feeling. He writes, 'The beautiful prepares us for loving something, even nature, without interest.'[30] Of course, this love must be an aesthetic feeling. But as we shall see, partly because of the disinterestedness but above all because of the freedom involved in such 'love', it makes possible a profound (and cultivating) analogy with morality.[31]

In the *Critique of Judgement*, Kant discusses the link between beauty and morality in two main, but widely separated, places. The first is §42, which follows up the 'empirical' interest in the beautiful that we discussed above with an 'intellectual interest'. The second is very near the end of the 'Critique of Aesthetic Judgement' (§59) wherein Kant claims that beauty is the 'symbol' of morality.

As we saw above at the beginning of this chapter, the problem surrounding the notion of 'intellectual interest' is understanding how we can claim a feeling for the beautiful as something like a *duty*. The 'empirical interest', precisely because it is empirical, cannot answer this question. We could only claim others' agreement as a duty if an interest immediately attaches to the beautiful, and attaches in a way that is universal and necessary. Kant begins §42 by remarking that it is sometimes claimed that there is an inherent and determining link between those who have an appreciation of the arts, and those who exhibit great moral virtue. However, he says, this is just wishful thinking, and on the evidence at least of 'virtuosi of taste' the opposite might well be suspected. Nevertheless, there might be a link between virtue and an appreciation of *natural* beauty. This is especially the case where that appreciation is both 'habitual' and discloses an immediate (although, as with the empirical interest above, *subsequent*) interest in the reality and preservation of such beauty. Reason in fact takes an immediate interest in natural beauty, Kant claims. This is because of two factors. First of all, there is an analogy between the aesthetic judgement of nature which is pleasurable without being founded on an interest, and the moral judgement of a maxim which determines a moral feeling again without a foundation on any interest *'yet it gives rise to one'* (§42). Secondly,

> . . . reason has an interest in the objective reality of ideas (for which, in moral feeling, it brings about a direct interest), i.e., an interest that nature should at least show a trace or give a hint that it contains some basis or other for us to assume in its products a lawful harmony with that liking of ours which is independent of all interest.

Beauty in nature shows a 'trace' of an absolutely general purposiveness with respect to our disinterested delight (initially aesthetic). Reason finds itself 'interested' in this because such delight (and its subjective grounds in cognitive harmony) is something like an exhibition of its rational ideas. And this interest is 'akin' to the interest in the moral because the delight (and, again, its grounds) so closely 'resembles' the moral feeling and *its* grounds. Nature in beauty gives a concrete indication of the real possibility of my moral purposes. As we shall see, such an indication ultimately must be taken, in the context of reflective judgement, to refer to a supersensible basis. Similar notions become hugely important in Kant's 'moral proof' in the 'Critique of

Teleological Judgement' (see Chapter 5). (See also Kant's generalisation of the notion of an aesthetic idea at the beginning of §51, mentioned above.)

Kant amplifies: 'whoever takes such an interest in the beautiful in nature can do so only to the extent that he has beforehand already solidly established an interest in the morally good' (§42). It follows that a failure to take an immediate interest in natural beauty puts one under the suspicion of a weakness of one's sense of duty. That is Kant's solution to why something like a duty attaches to our claims of universal communicability of aesthetic judgement. However, this solution is too narrow: it only applies to the beautiful in nature, and even then only when habitual and immediate. Even in §42, Kant can be seen as struggling to rectify this weakness when he writes of the 'analogy' between taste (*generally*) and 'moral judgement'. Not surprisingly, this notion of analogy shows up again in §59.[32]

The penultimate section of the *Critique of Aesthetic Judgement* famously considers again the relation between beauty and morality. Here, Kant claims that beauty is the 'symbol' of morality (§59). A symbol, he argues, is to be defined as a presentation of a rational idea in an intuition. The 'presentation' in question is an analogy between how judgement reflects upon the idea, on the one hand, and how it reflects upon the intuition that is symbolic, on the other. The notion of 'reflection' is important here. Reflection, as we know, indicates an ability of our general faculty of judgement, in the absence of a determining concept and thus thrown back upon its own subjective resources, to come to decisions concerning intuitions. By introducing the idea of an analogy between procedures of reflection, Kant is taking the emphasis away from the objective content of a concept, and placing it onto the subjective conditions of that meaning. Moreover, Kant stresses that this is a procedure of reflection, an activity, and this in turn suggests that it can cultivate or habituate our faculties to certain types of behaviour.[33] A straightforward analogy between two notions (rather than between the reflection upon those notions) would be an intellectual curiosity only, and have no implications for our habits of thought. Thus again, we see Kant philosophically underpinning the notion that taste should be related to and also, through culture, *promote* morality.

For example, if 'justice' is symbolised by a blind goddess with a scale, it is not because all judges are blind. Rather, 'blindness' and 'weighing' are concepts upon which judgement reflects subjectively in a way analogous to its reflection upon the concept of 'justice'. In treating beauty as the symbol of morality, Kant lists four points of analogy: (1) in the reflection upon these notions, both please directly and not through consequences or purposes; (2) both are disinterested; (3) both involve the idea of a free conformity to law (in the case of beauty, conformity of the imagination in, and in a sense *through*, its freedom with the lawfulness of the understanding; in the case of morality, conformity of the will); (4) both are understood to be founded upon a universal principle that does not involve determining concepts of the under-standing.[34] Through these connections, beauty is the symbol of morality – in other words, Kant writes, 'taste is basically an ability to judge the [way in which] moral ideas are made sensible' (§60).

Now, the interest of reason is to act upon nature in accordance with moral law, and in order to bring about the Good. However, there are a host of related problems with this notion that Kant feels we need to solve before we can satisfy ourselves philosophically of even the *possibility* of such action. Because of the importance of practical reason as the highest and most essential faculty of man, these problems lay claim to being the most significant in all of philo-sophy. One of these problems – the key *theoretical* problem as far as Kant is concerned – is called in the history of philosophy the 'free will problem'. This is something which Kant has dealt with over and over again, particularly in the famous antinomy concerning freedom in the *Critique of Pure Reason*.[35] The problem is how to understand the mere possibility of freedom within a universe entirely determined as necessary by natural law. Several closely related problems will culminate in Kant's discussion of morality and the final purpose in the 'Critique of Teleological Judgement' (see Chapter 5). There is thus no need for us to pursue Kant's solution here. It is only important to note, as we saw above with the antinomy of aesthetic taste, that the solution to Kant's antinomies always involves a change of ontological level, from appear-ances to things-in-themselves – that is, to the supersensible. The solution to the antinomy involves positing freedom as a *supersensible* causality.

The third of Kant's points of analogy (freedom) takes us to the heart of this problem with the possibility of morality. Moreover, freedom is defined partly by way of freedom *from* determining external conditions such as purposes or interests, and freedom *for* a self-given universal law.[36] The other three points of analogy are clearly also related to the general 'free will' problem. So, these points of analogy are reflections upon the very possibility of morality. It is not, then, Kant's point to claim that the aesthetic judgement on the beautiful is in an analogy with how moral judgements proceed. For these are just the procedures of reflection upon, respectively, the beautiful and the moral. Rather, the very *conditions* of the former mirror those of the latter. There-fore, even in its subjective conditions (especially in the spontaneity of the free, productive imagination, and the 'autonomy' of judgement as a whole) beauty *makes visible*, and is judged on the basis of something at least closely linked to, the supersensible basis of morality. This 'symbol' therefore is more than just a kind of similarity between two different things, for both can be seen (by way of the symbol) to be grounded in the same supersensible self. Imme-diately prior to this passage (§59), Kant explains (emphasis added),

> In this ability [taste], judgement does not find itself subjected to a
> heteronomy from empirical laws, as it does elsewhere in empirical judging

– concerning objects of such a pure liking it legislates to itself, *just as reason does regarding the faculty of desire*. And because the subject has this possibility within him, while outside [him] there is also the possibility that nature will harmonise with it, judgement finds itself referred to something that is both in the subject himself and outside him, something that is neither nature nor freedom and yet is linked with the basis of freedom, the supersensible, in which the theoretical and the practical faculties are in an unknown manner joined into a unity.

Kant here claims that the symbolism of morality in beauty, by way of the reference to and grounding in the supersensible, explains why aesthetic judgements are demanded of others as a duty. Anyone (contingently) incapable of aesthetic judgement must also be suspected of a decided weakness of virtue.[37] That is a broadened version of the claim made in the section on the intellectual interest in the beautiful. The claim can be broadened because we are no longer considering the naturally beautiful object in its purposiveness, but are now considering the actual procedure and ultimate grounds of the aesthetic judgement *on the side of the subject*. Kant sees the 'analogy' between beauty and morality as solving the problem that the intellectual interest only solved 'narrowly'.[38]

There are thus five general and inter-related aspects to the connection between aesthetic judgement and morality. First, as we saw in the first part of this section, there is an inner relation between the transcendental ground of aesthetic judgement in common sense and the vision of a society politically organised around the ideals of freedom and the morality of duty. Simply as a type of judgement, taste may have more general significance, insofar as it can bring its appeal to publicness to bear on other problems. Secondly, there is the mutual cultivation or empirical conditioning – for example, the sublime is only possible on the condition of moral culture, but also reinforces our feeling for the moral law. Again, this also suggests wider social issues concerning the embodiment in public life of these conditions of cultivation. Thirdly, this cultivation is not merely a question of establishing good empirical habits; rather, it is a question of grasping, both in theory and in practice, the true nature of the human subject. This means, above all, the ideas of both freedom and the self-givenness of the moral law. Accordingly, beauty (together with the actual process of judging beauty) is the symbol of morality. Beauty thus reveals a key element of the meaning of morality, as well as the supersensible basis both of itself and of morality, and reveals them as tightly linked. Fourthly, at least in the case of natural beauty, nature's purposiveness for our disinterested liking arouses the interest of reason which takes it as a purposiveness with respect to the total possibility of moral action. In the beautiful, then, nature shows itself to be ready and waiting, so to speak, for our moral purposes.

Finally, Kant will argue, however, that by combining the above points we can go still further than this. After the discussion of the 'Critique of Teleological Judgement' in Chapter 5, we will be able to see the full meaning of Kant's hypothesis that judgement mediates between theoretical and practical philosophy. Fulfilling the ultimate moral purpose of man requires the unification of these philosophies and the faculties that legislate for them. From the point of view of the overall system of critical philosophy, the faculty of reflective judgement shows the intimate connection between the supersensible as the mere horizon of theoretical philosophy and (from the point of view of practical philosophy) the supersensible as the positive ground of the possibility of the good in nature. This, as we shall see, changes the meaning of the apparently simple statement Kant made that, 'The morally good is the *intelligible* that taste has in view' (§59). We shall be returning to such material in Chapter 5.

SUMMARY: The actual experience of the sublime is subject to a contingency: moral culture. By this is meant both the training or sensitisation of our faculties to the ideas of reason, and the actual public culture that helps bring this about. The manner in which sublimity is encouraged in religious ceremony is one of Kant's examples. The sublime feeling and our feeling for the moral law are mutually reinforcing. The beautiful has to be seen to be similarly subject to the condition of cultivation, and also similarly related to moral feeling. This is both because reason takes a practical interest in the 'hint' of the purposiveness of nature in beauty, and because the grounds of reflection on beauty have close ties with the grounds of the reflection on morality (beauty, Kant says, is the symbol of morality).

CHAPTER SUMMARY: All art (as a human 'doing') presupposes a concept of a purpose. But the beautiful is purposive without a purpose. How is it possible for there to be fine art? Only as a product of genius, which is a natural talent for giving an original rule, and thus 'spirit', to art production – where rule here means 'aesthetic idea'. An 'aesthetic idea' is a presentation of the imagination that is 'unexpoundable' in any determinate concept, but the contemplation of which results in the purposive play of the faculties, as with natural beauty.

There is an 'antinomy' for aesthetic judgements, concerning whether or not they must involve concepts. The real issue here is the rational concept of the supersensible, as a foundation for the beautiful presentation, which is capable of reconciling the various contradictions in the antinomy. Though critically we must assume an idealism of beauty, for judgement itself the rational concept has validity. Thus, there is an immediate interest of reason in beauty, because it seems to give a 'hint' of the purposiveness of nature even for our moral judgement and its purpose.

Sensus communis, as a public sense or feeling, has to be taken as also referring to a real social notion: namely, the conditions of cultivation that make the actual, empirically contingent experience of the beautiful or sublime possible. Some of these conditions can be understood as the activities of critics and historians who can make several types of contribution toward helping one form aesthetic judgements. This makes actual public life quite significant in the development of an individual's abilities to form aesthetic judgements. For both the beautiful and the sublime, these conditions are in part explicitly moral; moreover, the cultivation of aesthetic judgement also contributes to our ability to feel and understanding the force of the moral law. Finally, the actual procedure of reflection in the aesthetic judgement (especially its autonomy) is profoundly akin to how we reflect upon the possibility of moral action.

5

The Critique of Teleological Judgement

The second part of Kant's book, the 'Critique of Teleological Judgement', is less often studied and referred to than the first. Even today, some Internet and CD-ROM versions of the 'whole' text do not include it, nor even indicate its absence. This is, of course, related to the fact that Kant's aesthetics has been hugely and more or less continuously influential, while his teleology sparked less interest (after initial enthusiasm from philosophers such as Schelling). This relative lack of interest probably stems from a number of sources.

First, Kant was fighting a losing battle by backing the issues of teleology at all, for its significance in the active scientific community was already slight at the end of the eighteenth century, and diminishing all the time. For many, Charles Darwin would put paid to it altogether by showing that the development of species need assume nothing of the kind. Secondly, the enthusiasm among many for Kant's epistemology as presented in the *Critique of Pure Reason* played a role. In the treatment of teleology, he *seems* to be retracting some of the key ideas of the first *Critique* – in particular, the absolute universality of the principle of causality across all natural phenomena. It became easy to read the 'Critique of Teleological Judgement' as the worst kind of back-tracking, and even as the product of Kant's 'dotage'. Thirdly, the rational philosophy of religion that is prominent here was also a losing bet, so to speak. The nineteenth century would be full of philosophers for whom theology and religion were no longer key issues. Even for those philosophers still addressing themselves to such areas, the terms of the debate tended to be entirely different after Romanticism and later German Idealism (Kierkegaard is an excellent example). If that were not bad enough, Kant's treatment of religious themes again could easily seem like back-tracking, for example, he here claims to be offering a proof of God's existence. Although this proof is clearly anticipated in the *Critique of Pure Reason*, it is often overlooked by zealous readers of that book. For such readers, this 'moral proof' smacks of precisely the metaphysics Kant so effectively destroyed just a few years previously.

Fourth and finally, in the Introduction to the whole text, Kant writes that, 'In a critique of judgement, [only] the part that deals with aesthetic judgement belongs to it essentially' (Introduction VIII). This is because, as we saw above, in aesthetic judgement the faculty of judgement is, as it were, on its own. As always, judgement involves the coordination of other faculties, and certainly the action of judgement has implications for our faculty of reason, but at its root aesthetic judgement is the purest form of reflective judgement. In teleological judgement, on the other hand, the action of judgement – although still reflective – is much more closely linked to the ordinary theoretical cognition of nature, and especially to reason. In its teleological function, judgement is not, let us say, laid bare in its purity. So one could be forgiven for thinking that the lengthy treatment of teleology is little more than an appendix to the real business of the book.[1] However, it would be wrong to ignore the 'Critique of Teleological Judgement' either on the grounds of its lesser influence, or on the assumption that its content is intrinsically less interesting. For in addition to a fascinating account of teleology in general, Kant gives his most sustained example of the relationship between reason and science. He also gives a fascinating discussion of the fundamental nature of the human mind (see pp. 149–54); and his most detailed treatment of the 'moral proof' which he evidently considered one of his main contributions to the philosophy of religion (see pp. 154–62).

Chapter 5 ends by pulling together a number of notions taken from throughout the *Critique of Judgement* in order to show how they comprise a solution to Kant's grand problem of the unity of philosophy.

Objective Purposiveness in Nature and Science

The word 'teleology' comes from the Greek word '*telos*' meaning end or purpose. In general, something is understood teleologically if its existence or activity is conceived as coordinated by and orientated toward some purpose. Traditionally, teleology involves the notion of a final cause: the purpose is conceived of as the cause of that which leads to it. The key difference between aesthetic and teleological judgements, then, is the 'reality' or 'objectivity' of the purpose for the object. The object of aesthetic judgement appeared purposive without a purpose, and purposive also only in the relation of the presentation to the cognitive faculties. The objects of teleological judgement do have or rather *are*, according to the judgement, purposes for which a concept or idea is to hand.

Kant immediately makes a distinction between two types of real purposes. The first type is an 'extrinsic' purpose which is the role a thing may play in being a means to some end. An example would be an object of art in the general sense: a shoe or a landscaped garden – something that was made for a purpose, and where the concept of the purpose is the reason behind it being made. We discussed these kinds of purposes in Chapter 2. And, just as in the

'Critique of Aesthetic Judgement', such ordinary examples are not (initially) troubling and are thus not what Kant has in mind. So, Kant notes that there is a second type of real purpose, an 'intrinsic' purpose in which a thing embodies its own purpose. These are what Kant calls 'natural purposes' (also translated as 'physical ends'), and the key examples are living organisms (§65).

Such an organism is made up of parts: individual organs, and below that, individual cells. Each has its function. The heart beats *in order to* circulate blood (and thus oxygen and nourishment) to all other parts of the body, including the heart itself. The lungs breath *in order to* take in oxygen, and expel carbon dioxide. These parts, however, are also 'organised'. That is, they seem to be determined to be the parts that they are according to the form or 'purpose' which is the whole creature. Their action is coordinated to keep the whole creature alive, to constantly repair and replenish it, and to enable it to perform higher functions.

Moreover, Kant says, the parts reciprocally produce and are produced by the form of the whole. Although the whole creature is made up of, and continuously produced by, such organs, still the heart only 'makes sense' as an organ, from the point of view of the 'sense' or structure of the whole creature. Nor is the idea of the whole separate to the organism and its cause (for then the creature would be understood as an art product.) A mechanical clock may be made up of organised parts, but this organisation is not the clock itself, but rather the concept of the clock in the mind of the craftsperson who made it. The organism intrinsically and continually *produces itself*, according to a structural 'idea' which is, again, the organism itself taken as a whole; the clock is not an organism because it has to be made according to an concept of it. So, living organisms are not fully explicable according to a synthesis of mechanical cause and effect relations.[2] What Kant is after is a definition of life, such that a living organism simply cannot be *fully* understood according to the mechanistic, synthetic cause and effect approach of the natural sciences. In order to come near the concept of life, we need to assume a teleological causation, such that the form of the whole organism (the purpose or *telos* of the organs) is represented as the cause of the organs and their operation. In summary, 'An organised product of nature is one in which everything is a purpose and reciprocally also a means' (§66).

How exactly does this principle relate to the sciences of nature? Such an account of organisms as teleological is not original to Kant, but extends back to Aristotle. Since the Renaissance there had been steadily increasing hostility to Aristotle's physics, which takes teleology as a key principle of all things, not just living things. But although hotly contested, this teleological notion remained fairly common in European *biology* throughout the eighteenth century and beyond. This is both because it remained a powerful tool for understanding precisely what is distinctive about living creatures, and because it was difficult not to see an analogous kind of interlaced hierarchy of the species, for example in what we now call the food chain.

Kant is careful to distance himself from the rationalist position which, he claims, takes teleology as a *constitutive* principle of knowledge. Importantly, he claims that such a teleological causation is utterly alien to any natural causation as our understanding is able to conceive it. Even calling it 'causation' is quite peculiar. If such a notion were constitutive, it would mean that the teleological approach would provide *knowledge* about how such organisms functioned. On the contrary, one can never identify or 'point to' the salient features of teleological causation, only to the organism as a whole. For whatever feature one identified could *also* be accounted for in terms of ordinary natural causation. Teleological judgement, then, does not judge the immediate intuition of an object, but rather judges it according to available empirical laws governing the workings of the organism's parts. Do these empirical laws of causation, considered reflectively as a possible whole system, suggest a law of production over and above them?[3] Something analogous to this problem arises in the case of our own purposive action (for example, my going downstairs to eat breakfast). For any particular feature of that action (placing my left foot on the first stair) can be explained 'mechanically', by the action of nerve impulses on muscles, muscles on tendons, tendons on bones, and so on. But the action taken as a meaningful whole seems to be less easily explicable in such terms.[4]

The radical distinction between teleological and mechanical causation entails that a natural purpose has to be understood to be *contingent* with respect to 'mechanical' natural laws. If the latter were taken as defining of nature (and Kant normally does), we would be left with the paradox that there are things in nature which are not natural. It is as if nature itself is split down the middle into two heterogeneous parts: the organic and the inorganic. Reason, however, always demands necessity in its objects – that is a condition of there being any scientific pursuit at all, as we saw in the Introduction to this book. Somehow, then, natural purposes must be conceived as necessary; that is, according to *some* idea of causation. But in addition to the ordinary 'mechanical' causation, there is only causation according to a purpose, final causation – and Kant writes at §65, 'there cannot be more than these two kinds of causality'. Accordingly, we use this 'remote analogy' to conceive of natural purposes. We naturally tend to understand organisms, in other words, by way of an analogy with our own purposive actions. But even this is inadequate. Kant states (at §65),

> In considering nature and the ability it displays in organised products, we say far too little if we call this an *analogue* of art, for in that case we think of an artist (a rational being) apart from nature. Rather, nature organises itself, and it does so within each species of its organised products [. . .]

Strictly speaking, therefore, the organisation of nature has nothing analogous to any causality known to us.

It is the immanence of the organising principle of nature to nature that
brings about philosophical difficulties. In fact, it cannot be proved that mere
mechanical causes are not responsible for natural purposes. But equally, it
can be proved that *our human cognition* is incapable of a concept of how a
nexus of mechanical causation might bring about natural purposes (§71).
Kant claims that, so far as our cognition of nature is concerned, calling this
an 'immanent organising principle' is just a name (and to some extent a
negative definition: it is *not* this, *not* that . . .) of a concept we – as human
finite intelligences – just cannot have. Instead, in order to satisfy reason's
demand for self-consistency and completion, we are given 'permission' (First
Introduction VI) to apply reflectively the idea of causation according to
purposes, which necessarily brings with it the idea of purposive action, of
something like 'an artist (a rational being) apart from nature'.[5]
Thinking in terms of the rational idea of causation according to purposes
reintroduces the idea of necessity. This at least *begins* to reconcile natural
purposes with our concept of nature as that realm of objects subject to the
law of causation, although only at the cost of creating still other problems, as
we shall see. But such teleological causation is not a category of the understanding, not a concept that could be exhibited in intuition. A purely *rational*
concept has no constitutive validity with respect to objects of experience.
Instead, Kant claims, teleological judgement even after the introduction of
this idea of reason is merely *reflective*, and its principle merely *regulative*,
writing at §78:

> Reason is tremendously concerned not to abandon the mechanism nature
> [employs] in its products, and not to pass over it in explaining them, since
> without mechanism we cannot gain insight into the nature of things. [. . .]
> On the other hand, it is just as necessary a maxim of reason that it not pass
> over the principle of purposes in [dealing with] the products of nature.

The teleological judgement gives no knowledge, as we already saw above,
but simply allows cognition to recognise a certain class of empirical objects
(living organisms) that then might be subjected (so far as that is possible) to
further, empirical study. Determinate judgements concerning natural cause
and effect and teleological judgements work together. The former do the job
of acquiring and applying empirical mechanistic laws for the parts of
organisms and their functions. The latter perform the job of identifying
the organism *per se* by way of considering whether the empirical laws do or
do not suggest a *systematic whole* in the way described above.[6] Thus
teleological judgements (which Kant often calls 'theoretical reflective judge-

ments' because of their relation to the cognition of nature) can guide or regulate what the former should look for, trying to ensure completeness. In effect, Kant is saying that, were it not for the reflective judgement and the principle of its functioning here, the ability to experience and then study something as alive (and thus the science of biology, for example) would be impossible.

Such judgements only apply (with the above mentioned constraints) to individual organisms on the basis of their inner structure, and do not constitute an attempt to account for their existence *per se*. Nevertheless, the judgements certainly raise the ground of existence as a possible question. By analogy, this suggests to reason the idea of the *whole of nature as a purposive system* based upon an indeterminate supersensible foundation. Recent ecological thought, for example, has often tended to think of whole ecosystems as if they are in themselves organisms, and species of plants and animals (as well as the physical environment they inhabit) are the 'organs' or 'cells'. Such an approach may be fruitful for understanding the inter-connectedness of the system, but may also be dangerous if taken too far – when it begins to see as *necessary* what in fact has to be considered (for the purposes of science) as *contingent*. In fact, the whole of nature is not given to us in this way, Kant admits, and therefore this extended idea is not as relevant to science as the narrower one of natural purposes (§75). Nevertheless, just as for the notion of an organism as natural purpose, the idea of nature as a purposive system may be fruitful in discovering phenomena and subsequently laws in nature that might not even have been recognised on a mechanical understanding alone. But although the judgement leads in that direction, it is hardly necessary or appropriate for a scientific investigation to pursue matters into the supersensible (§85).

SUMMARY: The second half of the *Critique of Judgement* deals with what Kant calls 'teleological judgement'. The first topic is what Kant calls 'natural purposes'. Kant had already sought to demonstrate in his *Critique of Pure Reason* that all nature (organic and inorganic alike) is determined by natural laws, especially those of the ordinary, 'mechanical' cause and effect type. However, the structure of living organisms is such that it is difficult to account for it on those terms. Instead, what should be the effect (the organism as a whole) of some set of causes (individual cells or organs) can be considered as the purpose, and therefore the cause. This type of entity can be conceptually recognised only by reflective judgement. Organisms judged in this way Kant calls 'natural purposes'. As far as the understanding is concerned, no such concept can be envisaged. As a substitute, then, we must use the rational idea of an intelligence acting according to purposes. The principle of the reflective judgement does not determine the object but serves science 'heuristically' as a guide to what science would not otherwise even be able to identify as an object of study.

'The Peculiarity of the Human Understanding'

Not surprisingly, if reason does not pay sufficient *critical* attention to the reflection involved, the result is an antinomy (§70). Just as in the antinomy of the 'Critique of Aesthetic Judgement', this happens when a faculty begins to 'reason', and posit a greater universality for its principles than can be critically authorised; in this case, when the principles of teleological judgement and of the understanding claim legislative authority over the same domain of objects. Formally, an antinomy is when two incompatible propositions seem both to be inescapably true. In this case, the antinomy is between the basic scientific principle of the understanding – to seek to treat everything as *necessary* by being subject to natural laws – and the teleological principle, that there are some objects that cannot be treated according to these laws, and are thus *radically contingent* with respect to them.

In a sense, Kant solves this antinomy before he even states it in §70, because he first presents it as two *regulative* maxims of judgement: that is, from a point of view immanent to judgement. The supposed antinomy is that, first, all production of things must be *judged* according to mechanical laws; but, second, some production of things cannot be so judged, and must instead be judged *reflectively according* to the idea of final causes. These 'do not seem quite compatible', Kant writes. Yet, because regulative, they are not strictly speaking contradictory, for the way something must be judged does not determine what it is. They only describe procedures that judgement is obliged to go through. Only when the maxims are taken out of the realm of the activity and procedure of judgement, and converted into 'constitutive principles concerning the possibility of the objects themselves' (that is, as if they were both laws prescribed by the understanding to nature), do we have an antinomy.

Kant's basic solution to this antinomy looks quite straightforward (§71): the problem is simply that reason has forgotten that the second of these principles is not *constitutive* of its object. By 'constitutive' he means that a principle seeks to account for the possibility of the object itself. There could only be an antinomy if *both* principles were understood to be so constitutive. The second half of the antinomy above, the principle of teleological judgement, is a principle of a *reflective* judgement. Kant writes (§71) that its principle is:

entirely correct *for reflective judgement* [i.e. judgement considered as a faculty with its own *a priori* principles], however rash and unprovable it would be *for determinative judgement* [i.e. judgement considered as a faculty in the mere service of the understanding]. [. . .] We make no claim that this idea has reality, but only use it as a guide for reflection.

The 'illusion' involved in the antinomy is the transformation of the regulative principle of teleology, with its idea of final causes, into a constitutive one. This, however, is not a fully satisfying solution, not least because it does not even begin to investigate the *ground* of this necessarily double approach to natural purposes. That is to say, Kant has made no mention of the supersensible, which in all previous antinomies was the hinge on which the solution depended. But §71 is only entitled 'Preliminary to the Solution', so we shall have to return to this material.

Kant continues for several sections the discussion of the antinomy and its solution, elaborating in interesting ways the implications. Sections 72–3 give a purportedly complete taxonomy and refutation of all other possible solutions to the problems identified by the above antinomy (Epicurus, Spinoza, and others). But Kant's own solution begins again in §74 and culminates in §77 with the treatment of the 'peculiarity' [*Eigentümlichkeit*] of the human understanding. At issue again is the faculty of teleological, reflective judgement and the manner in which it conceives purposiveness. Kant is at pains to point out that this manner is a necessity for human minds because of a peculiarity of such minds. This discussion recalls in particular the treatment of *idealism* in the 'Critique of Aesthetic Judgement' (see the end of Chapter 4). More generally, it recalls the conception of the principle of reflective judgement: the assumption that nature will present itself as purposive with respect to our faculties of cognition. In reflective judgement, in other words, the question is always how certain appearances or ideas must be thought of *by us* as human intelligences.

Now, in our understanding of the world (and any other understanding we could concretely imagine the workings of), the universal principle or law of nature that governs its production never fully determines any particular thing in all its real detail. Thus these details, although necessary in themselves as part of the order of nature, must be contingent with respect to *our* universal concept. It is simply beyond our understanding that any human-like intelligence could have a concept which, in itself, determines as *necessary all the features* of any particular thing.[7] As Kant explains it, rather than being made up from some contingent combination of parts, like the clock example with which we started, an object so understood would be a whole that conditions all its parts. A living organism (natural purpose) would be just such a whole. In the latter case, there is no room for contingency; it is as if the universal concept were somehow identical with the particular thing. It is for this reason that Kant is able to argue that a mechanical cause of natural purposes cannot be disproved, but that human cognition could never attain its concept. As we have seen, to even identify such purposes in nature, we have to apply (through reflective judgement) the rational idea of causality according to purposes, which is the closest we can come to grasping a natural purpose.

But why does Kant believe that the above propositions about what is 'beyond' our intelligence must be the case? This idea of purposive causation is of a *presentation* of such a whole, and the presentation is conceived of as a purpose which conditions or leads to the production of the parts, again like the clock example. The reflective principle of a natural purpose – when conceived as we must through the idea of a concept of a purpose conditioning action – already requires a *supersensible foundation* to be conceived which has intentions or purposes in mind.[8] The presentation of the whole is conceived of as distinct from – as an image of – that which it conditions. Ours, in other words, is an understanding which in its 'peculiarity' always 'requires images [*Bilder*] (it is an *intellectus ectypus*)' (§77). All of our thought and action, Kant says, necessarily proceeds through the detour of 'images' (derivative presentations of all kinds).[9] We human beings have a purpose, and *through* that purpose, we act; we have an intuition (which is in itself a phenomenon) of, say, a cat, which is determined to be a cat *through* a concept (and *vice versa*). Even when there is a sort of immediacy here – as for example when someone says, 'I didn't think, I just acted!' – one can make a perfectly understandable distinction between the purpose and the action. The action happens through an image of it, even if action and image are simultaneous.

Kant writes, 'Our understanding has to proceed from the universal to the particular' (§76). Figuratively speaking, a concept contains possible intuitive exhibitions of itself 'under itself' (*Critique of Pure Reason*, A25=B40). It is not a law somehow immanent to the particular, but a presentation or image of the particular as a type. For this is how experience is possible for us, by means of the detour of concepts (ultimately *a priori* concepts) which can serve to unify experience through acts of synthesis. Generally speaking, this was one of the chief results of the first half of the *Critique of Pure Reason*.[10] This 'fact' about our understanding 'has the following consequences: In terms of the universal [supplied by the understanding] the particular, as such, contains something contingent' (§76).[11]

However, any account of critical limits or conditions automatically entails for reason the *ideal possibility* of an alternative. Thus, for example, Kant's transcendental idealism raises the problem for reason, over and over again, of an unknowable supersensible foundation to appearances. Similarly, this peculiarity of our understanding poses the possibility of another form of intelligence, the *intellectus archetypus*, an intelligence which is not limited to this detour of presentations in its thinking and acting.[12] Such an understanding would not function in a world of appearances, but directly in the world of things-in-themselves. Its power of giving the universal (concepts and ideas) would not be a separate power from its power of forming intuitions of particular things; concept and thing, thought and reality would be one. From the point of view of such an understanding, what we humans must conceive as the *contingency* of particular natural forms with respect to the universal concept, is only an appearance. The whole notion of contingency assumes the separation of concepts and things, or purposes and actions, peculiar to the *intellectus ectypus*. A thing (or a property of a thing) is only contingent with respect to the concept of it, which is different from it by being *only* a universal; a particular action is only contingent with respect to a purpose, which is different from it.

For the *intellectus archetypus*, then, everything from the smallest detail to the most universal law is equally necessary. Specifically, the multiplicity of the laws of empirical particulars is no longer contingent. Thus, the possibility that natural purposes are in fact the outcome of the mechanism of nature – which for us was an unthinkable possibility because it required a production from the whole to the parts, and thus a concept fully commensurate, even identical to, the thing – is no longer 'unthinkable'. Natural purposes would indeed be necessary, in the same sense as events that we conceive of as subject to mechanical natural law. Thus, the notion of an *intellectus archetypus*, and the corresponding distinction *for us* between appearances and things-in-themselves, gives Kant a more complete way of solving the above antinomy. The idea we must use to conceive of natural purposes (the idea of production according to a concept of the purpose) leads us to the supersensible. But rather than see this as a problem, Kant now sees it as an opportunity to genuinely provide a solution to the antinomy. As with all his antinomies, the solution resides in a change of metaphysical levels: from appearances to things-in-themselves. Only by admitting the *possibility* of an *intellectus archetypus* can we conceive of a single ground for the necessity of both natural purposes and mechanical cause and effect. The thought/action of such an intellect would be the embodiment, so to speak, of a 'higher principle' (§78) which lies over and accounts for both natural purposes and mechanical cause and effect in nature.

Such a notion clearly takes us in the direction of theology, the study of the nature of the divine being, and of that being's relation to creation. But it is above all important to remember that, at this point, Kant is not claiming that there is, or must be, or that he can prove there to be, such a being. He is claiming only that it is a genuine possibility and that it solves a big problem that would otherwise *in principle* not admit of a solution. Moreover, throughout the first half of the 'Critique of Teleological Judgement', Kant is careful not to move too quickly into theological territory – he has other points to pursue: above all, the question of teleology as an immanent principle of nature: what must our idea of an organism be, how does this relate to science, and what are the more general implications of this idea?

Indeed, the first time that anything explicitly theological enters, it does so only to be dismissed as inadequate. The subject is the famous 'argument from design', a popular eighteenth-century argument for the existence of a creator. Kant discusses it at several points, for example under the heading of the 'physico-theological argument' in §85. This argument purports to prove the existence of a creator from the apparently designed quality of creation, and from the additional premise that a design requires a designer. David Hume, in his *Dialogues Concerning Natural Religion*, had already and quite comprehensively taken this argument to task.[13] Kant's take on it is revealing. First, strictly speaking, the argument taken as theoretically determining is quite unconvincing in so far as it takes a principle of reflective judgement (which does not even strictly speaking include a notion of design, §68) as evidence for a theoretical claim (the existence of God as creator). Kant had already dismissed the adequacy of *any* such theoretical approach to natural purposes in §§72–8. Moreover, it would have to supply a proof of the impossibility of an explanation of the apparently designed in terms of the immanent laws of nature (for example, §73), but there can be no such proof, as we have seen.

Secondly, the argument nevertheless carries modest plausibility for the human intelligence, because of the idea of purposeful action which we, as *intellectus ectypus*, must use in our conception of those natural purposes identified by reflective judgement. That is to say, the argument works (in a limited way) for reflective judgement: *we* can conceive the ground of natural purposes in no other way. Thirdly, however, even given the reflective validity stated above, the result is so indeterminate and vague a notion of a creator as to be completely useless for theology. The notion of an intelligent world-cause remains inseparable from the context of a reflection upon purposes in nature, and that context supplies nothing of use to theology.

But fourthly and finally, Kant claims that the argument, taken prior to any real analysis of it, carries conviction, but not for the reasons that are usually stated when the argument is reflected upon by philosophers. The argument secretly makes reference not just to natural purposes and the assumption that they entail a divine intelligence (that is the usual version), but to moral purposes as well, and the assumption that these entail a divine *wisdom*.[14] One would want to ask *why* a creator should create, if not for some value in the created world. That value (as we shall see below) must in principle be something like the moral value each of us finds in ourselves. This moral value, as a purpose in the world, is no longer merely empirical evidence. Kant then sets to work on this hidden side of the design argument, asking what about it carries such conviction, what is the nature of that conviction, and what implications does it have. The result is a new argument that Kant calls the 'moral proof'. It is this argument which occupies most of the second half of the 'Critique of Teleological Judgement'.

SUMMARY: Does not teleological judgement result in a contradiction: an antinomy? On the one hand, there is the demand that nature be fully determined according to natural laws; on the other, there is the assertion that certain phenomena cannot be so determined. The antinomy is only troubling if there is no possible hypothesis that shows the contradiction to be a natural illusion. The human intellect – what Kant here calls the *intellectus ectypus* – is unable to conceive of a natural purpose otherwise than as the product of an intelligence. Because of this, there is a contradiction *for us* between natural objects and events that are necessary according to natural law, and other objects or events that are purposes, and therefore contingent with respect to these laws. However, by contrast, we can at least conceive of a different type of intelligence – the supersensible *intellectus archetypus* – for which this distinction (and the contradiction that results from it) is no longer real. The hypothesis of the *intellectus archetypus* perhaps solves the antinomy, but again takes us to the possibility of a supersensible ground.

The Final Purpose and Religious Belief

In his 'General Comment on Teleology' at the end of the 'Critique of Teleological Judgement', Kant provides a neat taxonomy of arguments for the existence of God.[15] He claims that all such arguments, if they wish at all to achieve 'conviction' (§90), have to begin from something known. That is, a matter of fact (§91), either metaphysical or empirical. Theoretical philosophy can push itself towards theology either through the analysis of entirely *a priori* facts (this is the ontological argument) or through the analysis of *partly a posteriori* facts (including the cosmological argument, which Kant does not directly discuss in this context, or the argument from design). In the *Critique of Pure Reason*, Kant had already given the classic refutations of the ontological and cosmological proofs.[16] He continues that process here with his definitive criticism of the design argument as normally put forward, which we discussed on p. 153. That exhausts the possibilities from the theoretical point of view.

But there is one 'fact' which lies outside the competence of theoretical philosophy: the fact of freedom, which is exhibited in our consciousness in our possible morality. Might this 'matter of fact', carried to its furthermost implications, have anything to say of theological interest? To answer this question requires, first of all, a brief detour through the notion of what Kant calls the 'final purpose'.

From §78 to §82, Kant pursues the implications of the idea of nature as a purposive system for natural science in general, discussing, among other things, contemporary theories about evolution and epigenesis. In §82 he argues in this way: it might seem that certain features of nature have as an extrinsic purpose their relations to other features: the nectar for the honey, the river for the irrigation of land near its bank, and so on (ultimately, these might be seen as part of the intention or design of the intelligent cause of creation). Treating certain things or processes as means, Kant says, is a perfectly understandable way of speaking sometimes, and even helps us to think through certain natural processes, but has *no objective foundation in science*. There is always another way of looking at things from a different point of view, so that what we thought was a purpose is in fact only a means to something else entirely (the nectar is simply a way of attracting bees *for* the purposes of pollination).

It is sometimes even claimed (often on a religious basis) that human beings are the real, 'ultimate' purpose of nature, and all other things are, in the end, for the benefit and use of humans as an extrinsic end. By 'ultimate' is meant that, in the chain of extrinsic purposes, everything leads to human existence, and no further. This 'benefit' might be understood to mean human happiness – having food to eat as the top of the food chain, having coal to heat homes or generate electricity. Or, it could mean human cultural progress – that nature is not always bountiful demands the development of new and ever-refined skills, technologies, and forms of social organisation. Kant goes so far as to claim that even war, although terrible in itself, can be purposeful in this respect. Although, again, one can say some interesting things about both of these topics, it must be said that there is no way of making objective sense of such claims. As Kant writes, for nature conceived on the hypothesis of purposes, 'in the chain of [such natural] purposes man is never more than a link' (§83). Nature *per se* does not, then, contain or pursue any such extrinsic purposes, not even for man. But Kant is not quite yet finished with these kinds of problems, and introduces in §84 the notion of a 'final purpose'.

Kant defines a 'final purpose' as 'a purpose that requires no other purpose as a condition of its possibility' (§84). In an imagined chain of purposes (this *for* that, that *for* the other), it is the end of the chain.[17] By definition, then, a final purpose could not itself be extrinsic. Moreover, it is clear that, again, there can be no intrinsic final purpose *in nature* – all natural products and events are conditioned, including everything in the world around us, our own bodies and even our mental life. And, if we conceive of nature on the hypothesis of purposes, these purposes are always extrinsic, and there are always further links possible. We are, so far as nature taken in itself is concerned, part of a chain of causes (and perhaps also purposes). And all living beings, *qua* natural purposes, although certainly conditioned by themselves in an important sense, may also be conditioned as part of nature itself as a system of purposes. Certainly, such living things are also part of a system of 'mechanical' cause and effect within which they are completely conditioned. Thus, a purpose could only be the final purpose if it were inherently impossible for it also to be an extrinsic purpose. So, what kind of thing would such a final purpose be? Kant writes, speculatively, 'the final purpose of an intelligent cause [of the world] must be of such a kind that in the order of purposes it depends upon no condition other than just the idea of it' (§84).

As we have discovered on several previous occasions, for Kant human beings are not merely natural beings. Kant emphasises in several places – for example, in the last part of §91 – that it is the fact of freedom that forms the incontrovertible first premise of the argument he is about to put forward. The human capacity for freedom is a cause which acts with purpose (in the sense that I act *to* help someone in need, or *to* keep a promise, in the end to achieve the Good), and which determines itself according to the self-given moral law represented as necessary. Moreover, such freedom must be considered as independent of the chain of natural causation and even extrinsic purposes. For example, the issues of *why* I made the promise in the first place, or *what* I hope to get out of it are, at best, of secondary importance. My moral determination is not conditioned by its purpose (the Good). Kant writes, carefully, at §84:

> Now about man, as a moral being, (and so about any other rational being in the world), we cannot go on to ask: For what does he exist? His existence itself has the highest purpose, within it. [. . . Thus] if things in the world require a supreme cause that acts in terms of purposes, then man [*qua* free] is the final purpose of creation.

The human freedom for moral action is the only factual state of affairs we know (or could know) that fits the bill as a final purpose. Put more grandly, 'without man [as a moral being] all of creation would be a mere wasteland, gratuitous and without a final purpose' (§86). Thus, the question that really 'matters', Kant writes, 'is whether we do have a basis, sufficient for reason (whether speculative or practical), for attributing a *final purpose* to the supreme cause [in its] acting in terms of purposes' (§86). We can guess, straightaway, that whatever Kant says next, it will certainly not involve a 'speculatively' (that is, theoretically) sufficient basis.

Kant's 'moral proof for the existence of God' begins in §87. This proof first appeared in detail in the *Critique of Pure Reason* and again in the *Critique of Practical Reason*.[18] But the extent and detail of Kant's reflections on the matter in the *Critique of Judgement*, and their relation to the problem of teleology and reflective judgement, make this the most appropriate place to discuss the argument.

The rational idea of purposiveness, although never constitutive, seems to be relevant everywhere so far. We know that nature appears purposive in relation to our reflective judgements of it (for example the taxonomy of natural objects, and the laws governing them, all appear – and we must assume will continue to appear – to be condensing down to a finite and relatively orderly system (Introduction V)). We also know that nature appears purposive for aesthetic judgement (*as if* adapted to the harmony of the cognitive faculties, and thus beautiful; *as if* available for use to present to ourselves our supersensible 'vocation', and thus sublime). For teleological judgement (theoretical reflective judgement), there seems to be a necessity to view organisms as natural purposes, and indeed to view the whole of nature as a purposive system. Because these are one and all *reflective* judgements, they entail neither a theoretical nor a practical conclusion as to what might be *behind* these purposes. At best, this might be an assumption within and for judgement's own activity. Even where teleological judgements about purposes in nature lead us to consider the possibility of a world-author, this approach leaves quite *indeterminate* (and thus useless for the purposes of religion or theology) our idea of that world-author. But Kant is asking: is there any reason requiring us to assume nature is purposive with respect to practical reason? That is to say, is there a type of teleological judgement concerning moral purposiveness (a practical reflective judgement), and if so, with what validity does it function?

The moral law is conceived of as duty; acting from out of the *mere pure and universal form* of the moral law is everything, the consequences of action do not enter into the equation. However, as we saw above in discussing the Introduction to the *Critique of Judgement*, the practical faculties in general determine desire (that is, purposes motivating action) and the free will is the 'higher' faculty of desire. Thus, the moral law necessarily obligates us to set for ourselves a *final purpose*[19] of moral action, although not indeed as the ground of morality (as would normally be the case in desire, when the presentation of the result causes the action, and the action is then *for* such and such a purpose). This final purpose of our moral determination Kant calls the 'highest good' (*summum bonum*); conceived of as a state of *natural* beings, this means the greatest possible happiness for all moral beings. The purposes of our moral actions converge and reach their highest expression in this idea.

Kant is using this co-implication of moral law and the final purpose of moral action as an important premise of his argument.[20] The obvious question that arises is why, given the stress Kant always places on the absolutely unconditioned nature of moral freedom (unconditioned either by natural causes, or by purposes), should he feel able to make this claim. It would seem as if precisely the purity of the free will would make any connection to purposes immoral. Interestingly, Kant hardly seems to notice (and certainly does not dwell on) this 'obvious' problem.[21]

A possible solution to the above problem might rely upon the *psychological* impossibility of committing oneself to a necessarily pointless action, for example a game that cannot in principle be won. Kant might well agree with this thesis as a psychological point. However, he would have to reject this as a solution to the above problem, because such a psychological claim is utterly contingent. There is no reason to believe that it *must* be impossible for there to be someone whose perfectly sane, human psychology allows him or her to act willingly without an achievable purpose.[22]

Kant does write (at §87), however, that even speaking practically, we must consider ourselves,

> as beings of the world and hence as beings connected with other things in the world; and those same moral laws enjoin us to direct our judging to those other things [regarded] either as purposes or as objects for which we ourselves are the final purpose.

In other words, practical reason is a *human* faculty; moreover, one for which there are transcendental limitations on the manner in which its activity can be understood by us. Here, as always for Kant, being human is defined in terms of a unity of a lower, sensible nature which exists utterly caught up in a natural world, with a higher, supersensible dimension capable of moral action. Free will may determine itself unconditionally through the mere form of the moral law but it remains the faculty of will, that is the higher faculty of desire, and retains the essential link to purposes. Will, free or not, is by definition never without purpose; the general conception of the *intellectus ectypus* applies also to human action,[23] which must proceed through the detour of a conceptual presentation of its purpose.[24] It is only that the free will is not conditioned by its purposes and thus, in determining the moral course of action, we must cultivate an ability to 'abstract' from the purposes that are the 'promise' of the moral law, and act only in accordance with the law itself.[25]

Just as moral action must be possible through freedom, so the *summum bonum* must be possible through moral action. The impossibility of achieving this end would make a nonsense of moral action, not because it takes away the condition of such action, nor because of a psychological impossibility, nor even because such acts would somehow cease to be moral. Rather, it is because such impossibility would in effect mean that free will was no longer will, that practical reason was no longer practical. Kant is claiming that it is just part of the *meaning* of a human, and any other finite rational being's action – even a purely and formally determined action, that is one not *conditioned* by its purpose – to also posit the possibility of achieving its purpose.

But the possibility of the *summum bonum* as final purpose in nature is not at all obvious. Indeed, a cynic might claim that moral action makes no difference at all – that the good man is no more happy for it, and that 'nice guys finish last'. Kant argues (at §87):

> the concept of the *practical necessity* of [achieving] such a purpose by applying our forces does not harmonise with the theoretical concept of the *physical possibility* of its being achieved, if the causality of nature is the only causality (of a means [for achieving it]) that we connect with our freedom.

The obvious inference then is that the 'causality of nature' cannot be the 'only causality'; there must also be the causality of a moral author of the world which would make it at least possible for the *summum bonum* to be achieved. Without the postulate of such a moral author, who, as we saw above, must have our free morality in mind as *its* final purpose, our free moral action could not be presented as possible. Moral action, precisely as moral and as action, assumes within itself the existence of a God who, more than just an 'intelligence', acts with 'wisdom' making possible the system of rational purposes projected by the moral law. Of course, in acting morally we may not be conscious either of the *summum bonum* as final purpose, or of the necessary postulation of God as moral author of the world – we are just doing what is right. Nevertheless, when that duty is fully understood, these necessary implications will be found *within it*. God must exist as part of the meaning of any moral action.

Incidentally, because our free will for the moral law is the final purpose, and this requires the possibility *in nature* of the *summum bonum*, we have also uncovered nature's ultimate purpose (the last purpose within the natural realm). The ultimate purpose is the accordance of nature with the system of rational ends projected by moral law. Above, we saw Kant concluding that, in terms of nature itself, no such ultimate purpose could be demonstrated. This remains the case. Man is the ultimate end of nature only insofar as he morally deserves to be – that is insofar as man is not an entirely natural being (in the theoretical sense of the word 'natural').

That the postulation of God is 'within' moral action in this way automatically discounts the 'moral proof' from any *theoretical* validity. Theoretical philosophy must continue to operate within its legitimate grounds, treating so far as possible all of nature as intelligible in terms of mechanical cause and effect, barely tolerating the notion of natural purposes as a merely heuristic device, for which the supersensible is only a horizon of appearance, and certainly neither *requiring* nor demonstrating purpose or creator. This disclaimer is extremely important for Kant, as despite the link to morality and the 'fact' of our freedom, the moral proof does not make of religion anything but a matter of faith (for example §91).

This 'limitation' on the proof involves recalling that this argument, from start (freedom as the only possible final purpose) to finish (God as both intelligent and moral author of existence), is conducted utilising our faculty of reflective judgement with respect to the practical ideas of reason.[26] It is necessarily bound up with how things are cognisable by us, and not with how things can be determined to be in themselves.[27] To take one of many such examples, in speaking of God as a world creator, we are not in fact saying anything about God in 'himself'. We are at most speaking of God's relation to creation according to a reflective analogy. Kant argues (§90, translation modified):

> The very fact that I am to think of the divine causality only by analogy with an understanding . . . forbids me to *attribute* to this being an understanding in the proper sense of the term. [Kant continues in the footnote:] This does not result in the slightest loss to our presentation of that being's *relation to the world*, neither in the theoretical nor in the practical consequences of that concept. To try to investigate what that being is in itself shows an inquisitiveness that is as pointless as it is doomed.

Kant accordingly concludes that we can have no insight into whether for this possible God, there is a difference between acting according to purposes and acting according to moral purposes, as there is for us. Nevertheless, he writes (at §88):

> What we can say, however, is this: that *the character of our faculty of reason is such* that we cannot at all grasp how such a purposiveness as there is in this final purpose is possible . . . unless we assume an author and ruler of the world who is also a moral author.

Cognition involving reflective judgement thus concerns itself with how things must be conceived of by us. The theoretical sphere demands the actual or possible exhibition of an object in intuition for full conviction. Within this sphere, the results of reflective judgements generally have only a regulative or heuristic validity, or at best a sort of empty 'conviction' with respect to a completely indeterminate result (as in Kant's account of the design argument). Cognition involving reflective judgement is capable of achieving real conviction only in the practical sphere – not because it constitutes an object, but because it unravels the assumptions hidden within any moral determination of the *human* will, to reveal the purposiveness of nature for our moral faculty. This purposiveness is then *necessarily* supplemented by the rational idea of a supersensible intelligence acting according to *moral* purposes. The conviction in the conclusion borrows its force ultimately from the fact of freedom. This conviction is called faith [*Glaube*] (or 'belief'). Kant once famously wrote of his critique of the pretensions of reason to metaphysical knowledge, 'I therefore had to annul *knowledge* in order to make room for *faith*.'[28] At §91, he writes,

> As for objects that we have to think *a priori* (either as consequences or as grounds) in reference to our practical use of reason in conformity with duty, but that are transcendent for the theoretical use of reason: they are mere *matters of faith*. [. . .] To have faith . . . is to have confidence that we shall reach an aim that we have a duty to further, without our having insight into whether achieving it is possible.

Purposes – in particular here a system of rational ends – belong to moral action, although they do not condition it. But, Kant notes, achieving these purposes is at best only partly 'in our hands', whereas moral action is entirely so.[29] Moral action thus determines itself through the mere form of law, and puts its faith in the possibility of the corresponding purpose. The *summum bonum*, God as moral author (together with the immortality of the soul, a parallel proof of which is given in the *Critique of Practical Reason*) are all such objects of faith. For Kant, this stress on faith keeps religion pure of the misunderstandings involved in, for example, fanaticism, demonology or idolatry (§89). For example, it prevents us from claiming to know anything particular of God's purposes that would then authorise any manner of repellent practices. Similarly, it prevents us from imagining that God is in any way like ourselves, and thus trying to influence God's will with gifts or ceremonies.

The 'moral proof' and associated discussion brings to a close Kant's book. In some ways, of course, the moral proof forms the high point as well. For it marks the furthest any reason can go in uncovering the supersensible that lies behind the various purposive phenomena that Kant has been investigating throughout. Also, of course, it marks out a conception of religion with several characteristically Kantian elements. First, there is the all-important separation of the realms of knowledge and the realms of faith. Secondly, this is a *rational* religion, one not based upon fear or desire, although certainly leading to both reverence and thanksgiving. Thirdly, there is the fact that the only appropriate religious conception of God arises out of morality, and not the other way around, which for Kant would mean a religion of 'compulsion ('General Comment on Teleology'). In fact, all three of these points had been made many times before, but here Kant gives them one of the clearest and most forceful statements and defences. For this reason, at least, and although the moral proof has not so often been discussed in theological debates since, Kant's account of a rational religion and its relationships to morality, teleology, and transcendental philosophy more generally have all been enormously influential.

SUMMARY: Nature has no ultimate or last purpose, but if an intelligence were responsible for the creation of the world, what would be the final purpose of that creation? It could only be that which *in principle* could not also be a means towards some further purpose – that is, something unconditioned by purposes. The final purpose could only be human moral freedom. This leads Kant to his 'moral proof' for the existence of God. Although moral freedom is not conditioned by a purpose, as a human faculty, it necessarily has one and conceives of it as possible. The final purpose of our moral action is the *summum bonum*, the highest good for sensible beings or universal happiness. But such a purpose would hardly seem to be possible in nature, unless nature had been arranged so as to make it possible. Since the possibility has to be assumed, we must assume the arrangement and the arranger, an intelligence acting wisely according to purposes. This assumption has no theoretical validity, it is valid only as practical faith.

Kant's Conclusion: Judgement and the Unity of Transcendental Philosophy

As we know, Kant's *Critique of Judgement* is supposed to address a grand problem, and in a sense all other topics have to be subordinated to that problem. The problem is that of judgement's role in the unity of transcendental philosophy. Judgement, according to Kant, presents itself as that which mediates between the theoretical and practical domains. In particular, judgement must make the 'transition' between both the objects and the ways of thinking which make moral purposes compossible with nature conceived theoretically. The difficulty in reading Kant's text in this way is that he barely went beyond stating the problem in his Introduction(s).

If we are talking about reflective judgement in general, one might suspect that the moral proof is that solution. For in Kant's new version of that argument (compared with those in the first two *Critiques*), it is judgement's function of estimating nature purposively that makes practically necessary the transition from moral purposes to the existence of God. But Kant identifies *aesthetic* judgement as the hinge on which his grand problem is to be solved. This claim is made explicit in the First Introduction XI, and is indirectly asserted in Introduction IX, for example, where judgement 'mediates' 'without regard to the practical'. Indeed, in the *Critique of Judgement*, the moral proof is said to have only practical validity, and Kant certainly made this point in the *Critique of Practical Reason*.[30] Yet there he also leaves open speculative reason 'holding to' the reality of its ideas through the moral proof. It appears as if, between writing the second and third *Critiques*, Kant decided that the limitation on the moral proof was much moral radical. The moral proof, then, perhaps solves the problem, but only from the point of view of practical reason, which is as much as to say that the problem is not solved. It is for that reason that the third *Critique*, with its grand problem, had to be written. That which mediates between two sides cannot be over-constrained by one side, it must effect the mediation on common ground. Only then can one say that philosophy is truly unified.

Are there enough clues to construct a plausible version of what Kant had in mind? By way of conclusion to our whole treatment of Kant's text, we will now try to sketch out such a solution, in Kant's terms.

The proper object of the legislation of the understanding (under the condition of sensibility) is nature. This forms the condition of possibility of theoretical cognition. The proper object of the legislation of reason is freedom. This forms the condition of possibility of moral desire. The antinomy concerning freedom in the *Critique of Pure Reason* showed that these legislations were compossible 'in the same subject' under two constraints (see the discussion in the Introduction to this book): first, if we conceived of the subject as *appearance*, insofar as it is legislated for by the understanding; and, secondly, if we think the same subject as thing-in-itself insofar as it is free.

But since our will belongs to a sensible being in this world (a human being, the *intellectus ectypus*), the determination of the will *necessarily* involves a concept of purpose. The *moral* determination of the will thus involves a concept of moral purpose, the *summum bonum*. The problem of free will, therefore, is a wider problem than the mere possibility of free will in the subject. It includes the problem of the possibility of the achievement of the purposes of freedom outside the subject.

Judgement, Kant argues, 'mediates the connection between the understanding and reason' (First Introduction II). As a faculty of the transcendental subject, it lies between understanding and reason (in general), and as legislating for the faculty of feeling, it lies between the faculty of cognition and the faculty of desire. In the first case, judgement is the application of the categories of the understanding to intuitions and, here, especially other concepts. It is thus the instrument that allows reasoning – as the pursuit of both the relationships between propositions and of the furthermost conditions and implications of propositions – to happen. It is by no means clear, however, exactly how this relates to reason in its *practical* employment, that is as concerning the concept of freedom. In the second case, *if* judgement legislates for feeling (and Kant only 'supposes' this in his Introduction II), then that again would place it in a mediating role. For feeling is the manner in which concepts (of purposes) have a relation to the faculty of desire as sensible will. But, again, there are problems. First, this is only a hypothesis, and Kant needs to show that judgement contains an *a priori* principle that legislates for feeling (this he does in the deduction). Secondly, even granting the hypothesis, the link just detailed is only at the level of the sensible will [*Willkür*]. With respect to freedom, on the other hand, there is indeed a moral feeling connected to the determination of the will by the moral law, but not as its condition. In that case then, feeling does not lie *between* anything.[31] All Kant can do at this point is make some tentative gestures towards proving his thesis that judgement 'mediates' between the understanding and (practical) reason.

Reflective judgement gives itself an *a priori* principle of the purposiveness of nature for cognition in general. We saw this principle at work in the 'Critique of Aesthetic Judgement', especially in Kant's account of the presentation of the beautiful. There, on the foundation of this principle, our aesthetic judgements (or rather the feeling of pleasure characteristic of the activity of such judgements) about that which is 'purposive without purpose' exhibit the properties of tending towards universality, and of exemplary necessity. This principle can be seen either in a transcendental sense as a *subjective* principle of judgement's functioning as a faculty (for example common sense and the harmony of the faculties), which legislates for the mental faculty of feeling; or (on the side of the object, but only as an idealism) as the universal assumption of the purposiveness of the presentation of nature with respect to judgement as a faculty of cognition.

The second sense of aesthetic judgement's principle (the purposiveness of nature) has implications, for a new antinomy arises with respect to the critical account of aesthetic judgements. As before, the antinomies are solved by the critical distinction between appearances and things-in-themselves. The solution to the antinomy necessarily leads on to the rational idea of supersensible nature as the ground of nature's purposiveness, although this necessity is only for the activity of judgement itself. Kant then looks back over the antinomies of the previous two *Critiques*, and asks how the ideas of supersensible grounds posited in the solution to those antinomies relate to one another. He writes at §57, Comment II, that, for theoretical reason, aesthetic judgement, and practical reason respectively,

> we are led to three ideas: *first*, the idea of the supersensible in general, not further determined, as the substrate of nature; *second*, the idea of the same

supersensible as the principle of nature's subjective purposiveness for our cognitive faculties; *third*, the idea of the same supersensible as the principle of the purposes of freedom and of the harmony of these purposes with nature in the moral sphere.

These supersensibles are asserted here to be 'the same'. We know that beauty is ideal with respect to our theoretical understanding of nature; we know too that aesthetic judgement is separate from the practical. So what could this 'sameness' mean, and how can it be shown? (see Table 3 on p. 167 for a schematic version of the faculties and their supersensible grounds).

Kant writes, 'So there must after all be a basis *uniting* the supersensible that underlies nature and the supersensible that the concept of freedom contains practically . . .' (Introduction II). The latter concept is the *summum bonum*: happiness insofar as it is morally merited. Now, in the *Critique of Practical Reason*, an antinomy arises concerning this idea.[32] Either the desire for happiness is the *motive* of moral action, or moral action is the *cause* of happiness in the world. If the former is the case, then this 'moral action' is sensuously conditioned, and not in fact moral at all. If the latter is the case, then this causation must be subject to the laws of nature, and cannot be described as necessary *a priori*. Kant solves this problem by pointing out that the causation in question is the causation of a supersensible being. Ultimately, however, this solution requires the 'mediation' by a moral author of the world, thus leading Kant to an earlier version of his 'moral proof'.

However, as we pointed out above, the moral proof cannot be what Kant has in mind in saying that judgement brings unity to the two branches of philosophy. The full version of the above quotation runs (Introduction II).

> Hence it must be possible to think of nature as being such that the lawfulness in its form will harmonise with at least the possibility of [achieving] the purposes that we are to achieve in nature according to laws of freedom. So there must after all be a basis *uniting* the supersensible that underlies nature and the supersensible that the concept of freedom contains practically, even though the concept of this basis does not reach cognition of it either theoretically or practically and hence does not have a domain of its own, though it does make possible the transition [*Übergang*] from our way of thinking in terms of principles of nature to our way of thinking in terms of principles of freedom.

The 'way of thinking' nature is according to the principles of the understanding. These principles legislate for the way concepts can be used to cognise nature, and they demand above all that concepts only have a possible legitimacy to the extent that they can be exhibited [*darstellen*] in sensibility.

Perhaps, then, *this* is what Kant has in mind: that there could be no transition between the understanding and reason without the basis of that transition being in some way exhibited. This would be the 'common ground' we talked about above. The problem with the moral proof – that its validity is only practical – ultimately comes down to the fact that at no stage after the fact of freedom itself, are its concepts *in any sense* exhibited.[33] They are pure, rarefied possibilities for speculative reason. The objects of aesthetic judgement, however, are in a sense such exhibitions. Kant writes,

> This transition is from the *sensible* substrate of theoretical philosophy to the *intelligible* substrate of practical philosophy; [it is made] through the critique of a faculty (judgement) that serves only for [making this] connection. Hence this faculty cannot on its own provide an cognition or contribute anything whatever to doctrine; but its judgements – called *aesthetic* judgements (whose principles are merely subjective), since they differ from all those that are called *logical*, i.e., from those (whether theoretical or practical) whose principles must be objective – are of so special a kind that *they refer sensible intuitions to an idea of nature* in which [nature's] lawfulness is beyond [our] understanding unless [we] relate nature to a supersensible substrate. The proof of this lies in the treatise itself.
>
> (First Introduction XI, emphasis added)

Through the aesthetic judgement, the intuitions of the beautiful (and perhaps the sublime) are seen to 'say something'. They are certainly (initially) objects of nature, but at the same time are symbols of morality, 'hints' of a moral purposiveness in nature, revelations of our supersensible vocation, expressions of aesthetic ideas, and so on. Aesthetic judgement, it would seem, reveals the connection between nature (the object of the understanding, and the field of action of morality), freedom (the supersensible object of reason in the subject), and the ground of the moral purpose (the supersensible object of reason *outside* the subject).

Let us examine this 'exhibition' more carefully. The 'Critique of Aesthetic Judgement', being based upon an entirely subjective principle, had to distinguish itself rigorously both from an inquiry into our cognition of natural objects ('ordinary' experience, as we called it, and ultimately natural science), and from an inquiry into our practical 'experience' of the good. Nevertheless, throughout the work, Kant was on the lookout for, and in fact discovered, any number of 'transitions' between the aesthetic inquiry and these other inquiries. If judgement is going to mediate between the understanding and reason, then it must have a necessary relation to the objects of both.

These 'transitions' take two forms, which construct the two sides of a transitive argument: if A=B and B=C then A=C (all three are 'the same').

Table 3   *Objects and grounds of the higher cognitive faculties*

Ground	undetermined supersensible	determinable supersensible	determined supersensible – moral author
Object	nature as 'blind' mechanism	nature as the purposive without determinate purpose	nature as purposive with respect to moral purpose
Faculty	understanding, together with sensibility	aesthetic judgement	practical reason
Ground 'in' the subject	undetermined supersensible basis of the self	supersensible ground of cognition in its *free purposiveness*, and judgement as autonomous	freedom, as supersensible basis of morality

The principle of reflective judgement makes possible those acts of, let us say, pure reflective judgement (that is, aesthetic judgements). These judgements involve the coordination of the key faculties of the theoretical cognition of nature: imagination and understanding. But here, judgement as a whole is no longer simply in the service of understanding; if anything, it is the imagination that is dominant or, at least, most active. This coordination allows the subject to apprehend a form in nature that is purposive with respect to cognition. But it is purposive not just to any cognition, but to cognition in general, or as we put it in Chapter 2, the cognitive faculties 'freed' to express their 'essence' in activity or 'play'. Kant accordingly writes in the First Introduction VIII that,

> the faculty of [aesthetic] judgement . . . perceives a [certain] relation between the two cognitive faculties, a relation that constitutes the condition, which we can only sense, under which [alone] we can use the faculty of judgement objectively . . .

Certainly, the object of aesthetic judgement, the beautiful, is an intuition of some natural thing. But similarly the beautiful thing in nature is not just any object in nature. Rather, if we define nature in general as that which is cognisable, then the beautiful, by going straight to the heart of cognition, is *naturalness as such*. It stands in for all nature, and for all of nature's relations to cognition. That is why, for example, reason takes an 'intellectual interest' in the beautiful in nature. But such an interest, as we have seen, leads us necessarily to consider the supersensible grounds of nature.

The idea of the supersensible required by theoretical philosophy is of an utterly neutral ground of experience which authorises no claims about its mode of appearance. It is nothing but the mere horizon of phenomena. The supersensible for aesthetic judgement, as established in the antinomy of taste and thereafter, is different. Here, in accordance again with judgement's principle, aesthetic judgements 'refer sensible intuitions to an idea of nature in which [nature's] lawfulness [for our specifically human faculties] is beyond [our] understanding unless [we] relate nature to a supersensible substrate' (First Introduction XI). In contrast to the above neutrality, Kant will call this the 'determinability' of the supersensible object of judgement (Introduction IX). For instead of being the neutral ground, it grounds nature as precisely lawful in general, or purposive without purpose. But as grounds, they are the same, for the beautiful is both *purposive* and *naturalness as such*. Aesthetic judgement, freely or from out of its own grounds, has a necessary relation to the cognition of nature. This makes clear what Kant means when he writes,

> The understanding, inasmuch as it can give laws to nature *a priori*, proves that we cognise nature only as appearance, and hence at the same time points to a supersensible substrate of nature; but it leaves this substrate entirely *undetermined*. Judgement, through its *a priori* principle of judging nature [purposively, that is:] in terms of possible particular laws of nature, provides nature's supersensible substrate (within as well as outside us) with *determinability by the intellectual faculty* [i.e. reason]. But reason, through its *a priori* practical law, gives this same substrate *determination*. Thus judgement makes the transition from the domain of the concept of nature to that of the concept of freedom.
>
> (Introduction IX, translation modified)

The three ideas of the 'same' supersensible mentioned above, turn out to be arranged in a sequence: from an indeterminate supersensible object through determinability to determination. Judgement's principle of purposiveness for cognition necessarily leaves open the question of the purpose itself. Thus it makes the supersensible ready to receive a determination according to practical reason. So half of our 'transition' is complete: the object (both sensible and supersensible) of aesthetic judgement is the natural object and its 'indeterminate' supersensible ground (thus the object of the understanding 'in its lawfulness').

In themselves, aesthetic judgements are founded upon the faculties of cognition of nature, and therefore have an inner identity with the cognition of nature. But they do not produce objective cognition (knowledge). Similarly, such judgements are not in themselves practical. To ask that aesthetic judgement on its own were to *lead to* morality is to ask for the impossible, even the amoral. Judgement must be 'called', so to speak. And yet, Kant writes (§59), [aesthetic] judgement finds itself referred to something that is both in the subject himself and outside him, something that is neither nature nor freedom and yet is linked with the basis of freedom, the supersensible, in which the theoretical and the practical power are in an unknown manner combined and joined into a unity.

Simply by virtue of the defining form of our activity of reflection upon the beautiful (free and self-legislating, disinterested, universal, and so on) such judgements are a powerful 'symbol' for morality. That is, beauty is an 'exhibition' of both the meaning and grounds of morality. Through the analysis of genius, we were able to see that beauty in general is the 'expression' of aesthetic ideas, which are at least the 'counterparts' of rational ideas. Again, through the defining form of reflection (which is in agreement with 'nature' in the genius), these aesthetic ideas are innately capable of carrying a *moral* determination. Thus Kant can write, 'taste is basically an ability to judge the [way in which] moral ideas *are made sensible . . .*' (§60, emphasis added).[34]

The above notions make aesthetic judgement worthy, as it were, of a connection to morality and the ground of morality. Indeed, in the 'Ideal of Beauty', we saw beauty being put directly into the service of morality. Aesthetic judgement, freely or from out of its own grounds, has a necessary relation to our moral selves. This necessary relation allows aesthetic judgement (that is, on the side of the subject and its basis in the supersensible) to be 'called', as we put it above, to man's 'moral vocation'.

The 'Intellectual Interest in the Beautiful' extended this necessary relation to the side of the natural object and its supersensible basis. There, the naturally beautiful was taken to be a 'hint' of nature's own moral purposiveness. It is thus morality itself that takes up aesthetic judgement and completes the reference to morality, and thus brings into harmony all the higher cognitive faculties (§59). In the middle of his discussion of the 'intellectual interest in the beautiful', Kant writes (at §42), as if it were only a supplementary observation,[35]

Consider, in addition, how we admire nature, which in its beautiful products displays itself as art, [i.e. as acting] not merely by chance but, as it were, intentionally, in terms of a lawful arrangement and as a purposiveness without a purpose; and since we do not find this purpose anywhere outside us, we naturally look for it in ourselves, namely, in what constitutes the ultimate purpose of our existence: our moral vocation.

The sentence is strange and perhaps carelessly written. Even so, the following logic is unavoidable. The beautiful appears to be purposeful without a determinate cognition, but with an indeterminate purpose of furthering the interests of cognition in general. Although in any specific aesthetic judgment, there is no 'exterior' interest, nevertheless the interests of cognition in general are not ends in themselves (this of course recalls the discussion in §84). They will always be ultimately subordinated to the final purpose, which in principle has no further purpose conditioning it. Aesthetic judgement can be so subordinated because of its necessary relation to morality, and thus it is not subordinated merely according to an external demand (as in the moral proof) but at least partly from its nature.

In effect, the above quotation is asking 'Why is there beauty?' Ultimately, that question can only be answered 'Because it serves what ought to be' – but beauty does make itself ready, and its substrate 'determinable', for that service. As Kant writes, 'The morally good is the *intelligible* that taste has in view' (§59). Aesthetic experience reveals both the human subject as in its grounds capable of coordination towards the highest purpose, and nature's purposiveness (grounded in the supersensible) as ready for moral determination.

That was the second half of the transitive argument. The grounds and objects of aesthetic judgement (ultimately, the supersensible both in and outside the subject) are capable of determinability according to moral ideas. And they are capable of such determinability without losing the inner connection to the cognition of nature, which was the first half of the transitive argument. Judgement thus completes the transition between the understanding (and theoretical philosophy), on the one hand, and reason in its highest, practical employment on the other. Judgement's activity exhibits (in a broad sense) the possibility of nature's cooperation in our moral enterprise, and this exhibition is neither alien to the understanding nor to reason. The faculty of judgement thus unifies the branches of philosophy and their objects.

We started our Introduction by quoting Kant's *Logic* and its four questions of philosophy. There Kant claims that all four are united in the question 'What is man?', and also that all four must be co-ordinated towards the highest or final purpose of the human. With respect to the first unity, judgement reveals both a structure of subjectivity that describes alike both theoretical and practical thought (cognitive harmony is also a self-legislating autonomy), and also the innermost nature of human subjectivity (the *intellectus ectypus*). It can bring these two branches of philosophy and their objects into a unity. The *Critique of Judgement* thus gives us a major part of a fundamental anthropology. Furthermore, judgement solves the second problem of unity insofar as, in a way not essentially distinct from the first, it provides the means by which theoretical and practical philosophy can be coordinated towards the final end. For aesthetic judgement exhibits both in nature and in man's non-moral thought an inner propensity towards the moral (indeed it also cultivates that propensity). It is for these reasons that Kant can claim that the *Critique of Judgement* is the completion of his philosophical labours.

CHAPTER SUMMARY: The principle of reflective judgement is recast in teleological judgement: 'An organised product of nature is one in which everything is a purpose and reciprocally also a means' (§66). This refers to an unthinkable (for our understanding) relationship among the empirical laws governing a natural purpose, and thus leads inevitably to an antinomy between the necessity of natural law and the contingency of such a natural purpose with respect to it. Theoretical cognition works together with teleological judgement to achieve scientific results not otherwise possible. But the unthinkable situation is supplemented by reason with the rational idea an intelligence acting according to purposes as the supersensible basis of nature's purposes. From our human (or finite rational, *intellectus ectypus* contrasted with the *intellectus archetypus*) point of view the former can only be thought of as an intelligence acting according to purposes.

If there is a supersensible intelligence, for what *final purpose* does it act? That can only be man's freedom for the moral law. That law, as determining of the will of a finite being, carries with it the assumption of the possibility of its purpose (the good) in nature. The guarantee of that possibility again takes us to the supersensible, as the ground of that same purpose (estimated by teleological judgement) in nature. Thus, the 'empty' supersensible intelligence of physico-theology is further determined as wise, and thus as God, the moral author of the world. In short, reflective judgement supplies the means by which moral action can demonstrate the real possibility of achieving its final purpose in nature, which also constitutes a *practical reflective* proof of the existence of God as the ground of that possibility.

The final part of the chapter provides a summary of Kant's 'grand' argument concerning the 'mediating' role of judgement between theoretical and practical philosophy. This argument is hinted at in Kant's Introduction, but is never pursued in the text. The key issue is the 'sameness' of the ideas of the supersensible objects of theoretical and practical reason; these are shown to be the same through a transitive argument that proceeds *through* the supersensible object of judgement. Judgement thus solves the grand problem of the unity of philosophy, both in the sense of showing the necessity of a link at the level of the idea of the supersensible, and in the sense of making possible the subordination of theoretical reason to the practical, that is to man's 'highest vocation'.

Notes

Introduction

1. 'Cosmopolitan' is better, but without Kant's explanation of the concept it is confusing. A similar passage is to be found, condensed from his logic lectures, in CPR A804=B832. Kant defines a world-concept, in this sense, at A840=B868n, writing '*World concept* here means a concept that concerns what interests everyone necessarily.'
2. *Logic*, p. 29.
3. Kant rarely uses the term 'anthropology' in this sense, though he often uses 'human' [*Mensch, Menschlich*] in a fundamental rather than empirical sense. The phrase 'fundamental anthropology' is convenient and not too misleading.
4. Maybe, knowledge is its own good – still, that's a good.
5. *Prolegomena to Any Future Metaphysics*, p. 260.
6. I should apologise for taking a handful of liberties with Werner Pluhar's admirable translation of CJ. First, I have occasionally modified the translation for the sake of clarity out of context. All these modifications have been indicated. I have also systematically reverted from Pluhar's perfectly justified translation of *vermögen* as 'power' to 'faculty'. This is simply because most of the secondary literature the reader might consult uses the latter.
7. As a critical philosopher, that is, though certainly not as a scientist or moralist.
8. First Introduction XI.
9. Both in *Theoretical Philosophy*, pp. 301–60, 373–416.
10. An importantly analogous type of investigation is found in the Phenomenology of Edmund Husserl and his followers.
11. Or also 'freedom' [*Freiheit*] or 'autonomy' [*Autonomie*] with respect to experience and other sensible conditions.
12. For example CPR, B127.
13. See CPrR, p. 9n, Ak. p. 9.
14. Compare the treatment in the 'Comment' following First Introduction VIII.
15. For example CJ, the final part of the 'Comment' following §29.
16. Various translations can easily lead to confusions between (1) 'purpose' [*Zweck*]/ 'purposive' [*Zweckmäig*], (2) 'final purpose' [*Endzweck*], and (3) 'ultimate purpose' [*letzter Zweck*]. In particular, the adjective 'final' in the second of these should not be confused with alternative translations of the first (i.e. 'end'/'final') and second ('final end') terms. Please see Section III below, and Chapters 2 and 5.
17. For a clear exposition of these distinctions, see Kant's *The Metaphysics of Morals*. pp. 11–14, Ak. 211–14.

18. For example *Grounding of the Metaphysics of Morals*, p. 46.
19. Presentations (also translated as 'representations') are usually thought of as mental objects (things or activities in our minds) of which we are or can become aware. However, we might also wish to think of presentations as the aspect by which things (real or ideal) present themselves to us, or are apprehended by us, through a faculty (*sensibly*, through the faculty of sensibility; *conceptually*, through the understanding; *as this or that*, through cognitive judgement; *merely formally*, through the imagination in aesthetic judgement, and so on).
20. Kant's account of the cognitive faculties in the Introduction to CJ seems to be primarily oriented toward understanding their role in the theoretical cognition of nature. Thus the name, 'faculties of cognition'. The manner of explicating them might well be different if the focus was, for example, the higher mental faculty of desire. Thus, it is slightly misleading to call practical reason a 'cognitive' faculty as we do below. Compare the opening sentences of the Introduction to CPrR.
21. Practical reason is involved in determining action only, Kant argues, if the will is conceived of as free of any condition. Other types of action are only 'technically practical' (Introduction 1), and are determined by natural concepts.
22. Kant states that sensibility in general (even in its *a priori* aspects) is left out of the list of the cognitive faculties because he is there concerned only with mere thought, that is the mere employment of concepts. Sensibility cannot legislate – provide a principle for the use of concepts – for this reason. See CJ, the comments about 'intuition' at the beginning of First Introduction II.
23. Such as the chapter on Schematism in the CPR, A137–47=B176–87. Not surprisingly, then, the notion of schematism has a significant role in CJ, of which we can unfortunately only catch a glimpse here.
24. By 'constitutive' is usually meant something still stronger: that the faculty gives the laws according to which the objects are produced.
25. Kant, in fact, does not always make this distinction between concept and principle quite as consistently as he might.
26. CPR, A150–3=B189–93.
27. Compare Kant's brief discussion in the *Anthropology* §40 (where, incidentally, higher and lower are clearly a *relative* characterisation). Thus, he only rarely speaks of 'principles' of sensibility (e.g. CPR, A21=B35–6).
28. For example CPR, A21=B35.
29. CPR, A147=B187.
30. One *a priori* condition of scoring in basketball is the existence of a number system to keep score – that is logically required by the idea of scoring. It also makes it clear that *a priori* does not mean prior *in time*: it would be absurd to say that 'the numbers arrived just minutes before the game was to start'.
31. Forming the basis of an *a priori* physics. Accordingly, Kant wrote in 1786 the *Metaphysical Foundations of Natural Science*.
32. CPR, First Preface, Axii.
33. CPR, A51=B75.
34. CPR, B xviii.
35. CPR, A28=B44 and A35–6=B52.
36. Such knowledge takes the form of what Kant famously calls *synthetic a priori* knowledge. See CPR, 2nd edn Introduction IV–VI.
37. CPR, A84–5=B117.
38. This is strictly speaking a distortion of the structure, leaving out the important sections on the 'Transcendental Doctrine of Method'.
39. Where such philosophy steps over the bounds of possible experience, Kant will often call it 'speculative'.

40. CPR, A840=B868.
41. CPR, A808=B836.
42. CPR, A840=B868.
43. CPR, A810=B838.
44. Teleological judgements do have a 'concept', however: as we shall see, they apply a regulative idea of reason rather than a determining concept of the understanding.
45. (Kant sometimes includes indeterminate concepts under this heading of 'reflective'.) *Transcendental* reflection, as discussed by Kant in CPR, ('Amphiboly of the Concepts of Reflection', A260=B316) would be an absolutely preliminary decision concerning the cognitive faculty from which a given presentation originated. Such reflection generates the 'concepts of reflection', which can then be used to adequately discriminate between the faculties, and allow transcendental critique to begin. Arguably, then, reflection is the subjective condition of possibility of transcendental philosophy. However, this notion of an initial discovering of a concept for discrimination is clearly analogous to how reflection is used in CJ. In fact, aesthetic reflective judgement takes us (as we shall see in Chapter 2) not to a particular intuition or concept, but to the essence of imagination (the free production at will of forms of intuition) and understanding (lawfulness) as faculties. This suggests that aesthetic judgements might in fact be very closely related to this fundamental type of reflection.
46. Kant uses the concept of 'art' [*Kunst*] as a more general term; he therefore uses the phrase 'fine' (or 'beautiful') art [*schöne Kunst*] for art in the sense of paintings and symponies and poems. See Chapter 4.
47. Indeed, it is not even clear that we can give a determinate definition of what a novel in general is, much less a 'great' novel.
48. Kant would probably claim that 'entirely subjective' judgements are in fact rather wishy-washy determinate judgements, but that does not much matter here.
49. This argument is closely related to the argument concerning the regulative role of the ideas of reason in CPR (see the 'Appendix to the Transcendental Dialectic', beginning at A642 = B670). Roughly, the difference seems to be this: reason presents an idea of, say, the totality of empirical laws, and demands that cognition pursue it; judgement begins from the other side, as it were, assuming on principle the real possibility of such a totality in a form available to (purposive for) human cognition, and thus that reason's demand will not be entirely fruitless.
50. Kant can only claim that although free moral action is, by definition, not motivated by pleasure or pain, it is certainly accompanied by it.
51. The same could be said for critical philosophy as a whole.

Chapter 1

1. In Kant, 'experience' [*Erfahrung*] is a technical term meaning the objective immediate cognition of nature. Thus, Kant is normally careful not to talk about aesthetic experience (but see, for example, Introduction VIII, or the Comment following §38). Unfortunately, this leads to, if not a false, then an over-emphasised dichotomy between experience proper and our presentations of beauty. As if the latter could do without the horizon of the former! So, when here we talk about aesthetic experience, this is indeed a slightly loose way of speaking, but it is justified in order not to lose sight of the fact that beauty for Kant is not a completely other-worldly phenomenon. My expression 'mere experience' tries to further underline the point.
2. I say 'formally' because, as we shall see, everything important about such judgements happens before we ever get around to explicitly making such connections.

3. Which is quite different to the point Kant makes about 'ugliness' in §48.
4. Indeed, Kant will describe the sublime experience in very similar terms. See Chapter 3.
5. CPR, A70=B95ff (and see Kant's note to the title of the first moment). For each characteristic, there are three 'moments' or ways in which that characteristic can be satisfied. Importantly, these judgement-forms become the 'guide' for discovering the complete system of *a priori* concepts of the understanding.
6. It is often said that Kant is failing to properly address aesthetic experience from the start by trying to force it into these cognitive characteristics. However, Kant equally could argue that if aesthetic judgement did not relate to judgment (and cognition) more generally, it would fail to have any significance for our wider mental life, and would be inaccessible to philosophy.
7. Subjective taste is an evaluation not a description. Therefore, calling it 'right' or 'correct' is, strictly speaking, inappropriate.
8. One could disagree non-aesthetically: for example, you and I could agree that X is beautiful, but I believe that such beauty is not enough to make it art. I must be applying some exterior concept of what art is or should be. Kant is speaking of the aesthetic judgement that is behind or before any such 'exterior' concepts. The perpetual debate about the 'value' of contemporary art is a debate about the meaning of a concept, not about aesthetic experience.
9. 'Truth' is in inverted commas here because it too is subject to the 'as if'. Aesthetic judgements behave as if they are true, but do not have all the objective properties of propositions which can actually be said to be true or false.
10. Though unfortunately also that of a 'superior' European. See p. 103.
11. What Kant calls 'disinterestedness' is often taken to be a key component of what more recent aestheticians call the 'aesthetic attitude'.
12. What about fiction or poetry, however? Here form is only *secondarily* in space and time – a different typeset, for example, and the work looks quite different; a different reader and the tempo or even the rhythm can change. Kant seems to need a different conception of form here, which would include prosody to be sure, but would also include, for example, genre and perhaps even the conceptual and symbolic relation between different episodes or characters in a novel. The point about the notion of 'form' for Kant is both its contrast with mere sensible content, and its status of not being readily conceptualised. See Douglas Burnham, '*King Lear*, Narrating, and Surprise', *The Yearbook of English Studies*, Vol. 20. (London: Modern Humanities Research Association, 2000), pp. 21–33.
13. This claim is related to the primary/secondary qualities distinction first made by John Locke in *Essay Concerning Human Understanding*, ed. Nidditch (Oxford: Clarendon Press, 1975) BkII, ch. VIII. Kant rejects many of the metaphysical implications of Locke's famous account, but (partly for the sake of Newton) largely preserves it as an empirical and scientific claim.
14. See Kant's 'Anticipations of Perception' in CPR, beginning A166=B207.
15. Actually, Kant here concedes that colour and perhaps sound in itself can be beautiful, but only if it itself is pure – that is, can be apprehended formally (as a wavelength, or in a mathematical relationship with other colours or sounds).
16. Later, Kant will complicate this by writing about interests that can naturally combine with aesthetic judgements (§§41–2, see Chapter 4). But even there the key point remains: the interest does not form the grounds for or basis of the judgement.
17. This notion of self-containedness is a provisional description of what, when we explore the transcendental grounds of the judgement, will turn out to be *autonomy*.
18. A classic argument against strict formalism.
19. In the case of food at least, this must be an inexact science. As we saw in the discussion of determinate judgements in the Introduction, not all concepts need to be exact in order to be operative in judgements.

20. Here, Kant identifies the type of common sense he does *not* mean with the Latin expression *sensus communis*. In §40, however, he seems to want to reclaim this expression for the type he *does* mean, primarily because the notion of 'sense' is closer to a description of the operation of aesthetic judgement than of ordinary understanding (see our discussion in Chapter 4.) Fortunately, this terminological confusion does not seem to hide any deeper confusion.

21. The faculty of taste is a particular instance of the fundamental faculty of judgement.

22. According to Kant's treatment of the categories of the understanding in CPR – derived from the 'moments' of judgement – universality refers to something like the quantity of the inclusiveness of the extension of the set of objects refered to – in this case 'allness' (*Allheit*) (A80=B106).

23. CPR, A218=B266, translation modified.

24. Nor involving an 'absolute' ought (§18).

25. Kant is not being entirely consistent: is common sense, as a condition, actually narrower than the 'universal conditions of experience'? (compare *Anthropology*, pp. 237–8).

Chapter 2

1. Kant defines these terms slightly differently at the beginning of §10, putting the emphasis on the concept. The reason is that one can either think *beforehand* of a concept (of a non-existing object) as the cause of the future object; or one can think *retrospectively* of the existing object as somehow having been the 'final cause' of its own production, by way of a concept. Thus, 'purpose' sometimes refers to the concept (thus 'intention'), sometimes to the object. This ambiguity shows some carelessness by Kant, to be sure, but is not a mistake. It goes right to the heart of the difficulties human cognition necessarily has with the notion of purposes.

2. Kant does, however, feel living organisms have to be conceived of as purposive. We shall return to this slightly different problem in Chapter 5.

3. See Kant's note at the end of §17.

4. Sometimes, artists will allow randomness in the production of artworks, But even here, we can argue that while the internal purpose is certainly more 'loose', it is not simply absent: there was an intention to introduce randomness at just this point, and in just this way.

5. All of these purposes can be accomplished in non-artistic ways.

6. Kant is going to complicate although not retract this blunt thesis. See below, Chapter 4.

7. Kant says that this can be a source of apparent disagreements: if one critic judges an object as dependent beauty, and another as free.

8. On this matter, Kant feels beauty in art and nature are very different (see the discussion of regularity in the 'General Comment' following §22). We will return to related topics in Chapter 4.

9. We have here skipped the notion of normal idea, also introduced in §17. Note, however, that, like the normal idea, the 'visible expression' of the ideal of beauty is empirical. Therefore, it too will vary from culture to culture and time to time.

10. This notion, for the most part implicit in 'Critique of Aesthetic Judgement', is explicitly the case in Kant's account of teleological judgement (see Chapter 5).

11. See also in, for example, Introduction VI, §§1, 10.

12. At the beginning of §12, Kant talks about the feeling of respect in the moral law. Will is not caused or determined by respect for the moral law; rather, respect is the feeling of the immediate determination of free will by the law. If the former were the case, then the will would not be free (because it is determined by a feeling). Moreover, practical reason would

not be practical, but would be supplying just another concept of the good which in turn grounds a pleasure determining the will to act. No mere concept is immediately practical. The case is similar to the inner 'causality' of the pleasure in an aesthetic judgement. An illegitimate interest would arise if the purposiveness of the presentation, instead of being the ground of the pleasure, were to be caused by it (§13). The beautiful object would become part of my intentions, and I would have an interest. Further, if the pleasure were separable and caused by (rather than grounded in) the purposiveness in the presentation, then again this assumes some concept of a purpose. But there can be no such concept. The parallel between the two cases is not exact, of course. The aesthetic judgement is not practical: it does not act to bring about anything other than itself. If it is not to be practical, the judgement has to be what we called 'self-contained'.

13. Kant says further than this situation is 'analogous' to (but not the same as) a case of sensible charm. The cases are not the same, formally speaking, in that the pleasure is corporeal. The mind therefore is passive; the cognitive faculties are not doing the work.

14. There is a curious relationship here between this causality and the causality of the natural purposes Kant discusses in the 'Critique of Teleological Judgement' (see Chapter 5).

15. See §33, or 'General Comment' following §22. The significance of this term is that it immediately suggests a relation to Kant's moral theory. Compare *Grounding for the Metaphysics of Morals*, Ak. 440ff.

16. As we said at the beginning of Chapter 1, formally speaking this means connecting the feeling with the experience of the object.

17. This definition of an aesthetic judgement focuses on the beautiful, and not on the sublime.

18. As we noted at the end of Chapter 1, Kant will also speak of common sense as itself a faculty of feeling for the beautiful, spreading some confusion (§40).

19. This is the main root of the word normally translated as 'harmony'. Except for this root, Kant is inconsistent in his usage.

20. We might initially suspect that by 'accord' Kant has in mind the idea of unity in the Deduction in the first *Critique*. We could plausibly talk about a relation between the faculties which brings about unity of the manifold of sense, as prescribed transcendentally by the unity of apperception. However, Kant never refers to this work in this way, not even when discussing the task of Deduction in §36 and §38 'Comment'. We will be returning at length to what is meant by this 'proportion'.

21. Compare for example, First Introduction VIII.

22. Kant claims, in the 'Comment' following §22, that with the exception of poetry (the object of which is in itself not directly intuitive) there is no opportunity for the imagination to be free as an *activity*, because it is bound to the intuitive form presented (in the painting, building and so on). But, he adds, that form might be 'just the sort of form' imagination would have come up with *had* its activity been free. There is something quite bizarre about this claim. In order for a presentation to be fixed in that way, there would need to be a determinate concept operating which fixes the synthetic function of the imagination as it scans the object. But there can be no such concept *for the beautiful* (although, certainly, for experience to be possible at all, there must be 'background' concepts operating). The description Kant gives of painting and related arts in §51 seems more appropriate:

> [I]t [that is, taste] judges only the forms (without regard to any purpose) as they offer themselves to the eye, singly or in their arrangement, according to the effect they have on the imagination.

This suggests rather that the imagination must constitute and reconstitute the form, in a genuinely free *activity*, in accordance with the lawfulness of the understanding. Compare also the equally peculiar distinction between 'beautiful objects' and 'beautiful views' at the end of the 'General Comment' after §22; and Kant's discussion of the 'enduring vehicle' of the visual arts in §53.

23. As we pointed out in the Introduction, the faculties are not things, but mere abilities or activities. Nevertheless, there is a difference between an ability that has a certain *a priori* essence, expressed throughout all its activity, and an ability with a set of outcomes which is contingent.

24. However, Kant does say that in so far as objective judgements also have a subjective dimension, they can in addition be felt (§9, see also Introduction VI). One might be able to reconstruct Kant's argument on this basis, but that would be speculative.

25. Kant sometimes wants to make a distinction between the verbs '*urteilen*' and '*beurteilen*', but is not very systematic about it. While the former is always translated as 'judge', the latter is sometimes translated by 'judge' and sometimes by 'estimate'.

26. Might the same be true even of the presented form? Compare General Remark following §22, the more detailed discussion in §49, 51.

27. In the sublime, this role is fulfilled for aesthetic judgement by the other cognitive faculty we have not mentioned: reason.

28. That is, the concept designated by a set of German terms all ending in -*Stimmung* (voice).

29. Intriguingly, Kant writes that the imagination is 'prompted to *spread* over a multitude of kindred presentation [*sich über . . . zu verberiten*].' (§49, emphasis added). The context is the genius' production of fine art, but the point looks to be more general. This, in turn, is related to the holism of the aesthetic judgement.

Chapter 3

1. Kant's interest in travel writing suggests another reason: the world, as it is commonly expressed, was 'opening up'.

2. Presumably also in terms of its vast antiquity. Kant virtually omits any temporal dimension to the sublime.

3. These are also translated as 'mathematically' and 'dynamically'.

4. In CPR, Kant considers as parallel operations our thought moving *outward* to ever more encompassing presentations and moving *inwards*, to ever finer divisions (for example the first and second 'antinomies' A426=B454ff). But here he does not suggest a sublime of the incomprehensibly small, numerous, or complex.

5. Consider a similar example: an attempt to conceive the size of the solar system. This would involve the mediation of images of the solar system as if taken from outside it, and would probably also involve an act of will to suspend ordinary perceptual cognition and imaginatively position oneself as a possible perceiver of such an object.

6. Exactly what this means, however, will not be clear until the next section.

7. CPrR, p. 169, Ak 161.

8. Or even a presentation of the same.

9. It should be noted that 'transcend' and 'transcendence' are used here in the sense Kant gives them in the 'comment' to §57.

10. The concept provided by judgement, the 'absolutely large', serves as a quasi-sensible *schema* of the rational idea (§29 and 'General Comment' following). By schema, Kant means the entity or operation that mediates between the very different realms of pure discursive concepts on the one hand, and purely sensible objects in space and time on the other (see CPR, A137=B176). The notion of schematism is raised again with respect to an account of aesthetic judgement generally in §35. The significance of this here is at least twofold. First, by echoing an analogous process of mediation from the first *Critique*, Kant is re-emphasising the role of judgement (with its domain of feeling) as a mediating faculty. Secondly, the section on schematism in the first *Critique* is very brief and notoriously vague. For this

reason, among others, it is tempting to read the CPR as not requiring the notion of schematism at all. What is interesting about passages such as these is that they demonstrate that Kant evidently felt the notion of schematism to be central, and the range of application of it as a notion in transcendental philosophy to be broad. A less charitable interpretation, of course, would be that Kant was clutching at straws in an attempt to understand with his available philosophical tools a phenomenon (the sublime) which is either not an identifiable phenomenon at all (there is no feeling of the sublime, distinct from other more mundane feelings) or is not something Kant could grasp with such tools (for example having to do with the Freudian unconscious).

11. As with the notion of 'absolutely large', the notion of 'might essentially without dominance', which belongs only to judgement itself, serves as the schema of this idea of pure reason, freedom with respect to that which threatens dominance over the will. The two 'concepts' of judgement, as we have interpreted them, are not however an exact parallel.

Chapter 4

1. The question whether animals are capable of purposive action is a typical Enlightenment-period problem, and one that has never quite gone away. Kant's definition of 'life' suggests he believes they do (see the Introduction of this book). However, animals are not rational, that is they are not capable of formulating and acting according to *principles*.
2. Although, strictly speaking, an agreeable art is not fully free because it involves interest, although not perhaps for the artist.
3. Here again, one can see the influence of Rousseau's (and others') conception of nature that we first mentioned in the Introduction.
4. See, for example, the end of 'Comment I' after §57.
5. Although often read in this way, Kant's theory of art is not necessarily constrained to the *imitation* of nature in the first sense.
6. Such notions, above all, had considerable influence on the Romantic period.
7. The whole discussion of perfection is part of Kant's response to Baumgarten's understanding of art as perfection in sensible cognition.
8. For example, the theme of a 'cosmopolitan attitude' in the poem Kant discusses in §49, or again the 'king of heaven' just previously.
9. See also §§15–16, especially the idea of 'accessory' or 'dependent' beauty.
10. §47, and see also Kant's discussion of 'mannerism' at the end of §49.
11. 'Evaporate' [*verdunsten*] §43. The metaphoric link is on '*geistig*' in the sense of 'alcoholic', presumably taking us to the root of 'spirit' as 'breath'.
12. As we shall see below, however, the same is true of the beautiful in nature. Something similar was already explicitly the case for the aesthetic judgement on the sublime.
13. §49, and for further clarification see §57, 'Comment I'.
14. §50, and compare 'evaporates' in §43, §47 and *Anthropology from a Pragmatic Point of View*, §67, p. 241.
15. This is probably the philosophical difficulty in the 'Critique of Aesthetic Judgement' that has been most troubling. My reconstruction here takes its plausibility as an interpretation, and thus also its suitability for inclusion in this book, from its intimate connection with what I take as one of the most authentically Kantian claims in the whole of the third *Critique*: the notion that a cognitive faculty has its legislative domain. For judgement, to be sure, this is not a domain of objects, but rather of feelings. However, even that has necessary implications for the assumptions immanent to judgement that must be made about objects.
16. There is, however, a significant difference here. The object of nature, as part of a world of

experience, is constituted by the *a priori* activity of our cognitive faculties. It is therefore valid, but at one remove, so to speak, from the supersensible foundation. But the aesthetic idealism describes a judgement on the subjective presentation of a natural object; it too is valid, but now at two removes. Kant never fully deals with how aesthetic judgements are related to this underlying transcendental world-giving activity. As we shall see, however, teleological judgement deals with objects of nature, though only regulatively.

17. See the end of the 'Comment' following §38.

18. Arguably, at this point any assumption of the supersensible as ground is less important than simply establishing that there is an inner link between judgement and the *idea* of the supersensible. This would seem to be part of Kant's point in 'Comment II' following §57.

19. As we saw above, for example, this is an assumption of Kant's theory of genius: the purposive mental state is not embodied in the art work – how could it be? – but 'expressed' in it, that the viewer might also have such a mental state.

20. That is, it belongs to their 'nature', in the sense of the object of the science of *empirical* anthropology.

21. Actually, the passage is still more complex than this, for it holds up those 'nations' where this has been partly achieved as 'models', but not for imitation. Thus the problem of influence (see section B below) between artists is the same as the problem of trying to learn from the example of an earlier society. This is one of Kant's many oblique references to the common eighteenth-century (especially German) problem of if and how to 'imitate' the Greeks.

22. Kant, Immanuel. *Political Writings*. pp. 54–60, 93–30.

23. Compare CPR, A738=B766ff 'The Discipline of Pure Reason in Regard to its Polemic Use' for a related discussion of the 'cultivation' of reason and the idea of public debate and communication. Cultivation as a real process, both private but also public, must be a part of philosophical method, broadly conceived.

24. Because, on certain ways of understanding the transcendental method of philosophising, that method has to be conceived of as free or spontaneous reflection, it was not uncommon after Kant for philosophical activity itself to be seen as akin to art.

25. See our discussion in Chapter 2.

26. Arguably, Kant is describing something similar in asking critics to investigate how judgement 'actually proceeds' in §34, or asking the 'master' to 'stimulate the student's imagination' in §60; perhaps too he is beginning something similar to this in his brief and often highly metaphorical discussions of examples or art forms. See the example of Frederick the Great's poem in §49, or the treatment of painting in §51.

27. Or rather, Kant might say that the first form (the production of interpretations) *can* be aesthetic on one condition: that it recognises that the 'theme' only has significance as the mere point of focus of the aesthetic idea, and it is the way that this theme is aesthetically played out through the object *taken as a whole* that gives the work *qua* work any value whatsoever. The 'aesthetic idea' is the principle of the *unity* of the fine art object. That is, it is only because of the aesthetic idea that the work is one thing in the first place, and could thus be studied as having a meaning.

28. It might be thought to constitute an exception to this rule where the work, or the criticism of it, is taken to expound a truth of morality or justice (or lack thereof). But for Kant, far more important than a piece of moral 'information' – such as a moral maxim – is both the hard-won ability to be able to act in accordance with the maxim, and the revelation of the possibility of such action by the subject, in nature.

29. Arguments broadly similar to this were in fact used at the origins of the conservation movement in the United States in the nineteenth century.

30. 'General Comment' following §29; and compare 'admiration and love' §42, §59.

31. In addition to the following limited discussion, see, for example, §23ff of *The Metaphysics of Morals*.

31. Kant says as much in First Introduction III. The mental powers remain only in 'aggregate'.
32. CPrR, pp. 119–26, Ak 113–19.
33. Perhaps that is why teleological judgement does not ground but certainly 'reinforces' the moral proof (§88).
34. A similar claim is true of aesthetic judgements on the sublime. Such judgements begin with cognition and will in the realm of nature, and end by disclosing these faculties as being in the service of our supersensible 'vocation' – in particular in so far as our 'vocation' involves our transcendence to nature as free. However, the sublime does not involve any claims about nature, and is therefore not fully part of this transition.
35. And rather confusingly looking forward to the teleology.

Glossary

Every effort has been made in this glossary to keep the definitions as brief and simple as possible, avoiding those subtleties or ambiguities that are explored elsewhere in this book. Therefore, where any section of this book contains a lengthier but illuminating discussion, it is indicated. With regard to Kant's terminology, please also see Caygill, Howard, *A Kant Dictionary* (Oxford: Blackwell, 1995).

A priori—That which is completely prior to, or independent of, anything which depends upon experience (see especially p. 17).

Aesthetic—In the *Critique of Pure Reason*, Kant's treatment of space and time as *a priori* forms of intuition. In the *Critique of Judgement*, a description of our experiences of the beautiful or sublime (see especially p. 40ff).

Art [*Kunst*]—At its most general, anything produced by human purposive action (see also 'Fine art').

Autonomy—The property of a faculty which is both free and gives the law of its operation to itself (see especially pp. 73, 138–9).

Beauty [*Schönheit*]—An object that gives disinterested pleasure through the mere contemplation of its form (see especially pp. 72–4).

Choice—See 'Will'.

Cognition [*Erkentnis*]—Normally in Kant, thought which is directed towards knowledge of possible or actual objects, either *a priori* or through experience (see especially p. 11).

Common sense: [*Gemeinsinn*]—(At times identified with *sensus communis*.) The universally shared ability to feel pleasure in beauty; sometimes also identified as the *a priori* but indeterminate principle of aesthetic judgement (see especially pp. 55–60).

Concept [*Begriff*]—A presentation of a *type* of thing, or of a set of individuals that have properties in common.

Condition [*Bedingung*]—That which makes something else possible or actual – often, in empirical terms, a material cause; in transcendental terms, the principle provided by a cognitive faculty. Thus, the unconditioned would be that which requires nothing outside itself in order to be possible.

Constitutive [*konstitutiv*]—Of the relation between a principle and an object wherein the former gives the law of the latter's possibility; or, more loosely, as the ground of something being the case (see especially p. 14).

Contingent [*Zufälligkeit*]—That which could have been otherwise.

Critical/critique—One name for Kant's overall philosophical project – determining through transcendental analysis the limits and validity of a faculty or power (see especially pp. 7–8, 16ff).

Culture [*Kultur*]—Sometimes, 'cultivation'. Usually, the development or training of the employment of our faculties. Sometimes, or indirectly, the public aspect of this training (communal objects, institutions or practices) (see especially pp. 126–8, 134–5).

Deduction—A transcendental argument to show the validity of an *a priori* principle or concept with respect to some type of experience, normally by showing that the principle is a necessary or constituting condition of that experience.

Determinate [*bestimmend*]—Of a judgement wherein the concept involved is fully adequate to the subsumption of the particular. Thus, 'indeterminate': of a judgement wherein either there is no initial concept, or the involved concept is not yet sufficient to unequivocally subsume the particular. More generally, something is 'determined' if it has a definite set of properties and not others; in a passive sense, something 'is determined' if its definite set of properties are externally conditioned (see especially pp. 26–7).

Disinterestedness (or 'devoid of interest')—A feature of the aesthetic judgement wherein the judgement is not conditioned by any interest in the real existence of the object judged (see especially p. 50ff).

Faculty [*Vermögen, Facultät*, sometimes *Kraft*; also translated 'power']—An ability of the mind to produce some presentation or to act in a certain way: for example cognition, reason, or imagination (see especially pp. 9–15).

Feeling [*Gefühl*]—The faculty of immediate awareness of the state of one's being alive (health, well-being, and so on), and also an immediate partial determination of the will to act accordingly.

Fine art [*Schöne Kunst*]—An art both beautiful and 'inspired' (see especially p. 108ff).

Freedom [*Freiheit*]—The ability of the human will to act autonomously (see especially pp. 11–12).

Genius [*Genie*]—The ability of the artist by means of which he or she is inspired by 'aesthetic ideas' to produce works of fine art (see especially p. 110ff, and see also 'Idea').

Ground/foundation/basis [*Grund*]—Figuratively, that which underlies something. So, a set of reasons (for a rational argument) or motivations (for the will); a cause; or the thing-in-itself as that which is the ground of appearance.

Harmony—[*Zusammenstimmung* or similar, or *Harmonie*]—The activity of the cognitive faculties of imagination and understanding when in the presence of beauty (see especially p. 73ff).

Idea—A concept formed by pure reason which purports to permit cognition of 'objects' beyond the limits of possible experience. Also, an 'aesthetic idea' in Kant's discussion of the genius, is a presentation of the imagination to which no cognition is adequate (see especially pp. 13, 113ff).

Imagination—[*Einbildung(-skraft)*]—The faculty of forming a presentation of that which is not present (see especially p. 14).

Intention [*Absicht*]—(Sometimes, 'purpose' is used in this sense.) Having a concept of a purpose in mind that determines action towards that purpose.

Intuition [*Anshauung*]—An immediate presentation of a particular (see especially pp. 13, 19–20).

Judgement [*Urteil*]—Any act of subsumption of a particular under a universal, or a decision concerning whether a particular is, or is not, something (see especially pp. 12–13, 24, 26ff).

Knowledge [*Wissen*]—Cognition that is held to be true by the faculty of cognition, and that is either given *a priori* or in principle verifiable in experience (see especially pp. 11, 19).

Life [*Leben*]—Defined, insofar as it relates to the problem of feeling and purposive activity, as the ability to act according to presentations of purposes (see especially pp. 11, 33–4).

Natural purpose [*Naturzweck*]—A living organism when judged (by the teleological judgement) to be not just a complex physical machine (see especially p. 154ff).

Nature [*Natur*]—The realm of all objects of which experience is possible and which are determined by the laws of the understanding such as cause and effect. 'Nature' is sometimes used by Kant in other senses, for example, in the phrase 'the nature of something; if he is referring to human beings, this nature may include that which is not natural in the first sense.

Necessity [*Notwendigkeit*]—Of something that could not have been otherwise.

Pleasure [*Lust,* or *Wohlgefallen,* or 'liking']—A feeling of the furtherance of the purposes of life, which is also a determination of the will to act so as to maintain the current activity of the body or mind (see especially pp. 11, 33–4, 100).

Power—See 'faculty'.

Presentation [*Vorstellung,* or 'representation']—The manner in which the mind apprehends something, for example my concept of a 'horse' is a presentation of the general quality of being a horse; my intuition of 'Desert Orchid' is my immediate presentation of that particular horse (see especially p. 173n).

Principle [*Prinzipien, Grundsätze*]—A proposition stating the fundamental legislative or regulative contribution of a cognitive faculty to one of the faculties of the mind (see especially pp. 12–14).

Purpose [*Zweck,* or 'end']—A thing or action that was produced according to a concept of the thing or action (intention) (see especially p. 31).

Purposiveness [*Zweckmäßigkeit,* or 'finality', 'purposefulness']—A property of a thing or action by which it *appears* either to have been produced according to an intention, or to be a means to some further purpose (see especially pp. 31, 62ff).

Reason [*Vernunft*]—One of the cognitive faculties, with at least three 'employments': (1) merely logical, as that which forms or identifies logical connections between cognitive propositions – that is to say, forms proofs; (2) reason in its theoretical/ speculative employment, which seeks to pursue these logical connections even beyond the proper founds of cognition, and thus forms ideas; (3) as practical, supplying the principle of the moral law for the free will.

Reflective [*Reflektierend,* but related to *Reflexion*]—Of a judgement, meaning indeterminate judgement (see also 'determinate'). Kant also, however, uses 're-flective judgement' to describe the still more interesting case of a judgement that not only does not *begin* with a determinate concept, but also does not *conclude* by forming one. Both the aesthetic and teleological judgements are reflective in this latter sense.

Sensibility [*Sinnlichkeit*]—The faculty that provides immediate, particular presentations of all kinds, from sensations to pure intuitions, and including imaginings (see especially pp. 13–14).

Sublime, the [*das Erhabene*]—The experience of that which is absolutely large or mighty (see especially p. 88ff).

Summum bonum (or 'highest good')—Kant also speaks of the 'highest purpose'. The object of all morality: happiness combined with moral merit.

Supersensible [*Übersinnliche*]—That realm of 'objects', unexperiencable in principle, which is purported to be the ground of all objects of experience (see especially p. 121).

Teleology—The study of nature as judged to contain purposes. More widely, the study of judgements about final causes (see especially pp. 27–8, 143ff).

Thought/thinking [*Denken*]—Kant's most general term for any mental activity whatsoever involving a concept or idea.

Transcendental—Concerning that which forms the *a priori* conditions of the possibility of something (see especially pp. 16–20).

Understanding [*Verstand*]—The faculty of cognition which legislates for the cognition of nature by supplying *a priori* concepts (categories) (see especially pp. 12, 14–15, 19).

Universality [*Allgemeinheit*]—That which applies, or is the same, everywhere and always.

will/choice: [*Wille, Willkür*]—The determination to act, including the ability to choose an action from several possibilities, including non-action. As part of the lower faculty of desire, choice [*Willkür*] is always partly determined by inclination. As part of the higher faculty of desire, will is autonomous, determining itself according to the principle of the moral law (see especially pp. 11–12).

Selective Bibliography

Works by Kant

The standard edition of the collected works in German is *Kant's gesammelte Schriften*, edited by the Deutsche Akademie der Wissenchaften, Berlin: Walter de Gruyter. Equally widely available is *Werkausgabe in zwölf Bänden*, edited by Wilhelm Weischedel, Frankfurt am Mein: Suhrkamp. There are alternative, perfectly acceptable, translations of most of the following. Cambridge University Press, at the time of writing, is about halfway through publishing the complete works in English.

Aesthetics and Teleology, ed. Eric Matthews and Eva Schaper (Cambridge: Cambridge University Press, forthcoming).

Anthropology from a Pragmatic Point of View, trans. Victor Lyle Dowdell, intro. Van De Pitte, rev. and ed. H. Rudnick (Edwardsville: Southern Illinois University Press, 1978).

Critique of Pure Reason, trans. Werner Pluhar (Indianapolis: Hackett, 1996).

Critique of Judgement, trans. Werner Pluhar (Indianapolis: Hackett, 1987).

Critique of Judgement, trans. James Creed Meredith (Oxford: Clarendon, 1988).

Critique of Practical Reason, trans. and ed. Lewis White Beck (Oxford: Maxwell Macmillan International, 1993).

Grounding for the Metaphysics of Morals, trans. James W. Ellington, 3rd edn (Indianapolis: Hackett Publishing, 1993).

Logic, trans. and intro. Robert S. Hartman and Wolfgang Schwarz (New York: Dover, 1987).

Metaphysical Foundations of Natural Science, in *Philosophy of Material Nature*, trans. James Ellington (Indianapolis: Hackett, 1985).

The Metaphysics of Morals, trans. and ed. Mary Gregor, intro. Roger J. Sullivan (Cambridge: Cambridge University Press, 1996).

Political Writings, ed. Hans Reiss, trans. H. B. Nisbet, 2nd edn (Cambridge: Cambridge University Press, 1991).

Prolegomena to Any Future Metaphysics, trans. James Ellington after Paul Carus (Indianapolis: Hackett Publishing, 1977).

Religion Within the Limits of Reason Alone, trans. and intro. Theodore M. Greene and Hoyt H. Hudson (New York: Harper, 1960).

Theoretical Philosophy, 1755–1770, trans. and ed. David Walford with Ralf Meerbote (Cambridge: Cambridge University Press, 1992).

Other Primary and Secondary Works

For a treatment of various themes in Kant, see also the introductions to the above editions.

Caygill, Howard, *A Kant Dictionary* (Oxford: Blackwell, 1995).

Caygill, Howard, *The Art of Judgement* (Oxford: Blackwell, 1989).

Cohen, Ted and Guyer, Paul, *Essays in Kant's Aesthetics* (Chicago: Chicago University Press, 1982).

Crowther, Donald, *Kant's Aesthetic Theory* (Madison: Wisconsin University Press, 1974).

Crowther, Paul, *The Kantian Sublime* (Oxford: Clarendon Press, 1991).

Gibbons, Sarah L., *Kant's Theory of Imagination* (Oxford: Oxford University Press, 1994).

Guyer, Paul, ed. *The Cambridge Companion to Kant* (Cambridge: Cambridge University Press, 1992).

Guyer, Paul, *Kant and the Claims of Taste* (Cambridge: Harvard University Press, 1979).

Guyer, Paul, *Kant and the Experience of Freedom* (Cambridge: Cambridge University Press, 1996).

Henrich, Dieter, *Aesthetic Judgement and the Moral Image of the World* (Stanford: Stanford University Press, 1992).

Hume, David, *Dialogues Concerning Natural Religion*, ed. and intro. Henry D. Aitken (New York: Hafner, 1958).

Kemal, Salim, *Kant and Fine Art* (Oxford: Clarendon Press, 1986).

Kemal, Salim, *Kant's Aesthetic Theory* (London: St Martin's Press, 1992).

Locke, John, *Essay Concerning Human Understanding*, ed. P. H. Nidditch (Oxford: Clarendon Press, 1975).

Makkreel, Rudi, *Imagination and Understanding in Kant* (Chicago: University of Chicago Press, 1994).

McCloskey, Mary, *Kant's Aesthetic* (London: Macmillan, 1987).

Schaper, Eva, *Studies in Kant's Aesthetics* (Edinburgh: Edinburgh University Press, 1979).

Shell, Susan Meld, *The Embodiment of Reason* (Chicago: University of Chicago Press, 1996).

Wood, Allen, *Kant's Rational Theology* (Ithaca: Cornell University Press, 1978).

Zammito, John H. *The Genesis of Kant's Critique of Judgement* (Chicago: University of Chicago Press, 1992).

Index

Many of the following are *passim*; the page numbers given thus refer to passages where the notion is developed or applied.